Historical Archaeologies
of Capitalism

CONTRIBUTIONS TO GLOBAL HISTORICAL ARCHAEOLOGY

Series Editor:
Charles E. Orser, Jr., *Illinois State University, Normal, Illinois*

A HISTORICAL ARCHAEOLOGY OF THE MODERN WORLD
Charles E. Orser, Jr.

ARCHAEOLOGY AND THE CAPITALIST WORLD SYSTEM: A Study from
Russian America
Aron L. Crowell

AN ARCHAEOLOGY OF SOCIAL SPACE: Analyzing Coffee Plantations in
Jamaica's Blue Mountains
James A. Delle

BETWEEN ARTIFACTS AND TEXTS: Historical Archaeology in
Global Perspective
Anders Andrén

CULTURE CHANGE AND THE NEW TECHNOLOGY: An Archaeology of
the Early American Industrial Era
Paul A. Shackel

HISTORICAL ARCHAEOLOGIES OF CAPITALISM
Edited by Mark P. Leone and Parker B. Potter, Jr.

LANDSCAPE TRANSFORMATIONS AND THE ARCHAEOLOGY OF
IMPACT: Social Disruption and State Formation in Southern Africa
Warren R. Perry

A Continuation Order Plan is available for this series. A continuation order will bring delivery
of each new volume immediately upon publication. Volumes are billed only upon actual
shipment. For further information please contact the publisher.

Historical Archaeologies of Capitalism

Edited by

Mark P. Leone

*University of Maryland
College Park, Maryland*

and

Parker B. Potter, Jr.

*Sargent Museum of Archaeology
Concord, New Hampshire*

KLUWER ACADEMIC / PLENUM PUBLISHERS
NEW YORK, BOSTON, DORDRECHT, LONDON, MOSCOW

Library of Congress Cataloging in Publication Data

Historical archaeologies of capitalism / edited by Mark P. Leone and Parker B. Potter, Jr.
    p.   cm.—(Contributions to global historical archaeology)
   Includes bibliographical references (p.   ) and index.
   ISBN 0-306-46067-X.—ISBN 0-306-46068-8 (pbk.)
   1. Archaeology and history. 2. Archaeology and history—United States. 3. Material cul-
ture—United States. 4. Capitalism—History. 5. Capitalism—United States—History. 6.
United States—Antiquities. I. Leone, Mark P. II. Potter, Parker B. III. Series.
CC77.H53 1999   98-45788
930.1—dc21   CIP

ISBN 0-306-46067-X (Hardbound)
ISBN 0-306-46068-8 (Paperback)

© 1999 Kluwer Academic / Plenum Publishers, New York
233 Spring Street, New York, N.Y. 10013

10 9 8 7 6 5 4 3 2 1

A C.I.P. record for this book is available from the Library of Congress.

Printed in the United States of America

Contributors

Mark P. Leone, Department of Anthropology, University of Maryland, College Park, Maryland 20742-7415

Terrence W. Epperson, Cultural Heritage Research Services, Inc., North Wales, Pennsylvania 19454

Matthew Johnson, Department of Archaeology, University of Durham, Durham DH1 3LE England

Parker B. Potter, Jr., Sargent Museum of Archaeology, Concord, New Hampshire 03302

Paul R. Mullins, Anthropology Program, George Mason University, Fairfax, Virginia 22030

Charles E. Orser, Jr., Anthropology Program, Illinois State University, Normal, Illinois 61790-4640

Margaret Purser, Department of Anthropology, Sonoma State University, Rohnert Park, California 94928

Alison Wylie, Department of Philosophy, Washington University, St. Louis, Missouri 63130-4889

Preface

There is a series of issues to be addressed by any scholar studying capitalism. In addition, there are some issues which must be addressed by anyone concerned with capitalism's material culture and its archaeology.

If a scholar of the past chooses to focus directly on capitalism and embeds his or her work in an understanding of Marx, then the existence of classes and their inevitably antagonistic relationship is an assumption. Social stratification is known as *class* in analysis of capitalist societies and two ideas follow accordingly. First, classes based on wealth and power exist and have an unstable relationship, with a constant and confusing set of negotiations and shifts in power. The objective of this ever unstable dynamic is maximization of profit or accumulation of wealth. Second, while production is the objective of capitalism, a focus on production reveals how society operates to make production successful, and consequently, one must also focus on the place of power. A focus on power reveals that the constant quest for a monopoly on wealth entails the deliberate creation of poverty and the operation of popular opinion, ordinary beliefs, or *ideology* in the service of both power and profit. *Ideology* operates to convince many that their lives are stable, and hopeful, and that work and opportunity can yield an improved lot in a rational world where leaders are often thought to have the common good in mind.

In the context of power, capitalism creates identity for people. This is a complex issue that frequently calls forth denials of relevance from archaeologists. Such calls are false. Identity exists both for individuals and groups in a way that is important for archaeologists. Capitalism operates to achieve two parts for identity. On the one hand, identity can be assembled and added to, but on the other, some aspects of it are said to be fixed, usually in nature and biology; these, it is claimed, cannot be altered.

Anthropologists have understood from the beginning that identity is symbolic, that is, it is created in our minds and then reified. Therefore, identity is cultural. In addition, all cultures have mechanisms by which identity is created and made, and assumed by each member. As historical archaeologists, we are particularly concerned with how material objects were used to create and sustain the identities of racial groups and classes. An entire group of historical archaeologists also concentrates on the materials of gender. All of us, as authors, in this book are concerned with how identity is actively created from without, and also how it can be actively resisted, accommodated, reshaped, and neutralized within a group.

A third issue touches our definition as scholars. What are we to do with our knowledge? Indeed, how do we go about creating it, once we know that one way to create identity is to ground it in the past? If identity is thought to be fixed, as is the case with North American ideas of race and gender, then it is regarded as essential: there could never be an alternative to the way things are. Since capitalism acts to use biology and history to fix identities, our task should not be to cement identities in place, particularly when they are exploitative. Archaeologists normally disapprove of such use, but also normally do nothing to prevent it.

Most of the authors in this book believe that their job is to show that the past is created for use now, in situations defined by class relationships and the changing distribution of wealth. Therefore, their task involves assuming that consciousness of existing relationships, including those identified best through historical archaeology, is enough to call exploitative relationships into question. In order to achieve this, there must also be a strong role for philosophical analysis which shows that identities thought to be fixed are not fixed. There must also be a role for showing that identities known to be constructed are not false and, alternatively, that an awareness of the profound place of power in capitalism does not mean that those with less power are powerless to change or challenge the ways they are subordinated. Thus, we must understand that our work is embedded in social change and that, while we are being accurate and empirical, these are not our ultimate aims. Rather, change is our ultimate aim.

Douglas W. Schwartz, president of the School of American Research, and his staff organized a successful seminar in 1993. Thomas Patterson offered valuable advice at every phase of planning for the conference and volume. He has played a significant role in clarifying the definitions of capitalism used throughout the book. Charles E. Orser, Jr. editor for this series in historical archaeology, led the successful publication of this volume through Plenum Publishing Corporation. We are grateful to Eliot Werner, Plenum editor, for his ready optimism and helpfulness throughout the publication process.

Irwin L. Goldstein, dean of the College of Behavioral and Social

Sciences at the University of Maryland, College Park, and his staff have always sponsored an environment that promoted research and publication.

Nan S. Wells and Veronika Wells Leone always provided the supportive environment that made this book possible.

Nancy Jo Chabot was indispensable to the creation of this volume through her support.

Linda Konski and Andrew Tobiason, of the Department of Anthropology, University of Maryland, College Park, diligently typed and edited many versions of much of the material in this book. This volume was indexed by Julie H. Ernstein.

Contents

Chapter 3. Historical Archaeology and Identity in Modern America **51**

Parker B. Potter, Jr.

Chapter 4. The Contested Commons: Archaeologies of Race, Repression, and Resistance in New York City **81**

Terrence W. Epperson

Issues in a Historical Archaeology Devoted to Studying Capitalism

I

Setting Some Terms for Historical Archaeologies of Capitalism

1

Mark P. Leone

The essays in this book are adapted from presentations delivered in 1993 at a School of American Research Advanced Seminar in Santa Fe, New Mexico. This seminar was organized to explore the use of historical archaeology as a means for understanding the origins, development, and modern condition of capitalism. Historical archaeology is cross-disciplinary by nature and the seminar participants who have contributed were drawn from the fields of anthropology, American studies, cultural-resource management, history, and philosophy. We, the authors, are interested in finding ways to use historical archaeology to study processes relevant to the dominant Western economy of recent history.

By writing as historical archaeologists, we assume that a tie exists between the material culture of the past and the current condition of our own society. The field of historical archaeology offers knowledge of the ground, the artifacts within it, chronologies, written records, secondary sources, interpretive literature, and the agreed upon, but sometimes complex, ways of fitting these sources of knowledge together.

We not only believe our areas of knowledge to be filled with material connected to the origins of the present, but also see this material as capable of *illuminating* the present. This is a standard piece of rationale for the pursuit of archaeology. On the other hand, capitalism is a complex, pervasive, and historically recent phenomenon, which historical archaeologists often see as an appropriate target of inquiry. It is a system from which to interpret the past, as well in itself a perplexing development that archaeology may help illuminate.

CAPITALISM AND ITS PARTS

Our audience is historical archaeologists, so it is not necessary to define our common practice; however we will define capitalism. Capitalism is a set of social relations, including those that exist among people in a workforce who own neither land nor any other form of wealth by which to sustain themselves. People in a workforce sell their labor to earn a living. Resources, such as land, money, raw materials, and property of all kinds, are owned privately. Public lands and public wealth on which anyone can depend is limited; little is owned in common. Capitalist society is characterized by owners, governments, and their agents continuously introducing technical changes that alter the structure of labor, and pushing these changes into areas, cultures, and classes where they did not exist before, or where they become intensified. Owners and their agents expand markets in a deliberate search for customers, as well as for other peoples' resources, including labor, so as to bring them into the production process. In this system, production produces money, which is distributed according to a hierarchy of control. Wages are what workers receive for their labor—the rest is profit. Profit exists when the wealth produced through selling the worker's effort is controlled by the owner of the product, the capitalist. While these terms are commonplace, a critical investigation into the nature of capitalism requires clear definitions. The differences between wages and profit, and workers and capitalists, represent real differences in power, as well as degrees of ownership.

There is some agreement concerning when capitalism came into existence. There may have been places in the ancient Western world when capitalist production existed, and there may also have been non-Western places that could be described as capitalist. There is, however, much more agreement on two of capitalism's temporal characteristics. First, its immediate beginnings are in Renaissance Europe, and second, it is the dominant form of social relations in the West, and probably the world, today.

The debate about capitalism's origins is particularly important because of the intensity of the scholarly effort to understand the relations among people involved in it. If it existed in antiquity, China, or pre-Columbian Mexico, then it could be studied cross-culturally because it would not be uniquely Western. If it appeared and disappeared, then its seemingly inexorable spread out of Europe beginning in A.D. 1400 would merely have been an episode, not an inevitable social form. While there may be more than one origin environment, the one we can be sure of is the early modern West. Furthermore, capitalism has its own developmental history, which we will not explore here. Capitalism has gone through phases, such as merchant and industrial. We will not expand on these either, but we do acknowledge that our own analyses are connected to capitalism's development.

The social relations that accompany capitalism are central to it, but at the same time are not regarded as unique by all scholars. For example, social stratification, based on control of wealth and holding a monopoly on power, exists within capitalism. The strata are normally called classes, which specifies a dynamic, often antagonistic, relationship. However, many societies that are not capitalistic are stratified. We point out that classes exist in potential conflict with each other because the profits of some are derived not from their own labor, but from the labor of others. This relationship is exploitative, is visible to workers and laborers, and creates unstable social relations.

Things that are made, sold, bought, and used are seen as objects, not as extensions of social relations. Further, social relations are seen as objects. They all have prices associated with them, and their functions and prices are the sources of their primary identities. Capitalism is unique in that it attaches to people notions of skills and wages, which are valued according to the cost of the actual objects of production. Capitalism maintains this confusion between goods and social relations by treating both of these as though they were "things." This is why social relations are said to be objectified when people are paid wages for using skills, not for what they may actually need to live.

Human productivity, called labor, is bought, sold, bargained over, cultivated, discarded, honed, and in every way treated as a commodity. Human beings in capitalism are given (and often willingly assume) a multitude of titles and labels, such as renter, worker, consumer, educator, wage-earner, homemaker, mechanic, and taxpayer, which expand or contract depending on the shape, scope, and needs of the economy at a particular time. One of the functions of this process is to attach money to work. When work is compensated for with money, the tie effectively severs object from market value, on the one hand, and producer from owner, on the other. Such severed ties are the basis for profit accumulations, as well as exploitation, which produces poverty.

Analyses of capitalism stress the relations between wealth-producing and wealth-holding groups. Often referred to as classes, these groups are always defined as having at their core relationships which can become antagonistic or exploitative. This definition allows us to examine the sources of stress and conflict. These aims have three implications. First, functional relations that show smooth, if unexpected, interconnections among the parts of a society are not the end-products of our analyses. Early anthropology made its name by showing that odd, magical, and non-Western practices did indeed have significance to the working of mainstream society. Although valuable, this is not one of the implications of an analysis of the relations between classes. Second, even though stress, conflict, and violence, rather than function, are central foci of our investigations, provoking violence is not an acceptable vehicle of social change, although producing depressing results and unpleasant insights may be essential to building understanding and consciousness.

The third implication, the most important and complicated, is how capitalist society manages to deal with conflict. This is a crucial relationship that effects each essay in this volume, especially those dealing with slavery and the life of free African Americans. Since racism and slavery are social conditions that enabled the creation and exploitation of huge, legally homogenous labor forces, it is important to know how such practices were sustained without continual violence. Our essays are about the lives of urban and rural workers—people who were poor. We ask: How is poverty created and sustained without ever-present violence?

The concept used to deal with these questions is ideology. Its central role is in creating a world of meanings, credible in various ways to those within it, that hides the exploitative or inequitable relations that exist in everyday working life. The ideology of capitalism implies that most people live in a world where work produces profit for someone else, a world in which hope, happiness, and optimism are sponsored by assumptions that may not hold much reality. It defines a world of many negotiated meanings. The exploration of ideology is at the core of many of the chapters in this book.

The representation of past events and objects as history and archaeology is one manifestation of ideology. Stories concerning past people, events, objects, episodes, and anything else are often attempts to legitimize living, powerful relationships by creating precedent. This seems to provide an objective, separate existence in the past for present relationships, and the professionals who write about the past need to see the connection. An ability to see that a connection between past and present is not only developmental, but also can be initiated and drawn by the interests of a specific class, is essential to understanding the ideology of capitalism and is thus the responsibility of all archaeology.

It has long been recognized that ethnic and other biases exist in how histories are compared. We take the position that common, popular history is not simply incomplete, but is itself an artifact of class production. We see a great deal of archaeology as resulting from the ideology of Western history, and as disseminated differentially according to levels of social access. This assumption necessitates both the deconstruction of the given product—a particular history—and the construction of a new product—a revised history that does not wholly undermine the value of what has come before, but which bears the marks of the explicit reasons for its creation. Of course, we also see that those who study capitalism participate in it. We assume that our disciplines are products of a capitalist society and that using them requires a reflexive or critical perspective.

THE ROLE OF CONSCIOUSNESS

How does consciousness affect our scholarship and how does our work create consciousness of social reality? Our entire enterprise in this volume is built on the twin assumptions that illumination, or awareness of social reality, can lead to change, and that violence is not an acceptable vehicle for change. Will knowledge undo the realities brought about by racism, bias, stamps of inferiority, and language that produce fear and hatred? We think it will. In particular, knowledge of origins should accomplish this.

Tracing the roots and causes of current conditions, including their names, to their ancestral relations may yield one of two results. It can explain how people kept in inferior positions came to these positions. It can answer a question such as, how did "we" get to be in this condition here and now. Second, because such conditions, of both the inferior and the superior, are often embedded in circumstances asserted to be inevitable, the origins of that group asserting such inevitability can be impugned, since life for them, and for all, usually involves alienation and fragmentation. Thus, it can be argued that if they are responsible for modern conditions, they are also responsible for changing them.

Thus, an examination of origins offers two levers for freedom. One is a historical knowledge of the conditions of "unfreedom." The other is the ability to argue to those in a dominant position that the evils of the world are their fault and the fault of their glorified origins. The argument asserts that the founders of the republic, whose ideas are asserted to be the cornerstones of modern life, are responsible for these uncertain conditions. Thus, national leaders and the ancestors they claim created the misery of everyday life. This is the core of the argument made by Native Americans as a prelude to the passage of the Native American Graves Protection and Repatriation Act. Even though the argument vilified archaeologists, although not necessarily archaeology, the strategy required a strong insight into historical and archaeological knowledge in order to work.

In the face of such logic, we see the work of historical archaeology as inherently political and active. In addressing the question of what it means for historical archaeologists to do an archaeology of capitalism, a crucial and recurrent issue is to ask the following questions: Why do it? Who wants to know? What do they want to know? For the most part, those who want to know are often committed to dismantling the rationales, which are often racist and sexist, that entrench privilege. These rationales or concepts function as "taken for granteds" or as "default assumptions." They are assumptions that draw their power from having become common sense. They often look unquestionable to many, even when raised to consciousness and named, because in various ways they are presumed natural, inevitable, and essential about the world.

These concepts, which Gadamer described as "pre-judgments," define the horizons of our lives, thoughts, and actions. They allow us to efficiently sort and automatically deal with the majority of what we encounter in the world. They facilitate fast calculation, but are the ground against which anomalies emerge. In telling us what to expect, they are signposts and roadmaps, defining our own identities, locating us in the world as much as they locate those around us. They also canalize our actions of respecting or disrespecting others.

There is enormous value in not having to process every bit of incoming information as if it were new, but rather in having categories and automatic responses that let us deal with a world that we can regard as familiar. But the power of these rationales derives from cutting nature and society at the joints, so as to appear to grasp unchanging essences. They are supposed to capture those attributes that an entity must have to be what it is. Racist and sexist categories, and all the others that divide us against one another strategically, create hierarchies that ensure maximum differentiation. They are powerful in their various forms because they appear to become second nature.

Such rationales and assumptions appear to have no history. Once they emerge, immaculate of the history of the social negotiations that gave them birth, they are partly responsible for creating and maintaining the realities they purport to describe. They hold in place, and are in turn held in place by, the political economy of a class structure. Everyone who is categorizable as an inferior "Other" becomes in some sense exploitable or dispensable.

A historical archaeology of capitalism is at least in part an archaeology that promises to challenge essentialisms of these sorts—specifically those that have become crucial to the running of an exploitative system driven by the maximization of profit. It is an archaeology that may bring back into focus places and time periods in which entrenched categories were still in flux and contested, crystallizing around an organizing common sense that had not yet covered its tracks, and that had to use overt force to accomplish its ends, where its more mature offspring gives the appearance of working effortlessly. An African Burial Ground in Manhattan is an archaeology that testifies to the plasticity of racist constructs as they shifted opportunistically, strategically, from one category to another, lighting on skin color after religion, religion after legal status. These constructs "essentially" defined what it was to be the sort of person who had to be buried in "common" ground. If this artificiality, this arbitrariness, is recovered, will it help to dislodge the racism that structures all our lives and identities?

Once we have revealed the constructs as arbitrary, will that undo the reality of racism that they have created and sustained? Can we, indeed, use the "master's tools" to dismantle the "master's house?" Says Audre Lorde (1984: 112), in *Sister Outsider*:

> ... the master's tools will never dismantle the master's house. They may allow us temporarily to beat him at his own game, but they will never enable us to bring about genuine change. And this fact is only threatening to women who still define the master's house as their only source of support.

And that is the paradox of essentialism. Exploring unexamined labels that compose identity is a tool of the masters. These categories define us in terms of what we are not, and yet set us in strategic opposition to one another, ensuring that we do the job of division and control that maintains the privilege of others. It is a powerful tool that cannot easily be set aside. Says Mary Yee (1993: 34):

> This is a scary time in all our communities, as Western capital finds itself in crisis and needs to create scapegoats to divide a working class which is facing rising unemployment and economic insecurity.

Inevitably, however, such tools diminish whoever uses them. Essentialist categories, by their very nature, require a person being one thing, essentially. The challenge is to find ways of negotiating many views of the past and present so that we can embrace multiple fragmented identities that draw on the complexities of our experience, using these as resources. This is a challenge that can be best met by being clear about who wants to know, and why. That is, by being conscious of our political role and its possibilities.

WHO CREATES CONSCIOUSNESS FOR WHOM?

An effort to create consciousness also raises the issue of who can and should speak for various classes, ethnic groups, or gendered relationships, since what we do with the knowledge we produce could place the field in a quandary or revolutionize the public face of archaeology. The challenge is perhaps best captured in African-American archaeology, where historical archaeology has produced some of its most significant commentaries on capitalist society, as well as descriptions of the ability of people to resist it under persistently difficult conditions. The vast majority of that research has come from white, lower-middle- to middle-class archaeological workers, separated by race (but not usually by politics) from parallel groups of African Americans. The likelihood exists that some African Americans would interpret the material on African-American pasts differently and even pose quite different questions. Racism and its vitality in contemporary America make the political issue of who interprets African-American history particularly important because of who will believe and use it. "Voices" is a term that implies different groups, especially those not normally listened to or heard. It also implies speaking out for oneself. Voice implies hearing and listening, and thus raises the issue of creating large enough political alliances among differing constituencies to achieve desired change. We see archaeology, both speaking and being used to speak, as an important ally to those who want change.

Capitalism has been successful and expansive for over four centuries because it constructs and reproduces social relations that resist simplistic analyses. We cannot expect archaeological interpretation of capitalism's social base to be any more straightforward than the problems themselves. Consequently, the issues of consciousness and advocacy for peoples who have been persistently marginalized is a demanding enterprise. In African-American archaeology, for instance, such advocacy would attempt to create a relationship that white people and black people rarely have sustained. The voices of African-American experience, on the one hand, and of archaeological authority, on the other, are part of interpreting the African-American past. Answers to complex social problems will very likely entail many authorities in order to secure a resolution to a research question, because advocacy as we see it encourages dialogue across boundaries.

The tension over proprietorship of the heritage of colonized, marginalized, and stigmatized peoples, including African Americans, forces historical archaeologists to confront what social role we envision for our field. Since advocacy suggests that groups can formulate coherent social goals and plans of action that can be achieved by combining their resources, we also have to recognize that such concord between marginalized peoples and archaeologists is very rare and demands a persistent, sustained, and patient relationship in which archaeologists and any particular community construct a research agenda.

Advocacy is intended to create spaces for voices that have not used interpretations to achieve particular ends, yet we cannot predict how, or even if, those opportunities will be used. It is difficult to argue that historical archaeologists have spoken as activists for voiceless communities with any genuine efficacy, but we sometimes have had considerable influence as advocates for peoples who routinely are misrepresented or ignored by the dominant media. Unlike most social sciences, historical archaeology contains the beginnings of some promising collaborative projects and a growing self-consciousness of the field's potential roles. Yet learning to communicate with, and listen to, African Americans demands confronting three centuries of racism and forging a productive relationship in spite of such historical precedent. On the surface, we notice that archaeologists sometimes have been naive about the impact of racism on African America. We also know that history and archaeology generally have been irrelevant or inimical to the interests of African America, and we acknowledge that Black community members have good historical reasons to be suspicious of White society's sudden interest in African-American heritage.

Beneath the issue of advocacy, there are two other issues. One is whether sustaining consciousness through advocacy compromises academic freedom. The other is why one should be involved with the meanings of history of those who are not usually regarded as central to its main events and thrusts. The normal understanding of academic freedom involves the strong sense that scholars and teachers sometimes handle truths that are controversial and might bring social and political criticism and condemnation when spoken. As a kind of by-product for protection to say what appears necessary, there is a sense among scientists that their conclusions must be neutral and cannot be involved in taking sides in difficult political debates. Most forms of scholarship, including virtually all forms of science, claim a methodological ability to examine all or most sides of issues and disputes, and weigh them without reference to politics, prejudice, predisposition, or any other factor that would compromise getting at the truth.

Advocacy means taking sides in real, political, local, deeply felt debates. If one does this, does one violate codes of scientific practice on the one hand, or compromise the social privileges enjoyed by scholars within our society, on the other? Because this issue is intertwined with the postmodern critique of scholarship as inherently political by its own social nature, we ourselves see maintaining the balance between freedom and advocacy as very difficult. If advocacy does not achieve much along the road to social justice, and if it is done at some cost to academic freedom, what have we accomplished?

Advocacy for us is connected in two ways to life in a democratic society. Social justice or equality is a desired condition because of the commitment to individual freedom, and freedom, often called liberty in our founding documents, is essential to universal participation in government. This commitment has led to an understanding that representative histories ought to discuss everyone. Everyone helped make the past and, because writing and teaching history is a way of building social solidarity and communicating models for emulation, then all parts of society may expect to find themselves in history. It is good for the health of society and is not only a matter of fairness. This reasoning will help protect academic freedom because all are included in the academic project.

Much more powerful, however, is the matter of the actively disfranchised. A description of those whose past and current interests and conditions are absent from history denies society a handle on itself, since their subordination, oppression, marginalization, and inferiority, as well as their resistance to these processes and conditions, allows others no model for escape. Without the other side of history, modern society, especially a capitalist one, appears to absorb all its members into a homogenous, consensus history that masks the origins of inequity and thus its causes, as well as any models for changing it. If fairness to the disfranchised is reason for advocating their presence, then fairness to anyone demanding more honest democratic government is also a reason for advocacy and consciousness. There is no academic freedom if this role cannot be fulfilled.

If we choose advocacy, where do we push, what level do we push from, and what should the final product look like? It is easy, using the enormous effort spent by Habermas (1984; Kemp 1988: 177–201), to identify democracy as a goal. But that is a form of government and not a larger or smaller whole, like a community or a nation. Capitalism is powerful, not only because it is a process or institution, not only because it is an outside or exterior force, but because of what is called its totalizing or universalizing potential. Its ideology operates so as to convince people that they are individuals, have freedoms, earn what they are paid, have futures, and so on. It is very easy to see capitalism as having so many effects and to be so inclusive that it is a culture. Moreover, it is very important for us to use definitions of capitalism that allow us to describe its history, its absorptive capacities, and its ideology, and yet still set it apart as a particular phenomenon. Capitalism's processes are powerful and not easily found through scholarly description. Because capitalism's aspects are so complete that it appears to substitute for culture, we caution against replacing the need for seeing a society as having a culture.

CULTURE AND CAPITALISM

We will take a strategic position on the differences between capitalism and culture. Within anthropology we share the assumption that learned meanings and behaviors differentiate humans from all other creatures. We see culture as learned, comprehensive, and inescapable, with a history of four million years and a worldwide expression. It is, therefore, not conterminous with capitalism. While we see some cultures as having exploitative relations, we see capitalism as dependent on exploitation. While we see some cultures, but not all, as stratified, we see capitalism as creating classes in antagonistic relationships. And while we know that most cultures cannot be characterized as having economies that can be separated from the rest of their functions, we define capitalism as a relentless search for profit.

For most anthropologists, culture is the readily identifiable object of study; for us, as historical archaeologists, capitalism is an absorptive set of practices that can be found amidst existing social relationships. In order to deal with this distinction, we use the most basic definition of capitalism and see it as a social system in which the people who own and control the fields, factories, machines, tools, and money do not assume the brunt of the work. Other men and women, who must sell their labor as if it were a commodity, perform the work. Nonetheless, the owner of the machines and money—the capitalist—reaps most of the benefits from the labor of the workers. This way of seeing capitalism pushes its economic character to the front, without denying the totalizing efforts of capitalism. Since capitalism can masquerade as culture, it pretends to be something it is not. And since we seem to take our very essences from our economies and identify ourselves through what we have, we confuse our economy with our culture. We call our history capitalist and say that our architecture reflects capitalism and that the organization of our productivity is the heart and soul of capitalism. Yet these are cultural practices that have been rationalized and commodified in the service of profit, but are not wholly a product of capitalism.

How Do We Take Culture apart from Capitalism?

While we study culture and a particular kind of economic system within it, we know that the issues are worldwide, but the sources of archaeological information are almost always local. Thus, much archaeological interpretation depends on extremes, the local and the global. We use a set of scales to articulate how capitalism works and uses material things. The patterns of capital investment, the flow of human population, and the distribution of goods, technologies, and ideologies were fundamentally without borders by about 1850, and represent the action of capitalism. A more complex picture of the larger-scale economic practices working over this period enhances our understanding of the kinds of choices taking place at the smaller, and more archaeologically accessible, scales of households and communities, where it is vital to identify local, regional, and even national cultures where capitalism, and especially strategies for modifying or evading it, can be found.

There are archaeological cases that clearly document the active imposition of local sets of meanings that play off and manipulate labels stipulated at larger scales of production processes, exploitative practices, and advertising. We explore issues of control, resistance, and manipulation that emerge from data derived from different levels of meaning, from within cultures as well as between those effected by the process of market expansion that crosses cultures.

We have written archaeologies of niches of evasion, as well as impoverishment. Such groups and communities usually do not escape capitalism or stand outside it for long. From time to time, they may evade the dominant economic mode and ideological frame through barter exchanges, theft, or piracy. Any number of households, communities, and social groups practice a range of economic strategies and alternative definitions of success that operate in the interstices of capitalism; these are kin-based, labor-intensive, little capitalized, and opportunistic. For archaeologists, these strategies require that we look for comparable patterns of consumption and use, rather than the same, or even equivalent, artifacts. For example, we explore the patterns created by tenancy, squatting, and other strategies of evasion. These strategies were produced by people who believed that you don't buy what you cannot carry away; that it's better to mend what you own, so buy what's mendable; that you should never do just one thing to make a living; and that cash is not the only medium of exchange. The archaeological signatures of ephemeral ownership can be read in the seemingly haphazard assemblages of machinery, tools, and structures whose logic lay in functional flexibility, localized maintenance, and portability, rather than in technological sophistication promoted by national advertising.

Within capitalism, the scale of human groups through which material things pass can be understood through modern anthropology and historical archaeology because these fields operate successfully within and between households and communities, and with the ability to understand dialects, jargons, and new languages. We understand institutions like churches and the creation of national and ethnic identities. Most of our papers cross these scales, but rarely remark on the movement and never dwell on the crossing as a methodological difficulty, even though it often is. We focus, rather, on the impact of things at fairly specific levels: households, stores, communities, counties, colonies, or states, and occasionally regions, like the Chesapeake area or the intermountain West. Our essays illustrate considerable success in understanding the passage of goods into and out of households and the reasons the goods come and go. We can do this because of the idea of culture that allows us to see societies before capitalism and outside of it.

COMMODITIES AND AN ACTIVE ROLE FOR THINGS

In order to achieve our definition of historical archaeology of capitalism, we have adopted Marx's idea of commodity and Gidden's idea of the active role of things in shaping meaning in society. It should be clear that the significance of analyzing commodities must occur within the context of a specific culture and its classes if the precise meaning, and thus working of a thing's symbolic qualities is to be grasped. According to Marx, the commodity is, at first glance, "a very trivial thing," and easily understood.

Marx's most explicit discussion of commodity fetishism appears in the first chapter of the first volume of *Capital*, although it appears in various guises throughout his work (e.g., Marx 1973: 687), Marx says that careful consideration, however, reveals that the commodity is a "social hieroglyphic, and a very queer thing, abounding in metaphysical subtleties and theological niceties." A commodity is a mysterious thing because:

the relation of the producers to the sum total of their own labor is presented to them as a social relation, existing not between themselves, but between the products of their labor. This is the reason why the products of labor become commodities, social things whose qualities are at the same time perceptible and imperceptible by the senses.... There is a definite social relation between men, that assumes, in their eyes, the fantastic form of a relation between things. In order, therefore, to find an analogy, we must have recourse to the mist-enveloped regions of the religious world. In that world the productions of the human brain appear as independent beings endowed with life, and entering into relation both with one another and the human race. So it is in the world of commodities with the products of men's hands. This I call the Fetishism which attaches itself to the products of labour, so soon as they are produced as commodities, and which is therefore inseparable from the production of commodities (1967: 72, 74).

Marx's choice of the pejorative term "fetishism" was quite deliberate and carefully considered. According to Mitchell, "Marx was telling the nineteenth-century reader that the material basis of modern, civilized, rational, political economy is structurally equivalent to that which is most inimical to modern consciousness" (1987: 191). For Marx, commodity fetishism represents a double forgetting. On the first level, the capitalist comes to see "exchange-value" as an innate attribute of the object, forgetting that it was he who projected life and value into commodities through exchange. In the second phase of forgetting, the commodity becomes veiled in familiarity and triviality, what Marx called the "natural, self-understood forms of social life" (1967: 75). Therefore, the most magical aspect of the commodity fetish is the denial that there is, after all, anything magical about it (Mitchell 1987: 193). Thus we can more fully appreciate Marx's rhetorical strategy. His first move is to strip the commodity of its everyday familiarity and reveal its underlying complexity and magical power. In his second move, Marx provides a scientific account of the commodity's magic through the analysis of exchange value, allowing us to understand how social relations between people assume the form of relations between things.

Arjun Appadurai and the other contributors to *The Social Life of Things* reject the "production-dominated Marxian view of the commodity" and seek to collapse any distinction between capitalist and noncapitalist exchange relations. They focus instead upon the "commodity situation" in the "social life of any 'thing,'" the moment when "its exchange ability (past, present, or future) for some other thing is its socially relevant feature" (Appadurai 1986: 13; Tiersten 1993). In seeking to equate commodities in capitalist social formations with barter and gifts in non-capitalist contexts, the contributors to *The Social Life of Things* recapitulate only the first part of Marx's rhetorical strategy.

The work of Daniel Miller represents an even more radical rejection of the concepts of commodity fetishism and reification (1987; 1990). Miller rejects definitions of objectification as processes of alienation or reification in the work of Marx and Lukacs and returns to Hegel for an overwhelmingly positive definition of "objectification." Miller believes the concept of "work" should be expanded to include consumption, the act "which translates the object from an alienable to an inalienable condition." Although the commodity may indeed be "the product and symbol of abstract and oppressive structures," the work of consumption is "the negation of the commodity" (1987: 192). Miller's analysis of the liberatory powers of capitalist consumption leads him to some rather stunning conclusions:

> Just as money is the foundation for freedom, the state is the essential mechanism for the creation of equality (1987: 186)

and

> There is no a priori reason why modes of consumption cannot be the main vehicles by which modern populations construct ... a culture that is authentic and profound (1990: 77).

Finally, we need to situate the rejection of notions of reification and commodity fetishism within the context of a political economy. The erasure of distinctions between capitalist and noncapitalist modes of exchange, the insistence upon according "work" status to the act of consumption, and belief that the alienation and reification embodied in the production and exchange of commodities can be negated through the act of consumption are all symptomatic of the post-modernist moment of late capitalism (Harvey 1989). In *Postmodernism or the Cultural Logic of Late Capitalism*, Fredric Jameson writes that the "effacement of the traces of production" from the commodity is an ideal move for "a society that wants to forget about class" (1991).

If we are going to work toward an archaeology of capitalism, we need to be very clear about the specificity of this particular and peculiar mode of production. The concepts of reification and commodity fetishism are valuable tools as long as we remember that they are "dialectical images" and not "reified and separable abstractions" (Mitchell 1987: 163). If we are going to try to change the world, and not just study it, we should also know that consumption of commodities is not the path to liberation.

Commodities and commodified relations are not the same as artifacts or material culture. But our task as archaeologists is to tie the two together so that archaeological circumstances can be better under-

stood in the context of capitalist relations. The vast majority of archaeologists do not see a connection to be made between the things they
uncover in context from the ground and written records, and the production and market forces that gave them birth. The position we take
defines artifacts as mirrors of culture, as well as building blocks of
culture. Things are symbols of meaning, as well as personalized expressions of meaning. Artifacts are fetishized forms of exploitation, as well
as avenues to personal fulfillment. We see artifacts as products of
rational thought, as well as conduits of emotion. They are about borrow-
ing status, as well as about forming identity. Artifacts can be about both
economic base and superstructure. They are products of capitalism and
rebellions against it. They may or may not be commodities at any one
moment in their histories. These complimentary relationships suit our
purposes and highlight consumer studies. Such an orientation uses
Adam Smith and Karl Marx to study production and consumption.
Further, if we strip away the Frankfurt School's disdain for consumer
goods, we find that artifacts and commodities not only help in the
performance of tasks, but also make people happy. Some people are able
to reject advertising's packaged meanings and reshape things into
something intensely personal and meaningful, and personal meanings
are grafted onto objects that can been seen, touched, and held. Groups
defined by race, age, gender, geography, or ethnicity can supply their
own meanings and uses for things. Such exploration of artifacts is at the
heart of several chapters in this volume, including those by Mullins and
Purser.

Artifacts have both use and exchange value. Exchange value is
negotiated and calculated; it is money in the pocket and food on the
table. Use value is the ability of an object to supply some human want,
and according to Marx, these wants "may spring from the stomach or
the fancy." Our definition of what counts as material culture is as
inclusive as possible. One feature of inclusion is a shift to defining
material patterns based on consumption and use, rather than on production. As we draft an archaeology of capitalism, this shift provides a
powerful means of returning some sense of individual motivation and
action, and, therefore, of creating ways of analyzing objects whose
meanings are ambiguous. Patterns of consumption have proved particularly sensitive to the fundamental duality of capitalist material culture, best articulated during seminar discussions by Alison Wylie's
comment that the same symbols of belief act as tools of oppression as
well as resistance.

The existence of such patterns requires a reassessment of how we
interpret archaeological data. The most direct impact is in the physical
composition of individual artifacts, as opposed to artifact assemblages.

By now we are familiar with the complexity of artifacts composed of mass-produced parts, but disposed of locally in trash pits, that tell us about household purchasing selections based on different kinds of strategies for different goods. Further, after around 1830, meaning also became unstable over relatively short periods of time, helped on by advertising, and rapid communication.

All of this runs directly counter to the kinds of assumptions about meaning that we have made based on the overall formal and functional characteristics of material culture through the late eighteenth and nineteenth centuries. These assumptions grow from an initial premise that an increasingly homogeneous material culture became ever more widely distributed, purchased, and consumed in a context of ever more sophisticated corporate marketing and an ever more nationally organized popular culture. It is not so much that this scholarly picture is now false, but that approaches to artifacts that begin from consumption, rather than production, have created a picture that is also valid. We are capable of recognizing archaeological contexts in which different categories of material culture, such as bottles, tin cans, houses, and machinery, do not redundantly reflect the same set of meanings, but may in fact hold meanings that are in conflict, even within the same social group, depending on household, gender, class, or race.

We realize that there is no imperative to buy, emulate, or multiply possessions, nor is there any standard reason for commodities to dominate individual identity. In this book, we attempt to move well beyond commodities and commodification to the meanings that show why capitalism became so firmly planted among the poor and among the rich. We are also able to understand why the rich think of themselves as poor and incomplete from time to time.

Our job, therefore, as historical archaeologists is, first, to help identify the workings of capitalism, such as capital extraction, alienation, and supply and demand. Second, we need to see how these penetrate communities and change culture. Third, we can create an understanding of the social and economic implications of activities that make up daily life, such as looking at a clock, eating with a fork on a creamware plate, and going shopping. The practices of capitalism discipline people by the clock, by rules of etiquette, by the mass media, and by conventional histories.

Capitalism is worldwide and penetrating. However, no single research project, no allied set of projects, and no single research strategy can be adequate to the task of fully explicating it, archaeologically. Rather, the historical archaeology of capitalism, composed of many historical archaeologies of capitalism's effects, is a massive undertaking made up of many smaller parts.

Acknowledgments

This essay is composed of brief essays by the seminar participants on issues central to the seminar and of particular interest to us. Seminar participants were Terrence Epperson, Mark Leone, Ann Smart Martin, George Miller, Paul Mullins, Charles Orser, Parker Potter, Margaret Purser, and Alison Wylie. Their pieces were combined to form this introduction by the editors, who are responsible for any shortcomings.

REFERENCES

Appadurai, Arjun
   1986   Introduction: Commodities and the Politics of Value. In *The Social Life of Things: Commodities in Cultural Perspective*, edited by Arjun Appadurai, pp. 3–63. Cambridge University Press, Cambridge.
Harvey, David
   1989   *The Condition of Postmodernity: An Enquiry into the Origins of Cultural Change*. Basil Blackwell, Oxford.
Jameson, Fredric
   1991   *Postmodernism or, the Cultural Logic of Late Capitalism*. Duke University Press, Durham.
Habermas, Jürgen
   1984   *The Theory of Communicative Action. Vol. 1, Reason and the Rationalization of Society*. Beacon Press, Boston.
Kemp, Ray
   1988   Planning, Public Hearings, and the Politics of Discourse. In *Critical Theory and Public Life*, edited by John Forester, pp. 177–201. MIT Press, Cambridge.
Lorde, Audre
   1984   *Sister Outsider*. Crossing Press, Freedom, California.
Marx, Karl
   1967   *Capital: A Critique of Political Economy, Volume I The Process of Capitalist Production* [English edition of 1887, edited by Frederick Engels]. International Publishers, New York.
   1973   *Grundrisse: Foundations of the Critique of Political Economy* [1939] (translated by Martin Nicolaus). Vintage Books, New York.
Miller, Daniel
   1987   *Material Culture and Mass Consumption*. Basil Blackwell, Oxford.
   1990   Fashion and Ontology in Trinidad. *Culture and History* 7:49–77.
Mitchell, W.J.
   1987   *Iconology: Image, Text, and Ideology*. University of Chicago Press, Chicago.
Tiersten, Lisa
   1993   Redefining Consumer Culture: Recent Literature on Consumption and the Bourgeoisie in Western Europe. *Radical History Review* 57:116–59.
Yee, Mary
   1993   Finding the Way Home Through Issues of Gender, Race and Class. In *Returning the Gaze*, edited by Himani Bannerji. pp 3–37. Sister Vision Press, Toronto, Ontario.

Where the Questions Come From

II

As yet there are no standard questions in historical archaeology. Prehistoric archaeologists, on the other hand, inherit a set of questions formulated over the last century and a half. These questions are so well established and agreed upon that they are not only uncontroversial, but are also embedded in popular historical consciousness. Where do humans come from? How did humans occupy the whole planet? Where does culture come from? Where, why, and how were the first plants and animals domesticated? And the first cities and civilizations? We have not yet established parallel or analogous questions in historical archaeology.

This section proposes a way to postulate questions. The authors in this section assume that questions come from the scholar's social setting. They stress the aggressive use of a scholar's setting in American society in formulating questions. The authors in this book would argue, if asked, that the questions prehistorians ask are learned in graduate school as part of the process of professionalization that involves socialization into the habits and procedures of the field. They would also argue that these questions have their origin in nineteenth-century philosophical debates on the origins of Europe's most identifiable concerns and practices. In other words, these questions are socially situated, but this is not recognized by most American prehistoric archaeologists. As an alternative, the argument here is that historical archaeologists should use an understanding of the social nature of their work as an advantage, rather than denying it.

We propose a conscious use of that which is still largely maintained at an unexamined and unaware level in prehistoric archaeology. In the first essay, Alison Wylie urges a historical archaeologist to focus on vicious sequences of practices and identities; explore what people mean when they say some relationship is to be "taken for granted," suppressed, oppressed, and exploited. She argues that our subjects ought to be the concepts, opinions, and assumptions that have created the inequalities we find around us. And we should explore how these taken-for-granteds gained life and stayed alive. Thus, our questions stem from the conditions of life now, and are the job of the archaeologist

21

to formulate aggressively. Wylie begins by telling the scholar to address what he or she does not like in a society.

Parker B. Potter, Jr. makes these same assumptions and recommends the same process. In order to find how society operates to perpetuate inequitable relations, Potter looks for its contradictions—practices that are alive today that claim precedent and historical reality, but which actually have little or none. Public opinion, advertising, and daily speech contain unreasonable practices that are given weight because of their assumed ancestry or naturalness. When such practices create contradictions or logical conflicts, their arbitrariness becomes visible. Visible contradictions are where society's defense of itself falls apart, as when people argue that prejudice will be overcome by opportunity, that hard work will ameliorate poverty, or that the creation of wealth in general improves everyone's condition. These are ideological fragments that appear true, are questionable or even false, but which use their own citations of historical feasibility to achieve their ends. Potter says that a historical archaeologist's task is to write the accurate history of the operation of these assumptions in society. This will help create a level of consciousness that will allow some to challenge dominant practices.

Terrence W. Epperson argues that questions come from members of groups that have been exploited. Historic minorities know how they have been treated, know it's to the advantage of others to keep conditions this way, and know society's lies when they hear them. What they do not know, and what an archaeologist will explain, is when such conditions began and how these conditions operated to create the way things are. Historical explanations of exploitation offer illuminating liberation, which is why archaeology can be so powerful.

The ultimate reason to use Epperson's model for asking questions is to widen the participation of groups in a democracy. The reason is not just fairness, or a sense of "it's now their turn." The reason, as Habermas has argued, is that wide participation in democratic society protects democracy. Those excluded from the history of participation see participation cynically. And that is not participation; it is a commentary on democracy's failure.

2

Why Should Historical Archaeologists Study Capitalism?

The Logic of Question and Answer and the Challenge of Systemic Analysis

Alison Wylie

INTRODUCTION: DEMOCRATIZING FORCES

Since the early 1970s, advocates of the emerging field of historical archaeology have defended its worth and autonomy by appealing to the democratizing power of archaeological evidence over the alleged conservatism, the "inevitable elitism," of text-bound history. Historical archaeology is the key, many have argued, to making visible "the inarticulate" (Ascher 1974: 11), the "endless silent majority who did not leave us written projections of their minds" (Glassie 1977: 29), or were not of interest to those who did construct an articulate record of their activities and interests. While this sells short the radical potential of history, it does foreground the important contribution that archaeology can make to the investigation of periods for which we have documentary records. It captures what I take to be the central challenge facing historical archaeologists in the 1990s: that of realizing, of exploiting more fully, the potential of archaeological evidence to counter what Glassie describes as "superficial and elitist ... tale[s] of viciousness" ...

Alison Wylie • Department of Philosophy, Washington University, St. Louis, Missouri 63130-4899.

Historical Archaeologies of Capitalism, edited by Mark P. Leone and Parker B. Potter, Jr. Plenum Press, New York, 1999.

"myth[s] for the contemporary power structure" (Glassie 1977:29), which are by no means unique to history. Because these are tales specific to capitalist ideology, at once mediating and obscuring its contradictions, this is the challenge that defines a historical archaeology of capitalism.

Despite the conservatism of much historical archaeology as developed in the last twenty years, this critical potential has been realized, in some measure, in a number of burgeoning areas of research interest: in the important development of the archaeology of slavery (Singleton 1985; Potter 1991); in the archaeology of early Spanish exploration and settlement in the Americas (Deagan 1990; Thomas 1991); in research that has begun to document the enormous diversity of those who populated "the West" and the complexity of their interactions (see discussion in Wylie 1993); and in the archaeologies of colonial and neo-colonial societies, some of which are recovering a (largely suppressed) history of systematic oppression and displacement (see contributions to Schmidt and Patterson 1995). Most recently, these initiatives have been extended to women and to the gender dynamics that infuse the class structure of capitalist systems in historical contexts (e.g., Seifert 1991). Moreover, as archaeologists have developed a self-consciousness about the role they play in the construction and perpetuation of "vicious myths," historical archaeology has proven to be a disproportionately rich source of cases in which critics have been able to use archaeological evidence to expose the systematic erasure, distortion, and legitimation of dominant myths (e.g., Handsman 1989, 1990; Hall 1984; Leone 1981; Trigger 1980, 1991; Handsman and Richmond 1995; Schmidt 1995; Vargas 1995). This is, perhaps, unsurprising; entrenched presuppositions about historical contexts are especially potent, erasing or naturalizing the direct (causal) antecedents of the systemic contradictions we negotiate in the present.

These considerations suggest some preliminary answers to the question framing this collection of essays and the School of American Research seminar out of which they arose: Why should historical archaeologists study capitalism? They should study *capitalism* because it is this that we most need to understand if we are to recover alternatives to, and possibilities for, action in the present, in the context of a global political–economic system that is predicated on exploitative social relations "structured so as to maximize differentiation" (Fuss 1989: 117). *Historical archaeologists* should study capitalism because the archaeological record is, indeed, a primary source of information about the material conditions of life, and the social, ideological mediation of these conditions, that are constitutive of contemporary capitalist social formations.

Once accepted, however, several pressing questions arise about this specification of the "democratizing" mandate of historical archaeology. The one on which I will focus is: What does a commitment to the study of capitalism require of historical archaeologists methodologically? There are two parts to this question that I would like to disentangle for the purpose of discussion here.

First, there is the general question of how archaeological data are to be used to provide access to those aspects of the past that other sources leave out (from Deagan 1988: 8). This is often cast as a question about the proper roles of, and relationship between, the distinct traditions of research that have grown up around the use of documentary records, and of archaeological material, as primary sources of evidence relevant for understanding the recent past. When put in these terms, debate about the relative value and autonomy of these traditions is often overdetermined by the disciplinary politics of a struggle to define historical archaeology as a field that is distinct from, and is not subordinate to, history or prehistoric archaeology. In the first part of this chapter my aim is to draw attention to the epistemological and methodological issues that underlie these boundary-defining skirmishes. My thesis is that the debates over disciplinary identity turn on much more fundamental questions about the security and credibility of archaeological interpretation, questions that concern archaeology as a whole. Given a history of unflattering comparison with neighboring fields, practitioners in a hybrid field such as historical archaeology have been under particular pressure to address these questions; they ask, more specifically, how robust archaeological evidence is, compared to documentary evidence, as a ground for building and critically scrutinizing reconstructive and interpretive claims about the recent historical past of capitalism. I will argue that the answers historical archaeologists have given to these questions suggest a promising strategy of response to skeptical worries that has significance well beyond historical archaeology.

Second, there is the more specific question of how these strategies of reasoning about evidence can be used to get at capitalism, a paradigmatically large-scale (global) system of political–economic processes. Consideration of this issue has, again, been shaped by the politics of disciplinary self-definition, in this case by reaction against the untenable scientism of processual archaeology where its proponents insist on the primacy of questions about the structure and dynamics of large-scale cultural systems (cf. Deagan 1982). The point is routinely made that historical archaeologists had been developing a self-conception of their enterprise as "an interpretive human science," in quiet resistance to the nomothetic scientism of processual archaeology that existed well before post-processualism came to prominence (e.g., Beaudry 1996: 473). Not surprisingly, the contextual, symbolic, and structuralist approaches advocated by post-processual critics through the 1980s have found some of their most fruitful applications in historical archaeology. They give prominence to precisely the historical contingency and particularity of cultural life that had long been a central preoccupation for historical archaeologists (e.g., contributions to Hodder 1987), sharing, as well, the emphasis on seeing material culture as active (e.g., contributions to Hodder 1982; Beaudry 1993), and on the need to get at the "insides" of actions, which has distinguished historical archaeology from the outset (e.g., from Collingwood, as advocated by Hodder 1986; Leone 1982).

The danger is, however, that this prescient commitment to humanistic and critical initiatives encourages a return to particularism, fostering a historical archaeology of capitalism that is about capitalism only in the narrow sense that many of the periods and subjects of interest to historical archaeologists are, by default, components of a capitalist world system. If the archaeological study of capitalism is framed as a series of narrow case studies with no movement beyond concrete particularities, and no analysis of the encompassing processes and structural conditions that give rise to these particularities, it cannot be expected to provide an understanding of these subjects as capitalist. This worry is raised in especially compelling terms by Trigger (1989a: 33), who puts in historical perspective the network of structuring presuppositions that have set history in opposition to science and aligned it with "descriptive rather than explanatory" interests (1989a: 22).[1]

While a tendency in the direction of particularism is certainly evident in historical archaeology, as Trigger suggests, it is also clear that those committed to recovering local meaning and context are well aware of the issue Trigger flags; they resist the sharp opposition between generalizing (scientific) and particularizing (historical) options. Consider, for example, Beaudry's insistence that "the details of human

---

[1]Trigger situates this particularism in the context of developments in North American social science since the 1930s. It has roots in formative nineteenth-century debates about the relationship between the emerging social sciences, especially history, and the natural sciences; these earlier debates may be especially relevant to understanding these issues as they have been articulated by historical archaeologists.

life are as important as the broad generalizations" (1996: 483),[2] and her observation that "the reinvention of historical archaeology has permitted us to shift our attention from totalizing frameworks and to cultural actors" (1996: 496). She endorses a turn to particularism, not just as valuable in itself, but as the crucial basis for understanding larger socio-economic structures and dynamics. Indeed, Beaudry's objective, in exploiting interdisciplinary strategies for recovering (emic) meaning and agency (e.g., in connection with Lowell boardinghouses; 1993), is to get at recurrent contradictions between public corporate discourse and action, and dynamic tensions in working-class appropriations of, and resistance to, emerging middle-class ideals of leisure and domestic life. Citing Trigger, Beaudry rejects the opposition between generalizing and particularizing interests as artificial: "it is in the very particularity of individual experience that a broader understanding of the human experience is to be found" (1996: 496).[3]

In the same vein, Yentsch argues that researchers committed to the recovery of symbolic meaning can and should undertake to delineate not just "patterns" that may be contingent (indeed, accidental), but also

[2]For example, Beaudry argues that:

> ... [the] greatest potential [of historical archaeology] does not lie in its ability to contribute in a major and meaningful way to what are referred to as "important issues in history"—unless it is cultural, ethnographic history we are talking about—or to our understanding of sweeping and amorphous cultural processes. Rather, it is in its ability to inform us on the intimate and unheralded details of day-to-day life through the minute inspection of written clues as well as grains of dirt, artifacts, and features of all shapes, sizes, and descriptions, to help us bring to light and to understand the life history of one site and its inhabitants, and then of another, and another, such that we gradually construct a more and more complex mosaic by putting together our many individual cases, that we do best. (1996: 496)

[3]Several examples relevant to the more detailed argument I will make for refusing this dilemma come from the growing literature produced by feminist historical archaeologists. Here a concern to recover the concrete particularities of women's experience is motivated by the conviction that these often neglected particulars are valuable in their own right, and that it is in them that broader systemic realities are to be grasped. This nuanced commitment to particularism is typical of feminist work in many contexts. It arises as a resistance to discourses, academic and otherwise, that systematically obscure or deny the experience of women: "totalizing" and idealizing discourses that read women out or, when recognizing difference along gender lines, mark this as deviation from an androcentric norm. Under these conditions women's experience is a key resource for challenging taken-for-granteds about sex/gender systems; it is the basis for exposing, as partial, sexist or androcentric generalizations that regulate social relations as normative descriptions of how they (actually) are or must be (for further discussion of these issues, see Wylie 1992).

"structures," "relationships which determine the character of the whole [in which] ... the link with social process is visible" (1991a: 137). Both Yentsch and Beaudry echo Deagan's earlier discussion of the need for fine-grained studies that examine the "specific mechanisms of specific processes" as they operate within "a given unit" (1982: 162). They advocate a strategy of "generalizing within the case," to use a phrase of Geertz's (1973: 26), that fruitfully transgresses the opposition between particularizing and generalizing that we have inherited from nineteenth-century debates on the differences between scientific and nonscientific disciplines.

The key question for the historical archaeology of capitalism is, then, that of how exactly historical archaeologists are to move effectively from the investigation of concrete particulars to an understanding of encompassing conditions, that is, how they are to grasp the systemic and economic processes, the forms of life, and institutional structures constitutive of capitalist systems in their various manifestations, under which these particulars have arisen. This is the question of how historical archaeologists are to generalize within the sorts of instances of capitalism they can bring into view archaeologically. The role that historical archaeologists can play in challenging the "vicious myths" of capitalism thus depends fundamentally on the exercise of a very specific sort of (historical) sociological imagination (Mills 1959).

THE LOGIC OF QUESTION AND ANSWER

A number of compelling and largely convergent arguments have been put forward to show that archaeological evidence (and research strategies) must be used conjointly with historical evidence to get at aspects of the past that would not be accessible to non-archaeological modes of inquiry or, indeed, that would not be accessible using either mode of inquiry taken on its own.[4] Framed, as most such arguments have been, in the context of debates over disciplinary identity, they seem largely intended to counter the assumptions of "historicalist" researchers (Schuyler 1978); they establish that neither historical nor archaeological resources can be treated as secondary, dispensable supplements to the other. In particular, as Leone and Potter have argued (1988), archaeological evidence cannot be treated as "dependent" on historical resources, either in the sense of providing details that fill out

[4]Compare Deagan's argument that archaeology has unique "contributions" to make (1982: 153), with Beaudry's argument that "*archaeology* is not enough" (this is an amplification of Stone's discussion, "Artifacts are Not Enough," as cited in Beaudry 1996: 476).

the picture provided by the documentary record, or in that of being brought to life, interpretively, by the deliverances of this record. It is, in fact, precisely in the *independence* of archaeological and historical lines of evidence that the promise of historical archaeology lies. My aim here is to draw out an epistemological argument, largely implicit in the debates about disciplinary relations, for seeing the borderland position of historical archaeology as a resource, rather than a liability. In the final section of the paper I take up the further question of what, in particular, these strategies of inquiry have to offer the understanding of aspects of capitalism that have otherwise been systematically obscured.

The Argument for Conjoint Uses of Evidence

The case for regarding conjoint uses of historical and archaeological evidence as a particularly powerful methodological tool depends on (at least) three distinct, although interdependent, lines of argument. The first is a quite general argument to the effect that no evidential resource can be treated as a given or as uniquely foundational relative to other records or sources. However transparent the significance of a given body of data may seem to be as a "record" of particular past events and contexts, it has evidential import only under interpretation, and this interpretation is always open to question. More to the point, interpretive claims about the "meaning" of an archaeological or documentary record may vary a great deal in their security and in the degree to which their constructedness is obvious, but none can be granted automatic epistemic privilege; it is always an open question how tenuous a given evidential construct may be, relative to others.

Second, by extension of this argument, the case is made that no one evidential source can take epistemic priority over another as a matter of principle; therefore, documentary history must be recognized to be, in practice, on the same epistemic footing as historical archaeology. The relative security and significance of documentary, as opposed to archaeological, evidence must be assessed locally, with reference to the specific evidential resources each offers and their bearing on a particular set of research questions.

Third, arguments are offered to establish that, in some contexts and with reference to certain kinds of questions, archaeology may provide special resources for challenging taken-for-granteds about the historical past and learning about dimensions of the past that are otherwise inaccessible.

The first, anti-foundationalist arguments about evidence are by now a commonplace in archaeological contexts. The insight central to post-positivist thinking here and elsewhere is that reasoning from evidence is a "three-place relation." Any claim about the evidential significance of material identified as a record of the past (to take the case at hand) depends on mediating assumptions, variously described as background knowledge, auxiliaries, linking principles or, in archaeological contexts, middle range theory (MRT). In philosophical discussions these insights about the theory-laden, auxiliary-dependent nature of evidence are often described as a contextualist thesis. The import and credibility of evidence depends upon the contextual support provided by the "third term" in the equation, the background knowledge that establishes a link between the accessible (observable) material cited as evidence and the past (or otherwise inaccessible object of inquiry) on which it bears. This general contextualist thesis has the (anti-foundationalist) implication that the evidence archaeologists deploy in building or warranting claims about the past will be insecure to the extent that the data do not determine a unique "ladening" by interpretive theory, or that the ladening theory is itself evidentially unstable and open to revision. For some this is understood to establish that evidence is quite literally "constructed," and that extreme relativist conclusions are unavoidable (e.g., the hyperrelativism described by Trigger 1989b). If the background theories or linking principles mediating the interpretation of data as evidence are merely conventional, or are otherwise incapable of systematic empirical evaluation, then the resulting evidential claims cannot be expected to provide a robust empirical basis for assessing competing claims about the past. The danger arises that vicious circularity will compromise any appeal to evidence as grounds for evaluating reconstructive or explanatory accounts of the past (see, e.g., Kosso 1989, 1992); evidential claims may be open to reinterpretation in whatever terms are consistent with, or are deemed necessary to sustain, a preferred view of the past under investigation.

In fact, contextualism is compatible with a broad range of views about the epistemic status of evidence, including a number of different constructivist positions as well as various "mitigated objectivist" options of the sort that I favor. At one end of the spectrum, Binford maintains a form of foundationalism despite endorsing a general contextualist principle (e.g., Binford and Sabloff 1983, Binford 1983). He rejects outright the relativist implications that his sharpest critics believe contextualism entails because he assumes that the third term in the inferential equation, certain types of middle range theory, can provide a secure foundation for the interpretation of archaeological data as evidence. Although archaeological data may have no intrinsic, stable "meaning," the process of constituting them as evidence may be stabilized if archaeologists rely on interpretive principles that have the special kinds of security Binford attributes to middle range theory drawn from the natural sciences.

Few share Binford's confidence that contextualist theses can be circumscribed in this way; it seems unavoidable that evidence in the fields from which archaeologists draw linking principles is as theory-laden as in archaeology itself. Nonetheless, a great many reject the implication that a slide into corrosive relativism is unavoidable. Consider, for example, Leone and Potter's arguments concerning the role of "middle range theory" in the interpretation of archaeological data as evidence of the historical past (1988; also Leone and Crosby 1987).[5] This terminological affiliation with a broadly Binfordian view of "ascriptions of significance" signals a certain optimism about the capacity of well-chosen mediating theory to stabilize archaeological inference, and yet Leone and Potter's account of MRT-mediated reasoning is much more open ended than Binford's. In particular, they reject any tendency to privilege particular kinds of linking theory in the way Binford does,[6] and they offer a much more realistic account of the uncertainties inherent in interpreting archaeological data as evidence. An interpretive process based on well-established linking principles may make it possible to (tentatively) stabilize evidential claims, not because the mediating theory offers surrogate foundations but, as Leone and Potter suggest, because these claims are constructed using a wide range of mutually constraining sources. I return to this point below.

The important point here is that even a quite general (and minimal) contextual thesis, of the kind accepted by both Binford and his post-processual critics, and by the majority who hold intermediate positions, applies to any inference from a contemporary record to the cultural past. Whether evidential claims depend on documentary or material data,

---

[5]It is important for subsequent discussion to note that I use the term middle range theory rather differently than do Leone and Potter. I use it to refer specifically to the conceptual resources (background theory and interpretive principles) that link data, construed as evidence, to particular claims about the past, not to the processes of inference by which these resources are deployed. I note this because I suspect that much current debate arises, not over the question of whether archaeological data is theory laden or reasoning from evidence depends on myriad background assumptions (the original challenge posed by anti-processualists), but over the question of just how stable the inferences are by which this background knowledge is deployed.

[6]In the case of historical archaeology, the relevant middle range theory is often assumed to be background knowledge drawn from documentary history. By contrast, Binford typically conceptualizes middle range theory as a body of biconditional laws or lawlike statements of dependence between behavioral and material correlates that are directly drawn from (or emulate) the natural sciences.

and whether they are mediated by middle range theory drawn from the social, life, or physical sciences, the same three-place relation holds; in all cases evidence is an inferential construct (albeit, a construct of discernibly different degrees of security and robustness). In principle, then, historical archaeology is in no worse (and no better) a position epistemically than history or prehistoric archaeology. None provide direct, unmediated access to the past; all rely on interpretive linking principles to establish the evidential significance of their data as a record of the past under investigation.

On its own, however, a generic contextualism of this sort does little to level the disciplinary hierarchy that has put historical archaeology in the position of "handmaiden," in various senses, to document-based history (Deagan 1982, citing Hume 1964). A second argument is required to establish that, in practice (not just in abstract principle), document-based history depends on potentially unstable mediating assumptions and is, therefore, on the same epistemic footing as historical archaeology. I believe this is at least part of the point historical archaeologists make when they argue against any supposition that textual records have special veracity—that they provide direct (in some sense unmediated) access to past life, conditions of action, intentions, beliefs— as compared to archaeological sources. For example, when Beaudry insists on the importance of an "ethnographic" approach to historical documents, she foregrounds a vast network of background assumptions and interpretive inference that underpins even the most straightforward of the evidential claims routinely made by historians (1996: 476, 478).

The view of historical practice Beaudry articulates resonates with Collingwood's stern critique of "scissors and paste" history (1946). It was crucial to the emergence of history as a respectable discipline, he argues (surveying the entire sweep of Western historical practice), that by the nineteenth century historians should have come to recognize, finally, that the testimony of historical "witnesses" cannot be taken at face value; they must be rigorously cross-examined. In the process of systematic interrogation it may be possible not only to determine the efficacy of various primary sources, but to extract information from them that they never intended to disclose. This requires the historian to engage what Collingwood describes as the "logic of question and answer" (1946, 1939), essentially a hermeneutic (and dialectical) process of framing leading questions about why a given "witness" would report what they did in the way they did, which is alert to incongruities in testimony and, most important, between the testimony of different witnesses (preferably in different media). He draws elaborate analogies with detective work, by which he emphasizes both the need to take a vigilantly incredulous (critical) attitude toward historical documents,[7] as well as the importance of elaborating prospective answers to the questions historians raise, hypotheses about motivation, intention, informing beliefs, and circumstances of action—which yield concrete expectations about where additional evidence might lie that (if it survived) would provide a new and especially telling line of evidence for a particular reconstructive or explanatory model. The questions posed by an effective historical interrogator are capable of revealing much more than the text presents on its surface, precisely because they are informed by, and indeed are intended to test, a presumptive answer or set of alternative answers. These hypothetical answers depend, in turn, on a rich body of background knowledge concerning the possible, or likely, motivations, beliefs, and circumstances that shaped the actions and the testimony of historical witnesses.

Elsewhere, in discussions of "historical imagination" and the doctrine of "rethinking the past" (1946), Collingwood considers the crucial role played by interpretive resources (linking principles, background knowledge) in this process of interrogation; it is this component of the account to which Hodder appeals (1986: 95). Here the process of inquiry structured by the logic of question and answer is characterized as open-ended and dynamic in every dimension. As new evidence arises, questions and hypothetical answers are recast; given the outcome of previous investigations, inquiry may take surprising new directions, requiring that quite different bodies of background theory be deployed to anticipate, and make sense of, new ranges of data relevant to carrying the interrogation forward. Likewise, if there are changes in the relevant background knowledge—that is, in governing assumptions about what historical agents in a given context might have believed, intended, or been capable of doing, and in linking principles that allow insight into the processes of production, distribution, uses, symbolic valence, and associations of their material culture—questions and hypothetical answers will certainly have to be revised and evidence reassessed. Collingwood's account implies that historians at the top of their form work on all fronts at once, continuously seeking a balance, a point of equilibrium, between all the terms of the inferential equation—evidence, hypotheti-

---

[7]The similarity between Collingwood's account of systematic cross-examination of historical sources and the critical historiographic attitude recommended by Yentsch and Beaudry, among others, is clear when, for example, Yentsch urges historical archaeologists to "consider the past as a foreign land, a diverse countryside" (1991a: 149), and Beaudry advocates historical methods of reading documents "for what they reveal inadvertently as much as for what they say openly" (1993: 8).

cal answers, mediating assumptions—all the while recognizing that any balance they reach is subject to realignment as their work destabilizes one or another element of their projective questions and answers.

The model Collingwood presents of historical inquiry applies directly to archaeological practice. Indeed, Collingwood wrote about "history" not only as a philosopher, but also as an historian of Roman Britain who routinely applied the logic of question and answer to archaeological, as well as to documentary, sources and who urged that historians and archaeologists, like detectives, should use whatever resources they can to challenge their witnesses. The strategy he recommends is, most crudely, one of playing against one another the testimony offered by as many sources as possible, including historical and archaeological sources, as well as the insights afforded by one's own "historical imagination." On Collingwood's account, historical reasoning from documentary evidence is mediated, in practice, in all the same ways as is historical reasoning from archaeological evidence; it is no less dependent upon linking principles and background knowledge than archaeological interpretation.

Given this Collingwoodian thesis about the epistemological similarities between historical and archaeological reasoning, the third component of arguments for the conjoint use of archaeological and documentary evidence depends on a set of observations about the special resources that archaeology has to offer for the investigation of the capitalist past. These arguments foreground the special, if always contingent, capacity of archaeological research to challenge taken-for-granteds, or to bring into view otherwise unaccessible ("unrecorded") historical communities, conditions of life, and types of activities, including those that are systematically obscured by the rationalizing discourses of liberty, opportunity, and equality associated with capitalism. The most intriguing of these focus on the independence of archaeological from historical evidence. The argument is not just that historical archaeology is the only source of evidence relevant to many of the questions we might want to ask about capitalism, but that it confers a certain advantage in addressing these questions even (or, indeed, especially) when relevant documentary evidence is also available. The evidence provided by archaeology is particularly telling because it is understood to stand apart from, to have been produced independently of, and to provide a check on, the written records on which documentary history is based. At least some forms of archaeological evidence arise from precisely the sorts of activities historical witnesses are likely to suppress or ignore, whether because they are beneath notice or because they give the lie to a carefully constructed public face. Leone and Potter make this sort of case when, for instance, they argue that, once we "abandon the conceit that the documentary record was created for us" and the "submerged premise" that interpretation of the archaeological record is dependent on the documentary record, it becomes possible to exploit these records as "two *independent* sources of evidence" (1988: 14). A process of "analytical byplay" between documentary and archaeological data, of working "back and forth, from one to the other, using each to extend the meaning of the other" (1988: 14) opens up the scope of the logic of question and answer, offering greatly expanded resources for cross-examination than either could provide on its own.

Vertical and Horizontal Independence

The notion of "independence" between types of evidence that Leone and Potter articulate plays a central role in Binford's discussions of strategies for deploying middle range theory, and in an analysis I have developed elsewhere that parallels Leone and Potter's in many respects (Wylie 1989b; 1996); it is this independence that promises to stabilize reconstructive inference, not the security of mediating theory conceived as a surrogate foundation. The worry articulated by critics who regard relativism as unavoidable is that the background assumptions on which archaeologists rely to constitute data as evidence simply ensure that they will "find" (or construct) all and only the kinds of evidence they expect. One counter to this worry that Binford makes to critics is that if the background assumptions used to interpret the data as evidence are substantially independent of any of the hypotheses archaeologists might want to test against this evidence, then the general (contextualist) thesis of "theory-ladenness" does not entail vicious circularity (see, for example, Binford 1977: 1–13, and 1982a, 1982b; see also Kosso 1989, 1992). Associated with this "vertical" independence, as I have described it (1996), are a series of arguments about the importance of drawing on bodies of background knowledge whose credibility or security have been established independently of any archaeological uses of this knowledge. Where middle range theory is concerned, the position of being a consumer of results generated by other fields can be an epistemic advantage, rather than a liability, so long as the results of collateral research programs are applicable to archaeological problems. This seems to be one of the senses of independence that Leone and Potter have in mind in their discussion (1988). Independence of this sort is epistemically important because, if the fields from which archaeologists draw linking principles are conceptually and methodologically independent from archaeology, it is implausible that these principles will be shaped by the same presuppositions as inform the hypothetical "answers" about the past that they hope to evaluate against the evidence established using these principles. In this case the threat of a viciously circular interdependence between reconstructive claims and the evidence that (may) support them is mitigated, if not eliminated.

The most important sense of independence, however, that which Leone and Potter emphasize most strongly, is of independence between a number of different lines of evidence that may be presumed to bear on a given reconstructive model of the past; I refer to this as "horizontal" independence (Wylie 1996). The epistemological intuition at work here is that if several lines of evidence that depend on quite different ranges of background theory all converge in supporting the same a common hypothesis, the credibility of this hypothesis is enhanced much beyond a simple additive function, because it is implausible that such coherence could arise accidentally or as a result of compensating errors in each line of evidence. This is a modest version of the form of argument described, in the context of philosophical debates about scientific realism, as a "miracle argument": it would be a miracle that a number of (horizontally) independent lines of evidence should all converge on a given hypothesis if it were not an (approximately) accurate account of the underlying or antecedent conditions responsible for producing them. Whether or not such an argument establishes grounds for (one or another variant of) scientific realism, it certainly provides good reasons for regarding an hypothesis as *prima facie* plausible, in the absence of competitors that can assimilate the same range of evidence.

Leone and Potter draw out the crucial methodological corollary to this argument: when archaeological and historical evidence *fail* to converge, and there is reason to believe that they bear on the same set of events or conditions in the past, there is a compelling reason to suspect that some component in the chains of reasoning establishing each of the individual lines of evidence must be reexamined, or that the questions being put to the record (and the hypothetical answers that inform them) must be reframed. It is in the process of working back and forth between intransigent lines of evidence—reassessing background assumptions, reexamining the data, formulating entirely new prospective answers—that the capacity of archaeological inquiry to challenge settled assumptions about the past is most clearly realized. By Leone and Potter's account, horizontal independence is best achieved by playing off historical evidence against archaeological evidence. This is the rationale for fostering an historical archaeology that operates in genuine partnership with history; the disciplinary divisions that had been such a major stumbling block become an asset.

Causal, Inferential, and Disciplinary Independence

Juxtaposing Leone and Potter's account of hybrid practice in historical archaeology with Collingwood's account of historical inquiry, and with more general methodological proposals for exploiting independence in archaeology, I am struck by the parallels and puzzled by some residual questions about what exactly, we mean by "independence." In many of the cases where independence is invoked, it would seem that epistemically relevant independence can be realized without bringing into play a different kind of "record" or importing background theory from other disciplines. Indeed the distinction between what counts as historical and as archaeological, where records and practices of "reading" them are concerned, would seem to have been very substantially eroded by critical rethinking on both sides of the disciplinary divide in recent years (see, e.g., Patrik 1985). Moreover, one implication of treating material culture as textlike, meaning bearing, and actively structured and deployed, to varying degrees, for communicative purposes, is that a hyperconsistency may hold between aspects of both the documentary and the archaeological record.[8] Some of the material that survives archaeologically may well have served as another medium, alongside documentary sources, through which a common set of ideals and realities of social order are articulated. Indeed, in many cases there may be greater independence between (some) documentary sources when produced by historical agents occupying different standpoints, for different purposes or audiences, than between documentary and archaeological sources. Given this possibility, I would urge that the presumption of (horizontal) independence be treated as an empirical hypothesis: It requires substantiation on a case by case basis, and may well admit of degrees of instantiation.[9] It cannot be assumed, in advance, that the kinds of evidence typically associated with historical rather than archaeological inquiry are independent in any epistemically relevant sense.

To illustrate this point and disentangle several different senses of

---

[8]This is a point made in particularly compelling terms by Matthew Johnson (personal correspondence). It is always possible, he argues, that "certain forms of social practice may generate both documentary and material traces," consequently, "if certain classes of documents and artifacts are to be understood in this way then use of each as a 'check' against the other needs to be prefaced by an 'archaeological' (in Foucault's sense) analysis of the evidence under review" (personal communication 1993).

[9]In most general terms, the point at issue here is one Orser makes: "when capitalism becomes widely recognized as the proper focus of historical archaeology, its practioners will be freed from the reifications so commonplace in the formal, academic disciplines" (1988: 315).

independence that are at issue in historical archaeology, consider Hacking's now-classic analysis of how (horizontal) independence confers epistemic and methodological advantage in the context of research biological and natural sciences (1983: chapter 11). Hacking observes that, in the process of developing microscopes, scientists exploited a number of fundamentally different physical (causal) processes of interaction (or signal production) between the target and the receiving instrument. The great value of this proliferation of instruments (e.g., acoustic as opposed to optical microscopes) was that they allowed for a triangulation of signals, correcting and enhancing the information any one microscope could provide about the entities they allow us to observe: "we believe what we see [through microscopes] largely because quite different physical systems provide the same picture" (1983: xiii). The kind of independence Hacking notes here has at least three quite distinct components relevant for understanding appeals to horizontal independence in historical archaeology. I will refer to these as causal, inferential, and disciplinary independence.

The first and most obvious dimension of independence at work in Hacking's example is that which distinguishes the different physical systems (the processes or mechanisms) that produce the traces detectable by different kinds of microscope. In an archaeological context, a counterpart would be independence in the production of distinct kinds of record which ensures that errors or distortions transmitted in one source are not necessarily transmitted in others. A second is independence between the sources of inference—the bodies of background knowledge, technical expertise, and forms of disciplinary practice—that are deployed in reconstructing the pathway by which a particular kind of trace is transmitted and received. It is this inferential process, and the background knowledge on which it relies (in archaeology, middle range theory) that makes it possible to link what microscope users observe in a literal sense (the manifest trace, the image registered by the detecting instrument) with the entities the instrument is assumed to detect in an instrumentally extended sense (see Fritz on "indirect observation" in an archaeological contest; 1972). As in archaeological contexts, the crucial forms of inferential independence are those that ensure that a coincidence of images produced by different instruments is not an artifact of the instruments themselves, or the interpretive theories backing them. Often, as in the cases Hacking describes, one indication of such independence may be the fact that different instruments, and the background theory on which they rely, have been developed by institutionally, intellectually, and methodologically, distinct disciplines. This is a third sort of independence that often coincides with the other two. In at least some of Hacking's microscope cases, the traces generated by different physical systems of transmission (e.g., acoustic vs. optical phenomena) are detected and interpreted using bodies of background knowledge that derive from autonomous programs of research.

It cannot be assumed, however, that these three kinds of independence will always coincide. The same signal transmission process might be detected, or interpreted, using very different bodies of background theory, carrying the same distortion through different channels. Alternatively, apparently distinct bodies of background knowledge may share common assumptions so that persistent, compensating errors arise in the detection and interpretation of signals, even when they are generated by causally independent processes. Finally, error of this last sort may result when institutionally distinct disciplines are subject to common theoretical or methodological influences, so the understanding they produce of their distinct domains, which appears in other fields as auxiliary assumptions, is not as conceptually distinct as might be assumed.

The kind of (horizontal) independence archaeologists invoke incorporates all three dimensions of independence discernible in Hacking's microscope case; causal independence is assumed to be aligned with an independence in the content (or presuppositions) of background knowledge that is marked, in turn, by the distinctness of its disciplinary sources. Perhaps the most obvious archaeological analog is to be found in cases where different methods of physical dating are applied to material from a single archaeological context. Here there is substantial independence of the background knowledge on which archaeologists rely when, for example, they use tree-ring counts and measures of radiocarbon breakdown and magnetic orientation as the basis for determining cutting, burning, and deposition dates. In addition, the disciplines that supply the relevant interpretive principles and technologies of detection seem clearly independent of one another; it seems unlikely that the assumptions that might produce error in the reconstruction of a date using principles from physics will be the same as those that might bias a date based on background knowledge from botany. Finally, this independence in the content of the auxiliaries and in their disciplinary origins seems especially compelling because it is assumed to reflect a genuine causal independence between the processes that generated (and transmitted) the distinct kinds of physical trace exploited by different dating techniques.

In the case of independence between documentary and archaeological material, however, the argument is much more complex and uncertain. In some respects and in some cases the archaeological record can reasonably be assumed to be independent from the documentary record in all the senses described here. It may be entirely plausible that the contents of a trash heap and the various kinds of official history that appear in the documentary record are produced by such different means, for such different purposes, that they can be regarded as causally independent. The interpretation of these kinds of evidence may also require distinct bodies of background knowledge and interpretive techniques of the sort typical of documentary research, rather than that developed by archaeologists. In such a case historical and archaeological lines of evidence may be expected to provide a check on one another, conferring epistemic advantage on their conjoint use. But in many cases these various assumptions of independence cannot be made, and none can be assumed to entail the others. The handling of trash may reflect the same principles of decorum as writing for public record, and both lines of evidence may systematically obscure underlying contradictions. Indeed, there may be greater causal independence between different types of documentary record, for example, between legal transcripts as compared to personal diaries, than between certain kinds of archaeological and documentary record, for example, public architecture and official histories. In addition, however resolute (some) archaeologists and historians have been in maintaining boundaries between their disciplines, they are almost certainly subject to many common influences and rely on similar interpretive resources. For example, there seems no reason to believe that the politics structuring debate about how to mark the quincentennial would have had a fundamentally different impact on the historians, as opposed to the archaeologists, who study the history of various colonial powers in the Americas, or that the "romantic" presuppositions described by Trigger (1991) would have had shaped archaeologists' interpretation of Native American–European dynamics, but not those developed by historians. In consequence, historians and archaeologists may well overlook or misinterpret aspects of the different records they deal with in quite similar ways, consistently missing aspects of the subject that are unpalatable or unrecognizable given shared assumptions. The emergence of closely parallel feminist critiques in both fields makes it clear that the practice of deploying different kinds of evidence, even in conjunction with one another, is not in itself proof against pervasive androcentrism or sexism.

In short, questions about the conceptual, causal, and disciplinary independence of apparently distinct lines of evidence must be treated as empirically open, however incongruous their juxtaposition may seem. Disciplinary boundaries may not cut the world at its joints where different orders of causal production are concerned, and may not ensure freedom from the influence of a common stock of presuppositions that are capable of inducing compensatory errors in seemingly independent lines of evidence. It follows that, to determine epistemically relevant independence, two lines of inquiry are relevant: one to establish the extent to which the processes responsible for ostensibly different records were, in fact, causally independent of one another (itself evidence of internal contradiction and dissonance that will be of interest to the historical archaeology of capitalism); and another to determine the extent to which the background theories concerning these processes (the middle range theory used to read these records) are conceptually independent. This last will require reflexive critique designed to determine, not just the impact of standpoint-specific interests on how we understand the past, but the reach of these interests: how far they infuse the work of researchers in the neighboring fields on which archaeologists rely for the third term of their inferential equations when constructing the diverse lines of archaeological and historical evidence that are engaged in "analytical byplay." I suggest that this sort of reflexive critique must be an ongoing and central component of any interpretive practice in a historical archaeology of capitalism.

GENERALIZING WITHIN THE INSTANCE: CABLES AND TACKING

What the foregoing discussion shows is, most crudely, that cables of reasoning are better than chains (to use a Peircean metaphor; Wylie 1989). A chain of argument is as strong as its weakest link, while a cable of (independent) strands of arguments may be much stronger than its weakest constituent, indeed, stronger than the sum of its parts. It is important to note, however, that cables of interpretive argument can be used to establish the evidential significance of archaeological data at a number of levels of generality; whether these data are made to inform exclusively on local conditions or, through them, on global processes, depends on the questions historical archaeologists pose and the hypothetical answers they entertain. What should distinguish the historical archaeology of capitalism is a firm commitment to pose questions, and to entertain hypothetical answers, that move beyond the reconstruction of particularities, whether these are particularities of mind, social relations, or material conditions of life. The ambition of an archaeology of capitalism is to grasp the underlying processes, structures, and relations of production that are distinctive of capitalist systems. This is the second epistemological issue that I think must be central to the development of a historical archaeology of capitalism. What I offer here is a sketch of the structure of reasoning from evidence that this leap of theoretical imagination requires.

I have argued elsewhere for the usefulness, in an archaeological context, of the Geertzian metaphor of "tacking" back and forth between what he calls "experience-near" and "experience-distant" concepts in ethnographic inquiry (1989). My thesis is that this metaphor should be extended in several directions; the process of inquiry Geertz describes cannot, and should not, be conceptualized as a matter of moving only from our experience-distant (theoretical or abstract, or in essence, our sense-making, explanatory) concepts to "their" experience-distant (concrete, experience-embedded) concepts. Even conceived of as a dialectical process that proceeds along several lines at once (as a cable of interpretive argument), this strategy of tacking from familiar explanatory concepts to alien practices closer to the ground, as it were, leaves out the crucial processes of internal tacking that go on between abstract and concrete, distant and near, within both the source and the subject contexts. I want to suggest that, even if Geertz's designation of alien or unfamiliar is inappropriate for the capitalist world system of the recent past, this point about the architecture of the inferential process still applies. The logic of question and answer employed by historical archaeologists of capitalism must be bidirectional (dialectical), and must involve tacks on all dimensions. Of particular importance are the tacks by which explanatory concepts are formulated within the source context— the disciplinary and life world of the investigator.

On the account I propose, using this extended metaphor of tacking, the point of departure for a historical archaeology of capitalism is inevitably some experience-near preoccupation with contemporary conditions of life that impinge on us, whether or not this is consciously recognized. Often this concern arises from an activist commitment to understand how and why particular material and social conditions of life exist as we experience them *for the purpose of changing them*. In these cases the point of departure is an already developed experience-distant analysis of the damage done by "vicious myths" that systematically obscure the structural conditions that shape our lives.

I find recent feminist research in archaeology particularly interesting in this connection; the link between contemporary politics and a scholarly interest in the past is clear where archaeological evidence provides a growing contingent of feminist researchers a fresh source of insight into the processes that have created and entrenched contemporary sex-gender structures. But feminist standpoints are just one example of the experience-distant analyses that may give rise to fruitful tacking. On the principle that our understanding of historic capitalism will be strengthened to the extent that we can multiply the number of independent lines of evidence on which we base it, historical archaeologists of capitalism should be committed, above all, to expanding the range of standpoint-specific experience and interests represented in the community of researchers. At the very least, a diversity in the points of departure that researchers bring to the enterprise (and the associated experience-near/distant concepts that frame their research) broadens the range of sensitivities to gaps, silences, and systematic distortions on which the community can draw to critically assess its store of interpretive constructs. More constructively, such diversity expands the number of focal concerns that generate research questions, and the interpretive resources that can be used to comprehend the particularities of the archaeological record. This is just to say that our concrete experience of contradictions and systemic oppression under contemporary capitalism is an important catalyst for inquiry and a resource that we must exploit in the process of inferential tacking by which we build a historical archaeology of capitalism.

Given this starting point, the crucial inferential move that distinguishes an historical archaeology of capitalism is one that begins with the particularities of contemporary life under late capitalism and moves, within this source context, to the formulation of experience-distant concepts that grasp the principles of operation and, in particular, the dynamic contradictions inherent in capitalist systems. Lenin's sustained critique of bourgeois social science (specifically, its analysis if imperialism) makes clear what the study of capitalist systems requires: a grasp of the mechanics of these systems, the irreconcilable antagonisms inherent in them, and the causal mechanisms, the living connections, by which large-scale economic forces operate as the decisive factors shaping local social and political relations within these systems (Lenin 1975). Mindful of the inadequacy of standard accounts, Lenin urges us to frame an understanding of motive causes that is at once abstract, in the sense that it comprehends underlying causal mechanisms operating on a large scale, and also rigorously concrete, grounded in careful documentation of how these mechanisms operate in specific cases (e.g., 1975: 155); in this he recapitulates Marx's advice that, to grasp the contours and dynamics of capitalism, we must move from abstract to concrete (1970: 144). The social scientists Lenin critiqued had failed in their analyses, not because they lacked concrete data or had been unable to discern various trends and general patterns emergent in these data, but because they lacked any constructive, explanatory understanding of the encompassing dynamics and contradictions operating in the political–economic system as a whole. They remained mired in particulars, framing abstract explanatory concepts, in Geertzian terms, experience-distant concepts, by means of a process Lenin describes as speculative guesswork. Even if the specifics of Marx's and Lenin's analyses of capitalist systems are rejected, the wisdom of their methodological proposals remains. The distinctive mandate of the historical archaeology of capitalism is to make any analysis of the particulars of the archaeological and documentary record an occasion for the sort of concrete historical analysis sought by scientific Marxism. Its aim must be to understand the conditions of life to which these records testify as instances of causal mechanisms and processes that constitute (*qua*, are elements of, and causally drive) the expanding political economy of capitalism.

In the recent history of debate within historical archaeology, this objective has been articulated in response to, as an effort to extend, the initiatives due to Deetz, for example, whose delineation of a "Georgian world view" leaves largely unaddressed critical questions about how and why this world view should have manifested itself (differentially) in the period, places, and ways it has. Deetz, and many others working in a broadly structuralist tradition, make a very effective vertical tack within the subject context, linking the material manifestations of experience-near practices to an articulation of the experience-distant concepts informing them. Their critics object that they are less effective in making the diagonal tack between this tightly reticulated world view and its local manifestations to a body of abstract explanatory concepts (in effect, external experience-distant concepts) capable of bringing into view underlying features of the political economy on which this world view depends. They do not give an account of the conditions of life on which the entrenched world view depended and systematically obscured.

The move from archaeological investigation of a particular manifestation of capitalism to an archaeology of capitalism requires an inferential tack that puts documentary and archaeological evidence to work answering questions (in the Collingwoodian sense) about how key transformations came about in specific contexts: how some were systematically dispossessed of control over the means of production, while others accumulated control and capital; how relations of production were transformed and the population of those who had only their labor to sell came to be divided among themselves and differentially exploited. One such leading question has to do with the emergence of contemporary gender roles and relations of reproduction out of the conditions of subordination that Engels identified with the "monogamous" patriarchal family (1942: 138). Far from withering away, as Engels had predicted (1942: 145), the central categories and relations of these institutions have been elaborated, aligned with a segregation of domains of activity formerly unthinkable, and entrenched as natural. The result is a capitalist system in which women constitute an army of labor that, whether in reserve or not, has carried the burden of the continuous, unpaid "sex/affective" labor required to reproduce and sustain an exploitable labor force. As Caulfield put the point in an early, and especially compelling, discussion of family life under various systems of colonial exploitation, "in all of these systems, one factor is constant: women work two jobs, and are the lowest-paid workers when they do earn a wage" (1974: 78).

Some recent feminist work in historical archaeology exemplifies the diagonal tack back and forth between an abstract question about the structural dynamics at work in the formation of these new relations of (re)production and the concrete conditions of life they sustained. Consider, for example, Yentsch's movement back and forth between delimited generalizations of a pattern of appropriation of women's productive activities (household production), whenever these became capable of industrialization, and the specificities of archaeological evidence (the representation of types of wares in domestic assemblages over more than a century) that testify to a gradual, but ultimately decisive, shift in levels of domestic dairy production, as opposed to dependence on commercial dairy products (1991a). As I indicated earlier, Yentsch is clear on the point that this is a matter of distinguishing "structures from patterns," and of grasping underlying social processes that can be characterized as essentially and irreducibly material.[10] In a study that illustrates the capacity of archaeological and documentary particulars to resist the imposition of experience-distant concepts, Purser's "Paradise Ladies" demonstrates the fruitfulness of this tack as it doubles back (1991). Entrenched assumptions about what counts as a household and, in particular, about the location of women within households (literally and figuratively), prove empirically unsustainable when historical records reveal, under cross-examination, that much of the time women were simply not where they should have been given standard hypotheti-

---

[10]I resist, however, Yentsch's insistence that Marxist analysis must be abandoned as androcentric because it fails to "see change as beginning with culture" (1991: 137). I see no reason to assume that recognition of the ideological, cultural factors she stresses must be incompatible with a materialist analysis of the processes by which women working in a domestic sphere were systematically dispossessed of control over productive activities that produced cash income.

cal answers that reflect contemporary conceptions of household structure and gender roles.

CONCLUSIONS

What emerges from this dialectic of questioning is, ideally, a "jeweller's eye view" of large-scale causal processes specific to capitalism as they operate in particular contexts, events, and material conditions of life. Methodological strategies for exploiting independence between lines of evidence will serve the historical archaeology of capitalism only insofar as all are constructed as evidence relevant to questions about the nature of these processes. The insight central to Binford's early programmatic arguments still holds, if not with quite the implications he intended: the main limitation on what we can understand of capitalism archaeologically lies in the conceptual tools we bring to the task (1962). These tools are, first, background knowledge and linking assumptions (the components of MRT) that allow the interpretation of data as evidence relevant to questions about capitalism and, second, abstract, experience-distant, concepts that delineate the fundamental structures, mechanisms, and processes of capitalist systems that may (or may not) be instantiated in particular concrete instances. Given the vagaries of thoroughly constructive interpretive practice, however, any account of how capitalism operated in a given context will be established, not as a final conclusion, but as a tenuous point of "reflective equilibrium" (Rawls 1971, Daniels 1979) between the explanatory concepts that characterize the underlying, large-scale processes of capitalist systems, and the concrete particulars in that they are instantiated. These tentative answers are always open to re-equilibration as the framing assumptions that link explanatory concepts to concrete particulars are refined and new lines of evidence are elaborated that draw on quite different sources. The process of inquiry on this model is, then, dynamic and open-ended on many dimensions, but is not radically indeterminate.

REFERENCES

Ascher, R.
    1974   Tin*Can Archaeology, *Historical Archaeology*. 7.1:7–16.
Beaudry, M. C.
    1993   Public Aesthetics versus Personal Experience: Worker Health and Well-Being in
           19th-Century Lowell, Massachusetts. *Historical Archaeology* 27.3:90–105.

1996   Reinventing Historical Archaeology. In *Historical Archaeology and the Study of American Culture*, edited by L. A. De Cunzo and B. L. Herman, pp. 473–497. Winterthur Museum, Winterthur, Delaware, distributed by University of Tennessee Press, Knoxville.

Binford, L. R.
1962   Archaeology as Anthropology. *American Antiquity* 28:217–225.
1977   General Introduction. In *For Theory Building in Archaeology*, edited by L. R. Binford, pp. 1–13. Academic Press, New York.
1982   Objectivity—Explanation—Archaeology—1981. In *Theory and Explanation in Archaeology*, edited by C. Renfrew, M. J. Rowlands, and B. A. Segraves, pp. 125–138. Academic Press, New York.
1983   *Working at Archaeology*. Academic Press, New York.

Binford, L. R., and J. A. Sabloff
1982   Paradigms, Systematics, and Archaeology. *Journal of Anthropological Research* 38:137–153.

Caulfield, M. D.
1974   Imperialism, the Family, and Cultures of Resistance. *Socialist Revolution* 4.2:67–85.

Collingwood, R.G.
1939   *An Autobiography*. Oxford University Press, Oxford.
1946   *The Idea of History*. Oxford University Press, Oxford.

Daniels, Norman
1979   Wide Reflective Equilibrium and Theory Acceptance in Ethics. *Journal of Philosophy* 76:256–282.

Deagan, K.
1982   Avenues of Inquiry in Historical Archaeology. In *Advances in Archaeological Method and Theory*, Vol. 5, edited by M. B. Schiffer, pp. 151–177. Academic Press, New York.
1988   Neither History nor Prehistory: The Questions that Count in Historical Archaeology. *Historical Archaeology* 22.1:7–12.
1990   Accommodation and Resistance: The Process and Impact of Spanish Colonization in the Southeast. In *Columbian Consequences*, Vol. 2, edited by D. H. Thomas, pp. 297–314. Smithsonian Institution Press, Washington, D. C.

Engels, F.
1942   *The Origin of the Family, Private Property, and the State*. International Publishers, New York.

Fritz, J. M.
1972   Archaeological Systems for Indirect Observation of the Past. In *Contemporary Archaeology*, edited by M. P. Leone, pp. 135–157. Southern Illinois University Press, Carbondale.

Fuss, D.
1989   *Essentially Speaking: Feminism, Nature and Difference*. Routledge, New York.

Geertz, C.
1973   Thick Description: Toward and Interpretive Theory of Culture. In *The Interpretation of Cultures*, pp. 3–30. Basic Books, New York.
1979   From the Native's Point of View: On the Nature of Anthropological Understanding. In *Interpretive Social Science: A Reader*, edited by P. Rabinow and W. M. Sullivan, pp. 225–242. University of California Press, Berkeley.

Glassie, H.
1977   Archaeology and Folklore: Common Anxieties, Common Hopes. In *Historical*

Archaeology and the Importance of Material Things, edited by L. Ferguson. Special Publication Series No. 2:23–35, Society for Historical Archaeology.

Hacking, I.
1983   *Representing and Intervening*. Cambridge University Press, Cambridge.

Hall, M.
1984   The Burden of Tribalism: The Social Context of Southern African Iron Age Studies. *American Antiquity* 49.3:455–467.

Handsman, R. G.
1989   Native Americans and an Archaeology of Living Traditions. *Artifacts: The American Indian Archaeological Institute* 17.2:3–5.
1990   The Weantinock Indian Homeland Was Not a "Desert." *Artifacts: The American Indian Archaeological Institute* 18.2:3–7.

Handsman, R. G., and T. L. Richmond
1995   Confronting Colonialism: The Mahican and Schaghticoke Peoples and Us. In *Making Alternative Histories: The Practice of Archaeology and History in Non-Western Settings*, edited by P. R. Schmidt and T. C. Patterson, pp. 87–118. School of American Research, Santa Fe.

Hodder, I. (editor)
1982   *Symbolic and Structural Archaeology*. Cambridge University Press, Cambridge.
1987   *Archaeology as Long-Term History*. Cambridge University Press, Cambridge.

Hodder, I.
1986   *Reading the Past: Current Approaches to Interpretation in Archaeology*. Cambridge University Press, Cambridge.

Kosso, P.
1989   Science and Objectivity. *Journal of Philosophy* 86:245–257.
1992   Observation of the Past. *History and Theory* 31.1:21–36.

Lenin, V. I.
1975   *Imperialism, The Highest Stage of Capitalism*. Foreign Languages Press, Peking.

Leone, M. P.
1981   The Relationship Between Archaeology and the Public in Outdoor History Museums. *Annals of the New York Academy of the Sciences* 376:301–314.
1982   Some Opinions about Recovering Mind. *American Antiquity* 47:742–760.

Leone, M. P., and C. A. Crosby
1987   Epilogue: Middle-Range Theory in Historical Archaeology. In *Consumer Choice in Historical Archaeology*, edited by S. M. Spencer-Wood, pp. 397–410. Plenum Press, New York.

Leone, M. P., and P. B. Potter
1988   Issues in Historical Archaeology. In *The Recovery of Meaning*, edited by M. P. Leone and P. B. Potter, pp. 1–22. Smithsonian Institution, Washington, D.C.

Marx, K.
1970   A Critique of Political Economy (introduction). Reprinted in C. J. Arthur, *The German Ideology Part I*, International Publishing, New York.

Mills, C. W.
1959   *The Sociological Imagination*. Oxford University Press, Oxford.

Orser, C. E.
1988   Toward a Theory of Power for Historical Archaeology: Plantations and Space. In *The Recovery of Meaning*, edited by Mark P. Leone and Parker B. Potter, pp. 313–343. Smithsonian Institution, Washington, D.C.

Patrik, L. E.
1985   Is There an Archaeological Record? In *Advances in Archaeological Method and Theory, Volume 8*, edited by M. B. Schiffer, pp. 27–62. Academic Press, New York.

Potter, P. B.
1991   What is the Use of Plantation Archaeology? *Historical Archaeology* 25.3:94–107.
Purser, M.
1991   Several Paradise Ladies are Visiting in Town: Gender Strategies in the Early Industrial West. *Historical Archaeology* 25.4:6–16.
Rawls, J.
1971   *A Theory of Justice.* Harvard University Press, Cambridge.
Schuyler, R. L.
1978   Emergence and Definition of a New Discipline. In *Historical Archaeology: A Guide to Substantive and Theoretical Contributions,* edited by Robert L. Schuyler, pp. 1–2. Baywood, Farmingdale, New York.
Schmidt, P. R.
1995   Using Archaeology to Remake History in Africa. In *Making Alternative Histories: The Practice of Archaeology and History in Non-Western Settings,* edited by P. R. Schmidt and T. C. Patterson, pp. 119–148. School of American Research, Santa Fe.
Schmidt, P. R., and T. C. Patterson (editors)
1995   *Making Alternative Histories: The Practice of Archaeology and History in Non-Western Settings.* School of American Research, Santa Fe.
Seifert, D. J. (editor)
1991   *Gender in Historical Archaeology.* Special issue, *Historical Archaeology* 25.4.
Singleton, T. A. (editor)
1985   *The Archaeology of Slavery and Plantation Life.* Academic Press, New York.
Smith, B. H.
1991   Belief and Resistance: A Symmetrical Account. *Critical Inquiry* 18:125–139.
Thomas, D. H.
1991   Cubist Perspective on the Spanish Borderlands: Past, Present, and Future. In *Columbian Consequences: The Spanish Borderlands in Pan-American Perspective, Volume 3,* edited by David Hurst Thomas, pp. xiii–xix. Smithsonian Institution Press, Washington, D.C.
Trigger, B. G.
1980   Archaeology and the Image of the American Indian. *American Antiquity* 45: 662–676.
1989a   History and Contemporary American Archaeology: A Critical Analysis. In *Archaeological Thought in America,* edited by C.C. Lamberg-Karlovsky, pp. 19–34. University of Cambridge, Cambridge.
1989b   Hyperrelativism, Responsibility and the Social Sciences. *Canadian Review of Sociology and Anthropology* 26:776–797.
1991   Early Native North American Responses to European Contact: Romantic versus Rationalistic Interpretations. *Journal of American History* 4:1195–1215.
Vargas, I. A.
1995   The Perception of History and Archaeology in Latin America: A Theoretical Approach. In *Making Alternative Histories: The Practice of Archaeology and History in Non-Western Settings,* edited by P. R. Schmidt and T. C. Patterson, pp. 47–68. School of American Research, Santa Fe.
Wylie, A.
1989   Archaeological Cables and Tacking: The Implications of Practice for Bernstein's "Options Beyond Objectivism and Relativism." *Philosophy of the Social Sciences* 19: 1–18.
1992   Reasoning About Ourselves; Feminist Methodology in the Social Sciences. In *Women and Reason,* edited by Elizabeth Harvey and Kathleen Okruhlik, pp. 225–244. University of Michigan Press, Ann Arbor.

1993   Invented Lands/Discovered Pasts: The Westward Expansion of Myth and History. *Historical Archaeology* 27.4:1–19.

1996   The Constitution of Archaeological Evidence: Gender Politics and Science. In *The Disunity of Science: Boundaries, Contexts, and Power*, edited by Peter Galison and David J. Stump, pp. 311–343. Stanford University Press, Stanford.

Yentsch, A.

1991a   Engendering Visible and Invisible Ceramic Artifacts, Especially Dairy Vessels. In *Gender in Historical Archaeology*, edited by Donna Seifert, *Historical Archaeology* 25.4:132–155.

1991b   Access and Space, Symbolic and Material, in Historical Archaeology. In *The Archaeology of Gender*, Proceedings of the 1989 Chacmool Conference, edited by Dale Walde and Noreen D. Willows, pp. 252–262. The Archaeological Association of the University of Calgary, Calgary.

Historical Archaeology and Identity in Modern America

3

Parker B. Potter, Jr.

INTRODUCTION

This book is about the historical archaeology of capitalism. However, historical archaeologists don't dig up capitalism *per se*, and most Americans don't give much thought to capitalism *per se*. Archaeologists dig up broken dishes (and all sorts of other things), and modern Americans (including archaeologists) live all sorts of lives. Of course, a great deal of material culture can be interpreted as a commentary on the economic (and cultural) regime under which it is (or was) produced, just as many aspects of contemporary daily life can be interpreted as commentaries on the economies (and cultures) in which they take place. So, when one of Mark Leone's crew members in Annapolis digs up the fragments of a creamware plate and then uses those fragments as visual aids for a site tour given to a group of out-of-town visitors, what's really going on is the spectacle of capitalism coming face to face with itself.[1]

An increasing number of historical archaeologists, including many in this volume, have begun to describe what several different versions of capitalism—and resistance to capitalism—look like "in the ground." The aim of this chapter is to begin to describe what capitalism looks like in the mirror, to some of the people (myself included) who live so close to capitalism and so enveloped by it that we are barely aware of it. Once identified, these expressions of contemporary capitalism in the

[1] In this chapter I take as given the proposition that the practice of archaeology is, at all times, a public performance, whether or not any particular project has a formal program of public interpretation.

Parker B. Potter, Jr. • Sargent Museum of Archaeology, Concord, New Hampshire 03302.

Historical Archaeologies of Capitalism, edited by Mark P. Leone and Parker B. Potter, Jr. Plenum Press, New York, 1999.

lives of some modern Americans can be used as points of articulation between those lives and all the programs of site selection and artifact analysis we archaeologists are so busy designing in our attempts to learn more about early capitalism(s).

Because a substantial portion of this chapter is autobiographical, or self-reflective, I need to be very clear about what I can and cannot see in the mirror that I mentioned. I am a product of the middle class who has reproduced, with reasonable fidelity to the original, the middle-class life my parents led; while in Santa Fe attending the seminar on which this book is based, I phoned back to New Hampshire several times to check with Nancy Jo Chabot on the status of the offer we had made on the house we now own (in partnership with an obliging mortgage company). I am of the middle class. The expressions of capitalism to which I direct my archaeological work have been identified from a middle-class perspective. The audience for which I have created archaeological interpretations is largely middle class. That history cannot be changed, and I cannot write myself into the more recent history of "Archaeology in Annapolis," which includes Mark Leone's redirection of the project away from an audience composed of white, middle-class, adult tourists and toward an audience composed of African-American residents of several economic classes and various age groups. What, then, should I—and you—do about the middle-class perspective that permeates my work?

We could dismiss me on the basis of the long-held and well-substantiated position that the middle class has not been, and will not be, a force for revolutionary social change. Or, we could hear me out, on the basis of the observation that not all revolutionary change springs from revolutionary intentions. This position is a variant Romer's rule, which states that in any evolutionary process, biological or cultural, "an innovation that evolves to maintain an existing system can play a major role in changing that system" (Kottak 1994: 289). In vertebrate evolution, according to Romer, land-dwelling vertebrates evolved from fish as "fins gradually evolved into legs, not to permit vertebrates to live full-time on the land but to enable them to get back to the water when particular pools dried up" (Kottak 1994: 289). Amphibians "happened" as a result of evolution helping fish to be nothing more than more effective fish. If we accept the idea that the middle class cannot be radicalized, we must also acknowledge the failure, on the world stage, of any number of revolutionary movements that have originated in precisely the economic classes that are supposed to be the "proper" breeding grounds for revolution. That said, there may indeed be value in working from and toward a middle-class perspective, not to turn the middle class into something it isn't, but to push the middle class to the limits of its paradigm. It may be that by "perfecting" itself through consciousness, the middle class will become something else entirely. On that basis, a principal goal of my historical archaeological work has been, and will continue to be, to provoke better-informed, more thoughtful discussions among middle-class Americans about important social and economic issues, issues that might not have been given a second thought if not for my provocation.

Returning to the main thread of this introduction, the historical archaeology of capitalism, especially as this research project is presented to the public, can't just be about capitalism. Nobody experiences capitalism, but virtually all Americans experience a host of phenomena that are products of capitalism. These expressions of capitalism in American daily lives include, but are certainly not limited to, worries about job security, vacations, profit sharing, concerns about property values, union membership, and pleasure with, or dissatisfaction over, consumer goods. Furthermore, modern American lives are filled with categories such as work, leisure, family, money, home, gender, and dozens more that are determined, more or less strongly, by the character of particular participations in a capitalist economy and the culture that surrounds it. Any of these phenomena and categories may be used as the basis for a historical archaeology of capitalism, all of these things have histories that could be explored archaeologically and interpreted publicly.

My particular choice as a proximate target for a historical archaeology of capitalism is the issue of socially defined local identity, and I am taking it as a given that both individuals and social groups in modern America need identities and need to be able to participate in the process of identification. I have chosen to focus on identity because I have encountered this issue, in various shapes, over the course of 17 years of historical archaeological work in a variety of settings, from Virginia to Maryland to New Hampshire. Local identity problems I have encountered include: the suggestion, made by eastern Virginians, that western Virginia has no history; a local "amnesia" that allows the town of Lexington, Virginia and Washington and Lee University to "forget" their common heritage in the midst of "town/gown" conflicts; the 300-year struggle of Annapolis, Maryland to derive identity from outsiders without giving up power or authority to them; and New Hampshire's curious and longstanding self-definition as a refutation of Massachusetts.[2] An important similarity among these four identity problems is that at the

---

[2]In the interest of full disclosure, I should indicate that my explorations of these three issues have been conducted from three specific standpoints: 1) as a student, employee, and alumnus of Washington and Lee University, 2) as a long-term visitor to Annapolis, and 3) as a citizen of New Hampshire employed by the state government.

center of each is the dual process by which an individual makes or recognizes a connection with a particular geographic locale and then identifies with other individuals deemed to have similar and similarly strong connections to the same place. At least in my experience, as both a person and a scholar, group identity based on personal/individual ties to a place seems to be an important organizing force in modern American social and political life. And while this may or may not represent a displacement of class relations as a focus for both individual and group identity, to the obvious benefit of the ruling class, an important part of my project is to (re)establish the ties between issues such as local identity and the capitalist economies in which these issues have been played out. Finally, in each of the situations noted above, I have found four common elements: 1) problems associated with identity near the center of local discourse and dispute; 2) an ideological aspect to these disputes; 3) a relatively direct connection to one or more elements of modern capitalism; and 4) archaeological remains that could be used as an initial topic of discussion, leading to a better informed and less ideologically charged local dialogue about identity.

This chapter ends with two case studies in the historical archaeology of identity, each outlined in terms of the issues raised in the preceding paragraph. But before turning to these case studies, I discuss in more detail the general problem of identity in modern American life, and I do so in two ways. First, I place my own life under a microscope as a way of introducing several important aspects of the study of identity in a modern capitalist society. After that, I propose three possible historical archaeologies of identity, based on the work of Stanley Aronowitz, Dean MacCannell, and Daniel Miller. However, each of these possible historical archaeologies is ultimately generic, and this flies in the face of one of the more important contributions of critical archaeology—the rehabilitation of the local and the particular as valid objects of archaeological research and concern (Potter 1994: 27–28). Thus, I conclude this chapter with the two case studies mentioned above.

AUGUST, 1993

During the week in which I was most intensely occupied with the initial writing of this essay, I spent many of my after hours engaged in a variety of activities that seemed to make the life I was leading into an illustration of various key points made in several books I had turned to for assistance in writing about the establishment of identity as a topic for historical archaeological research and interpretation. Rather than ignoring these parallels, I chose to incorporate them into this text, mainly as an explanatory aid for readers, but also because I was intrigued with the idea of seeing/making a connection between my work life (including this essay) and the rest of my life. Without ever intending to put myself in any of these books, I found myself in *The Tourist*, and *Empty Meeting Grounds* (MacCannell 1976; 1992), *The Politics of Identity* (Aronowitz 1992), and *Material Culture and Mass Consumption* (Miller 1987). I will explain how.

At either end of the week, I spent three afternoons at Sand Bank Farm in Contoocook, New Hampshire, helping John Rowell milk his herd of Ayrshire dairy cattle, which includes two cows that Nancy Jo and I own. We bought these cows (as heifers) and brought them to Sand Bank Farm in part as a very small-scale project in landscape preservation, reasoning that high-producing cows would do better than low-producing cows at keeping pasture land open and the condominiums at bay. Since we added our cows to the herd, I have helped with the milking and barn chores nearly every Saturday, and during June and July I spend up to 10 hours a week helping bring in the hay crop. But while I take a certain pride in the quality of my commitment to New Hampshire dairy farming, my point here is not to demonstrate how good farmer I am; *why* I do these things is much more important than what, precisely, I do on the farm.

Throughout that same August week, I made five visits to the annual Craftsmen's Fair sponsored by the League of New Hampshire Craftsmen. At the fair I bought three carved wooden spoons, two etchings, and a silk screen print; I introduced one printmaker in search of a press to several others who I hoped could help her out; I started organizing a joint educational and promotional project involving many of the several dozen printmakers who belong to the League of New Hampshire Craftsmen; I helped staff the sales booths of several friends who are printmakers; and I observed the distribution of a newly published booklet I had written on the work of printmaker Matthew Smith (Potter 1993a).

All of these activities, it could be argued, represent more than recreation, shopping, or socializing. Rather, I have come to understand them as parts of a distinctly post-modern search for identity that is perhaps best understood as *bricolage* (Tilley 1990: 26–29), a patching together of after-hours activities and roles in an attempt to create what the workplace no longer does, a sense of craft and a place in society (see Aronowitz 1991: 10–75).

Down on the Farm

In milking the cows, I may be Dean MacCannell's tourist, spending the hours away from my bureaucratic desk job seeking to at least glimpse the authenticity inherent in non-alienated work, authenticity that is generally missing from the working lives of proletarian wage laborers, operatives in service industries, and agents of the state. And while my situation on the farm is clearly out of the ordinary, what drives me to go to the farm is not. My hunch that I am MacCannell's tourist is borne out by the existence of several New Hampshire "bed and breakfast farms," where the chance to help with the chores is a part of what visitors pay for and get along with their breakfast and bed.

My joint ownership of two cows, purchased at cattle auctions where I outbid a barnful of "real" dairy farmers, allows me special parking privileges at the Hopkinton State Fair, and, more importantly, the opportunity to parade my animals around the show ring while wearing the official uniform of a dairy exhibitor. As strange as it may sound, I treasure the ribbons our cows have won, and all year long I count the months until the next Hopkinton Fair. When I get to the fairgrounds, I get to go backstage, and I get to be on stage. I am not restricted to the audience. At the very least, my purchases of Cotrell's Everett Margo and Ardrossan MRE Miss Jackie are instances of "possessive individualism" (Macpherson 1962), a social and psychological process by which "the individual comes to be defined by the things he possesses" (Handler 1988: 153). Seen in this light, my cattle holdings could be interpreted as a MacCannellesque search for authenticity dramatically extended through several episodes of elaborate role-playing.

However, Daniel Miller (following Wilson 1985), rejects the seemingly essentialist underpinning of possessive individualism (Miller 1987: 174–175) and would probably see my cattle ownership as an example of "creative recontextualization," which is defined as a positive, active aspect of consumption, "a long and complex process by which the consumer works upon the object purchased and recontextualizes [or reappropriates] it, until it is often no longer recognizable ..." (Miller 1987: 190). While this term is typically used to describe the social redefinition of material culture that is mass produced by alienated labor, it seems to apply fairly well to me and my cows. Viewed from the standpoint of creative recontextualization, I am not a desk-jockey playing farmer, but rather, Margo and Miss Jackie play an important role in my otherwise non-agricultural life. While possessive individualism sees me as defined by my cows, creative recontextualization sees my cows as redefined by my ownership of them. As Miller says, "[t]he object is transformed by its intimate association with a particular individual or social group, or with the relationship between these" (Miller 1987: 191). In either case, however, the process taking place is one of identity-building; at some level, perhaps a very superficial one, my farm "work" ties me to the place where I live and to other people who are tied to this place in the same basic way.

Out at the Craftsmen's Fair

My most direct link to the exhibitors at the 1993 Craftsmen's Fair is the money I gave to Dan Dustin in exchange for three hand-carved spoons, to Mary Margaret Sweeney and Judith Ann Eldridge for hand-pulled, limited-edition etchings, and to William Mitchell for a hand-made, limited-edition silk screen print. As best I can tell, these transactions represent neither possessive individualism nor creative recontextualization. But if my purchases at the craftsmen's fair are different from the successful bidding that won me Margo and Miss Jackie, they are very different from what I do in the shoe store at the local mall.

What Americans do in malls, "the proliferation within our own country of consumerism" (Aronowitz 1992: 242), is a result of an economic system in which "most people are left defenseless by free time, thrown to the twins of buying and eating" (Aronowitz 1992: 249) or are "caught in the vise of consumption and overtime, as in the case of autoworkers" (Aronowitz 1992: 71). The name of this vise (vice?) is Fordism, defined as "the managerial strategy of simultaneously chaining labor to a series of externally determined repetitive tasks and providing workers with the means to sustain the circulation of the products they make" (Aronowitz 1992: 238). MacCannell (1992: 67) characterizes this situation even more darkly:

> It is characteristic of cannibal solidarity that is based on mutual complicity, on getting everyone involved in the economy of guilt.... Consumers in capitalist societies know that they do not need what they buy, but they also know that the entire system on which their, and their brother's, livelihood depends requires that they continue to consume what they do not need.[3]

Since moving to New Hampshire in 1987, I have learned to take great pleasure from putting money into the same pair of hands that had recently made the object I was buying, seeing this act as a way of sidestepping the treadmill identified by both Aronowitz and MacCannell. However, this pleasure was somewhat tempered by my discovery of the following passage, midway through the Craftsmen's Fair:

> Through the emergence of the arts and crafts movement, Morris succeeded in establishing a craft tradition in which the individual could retain some

[3]Miller, in contrast to both Aronowitz and MacCannell, rejects this rather strict reading of Marx (Miller 1987: 144) and follows Abercrombie et al. in rejecting the dominant ideology thesis.

control over every stage of manufacture from design to execution, and
thereby gain a far more satisfactory relationship with the product. Unfortunately, because this tradition tended to ignore the problem of consumption,
the main impact of this craft revival was to promote a conspicuous handmade
image, explicitly separate from the products of mass consumption, and
immediately recognized as a quality or luxury product which signified, and
thereby helped reproduce, the new moneyed elites. The impact of Morris's
ideas as channelled through the sphere of consumption, provided an effective means for the further development of precisely those class differences
which in turn helped reproduce the conditions for the exploitation of labour.
(Miller 1987: 140)

So, at the moment I am somewhat unclear about the status I have
achieved as a result of my purchases from New Hampshire's local
crafters; I am either a patron of the arts or, following Miller, an unwit-
ting bourgeois tool of capitalist interests (Miller 1987: 167). For now, the
best I can do is wonder about my place in the following two sentences:

For all the verbal attacks on modern goods, the more effective critique of
practiced asceticism is rarely encountered; that is to say, the private practices of many academic critics, amongst whom there are very few Gandhis
and Tolstoys, may well contradict the substance of their argument. As
anthropologists who have examined consumption have confirmed, it is impossible to isolate a range of "authentic" goods serving "real" needs. (Miller
1987: 188)

In addition to my problematic, though pleasurable, role as a buyer at
the 1993 Craftsmen's Fair, I played several others.[4] By introducing
Martha Scott, the printmaker without a press, to fellow printmakers
Christopher and Denise Morse, Matthew Smith, and Judith Ann Eldridge, and by trying to organize an exhibition containing the work of
these five printmakers and a dozen others, I was acting as some kind of
"impresario," gaining a measure of identity through my association with
this group of artists. Miller's (1987: 212) perspective on this type of
activity is fairly clear:

extensive quotation from oral history often complements the ethnography
in showing the satisfaction gained from controlling one particular domain of
self-productive activity.... because social groups work best as a kind of
practical kitsch, amalgamating and juxtaposing a wide range of activities

[4]Of course, no discussion of the dark side of consumption would be complete without a
mention of fetishism, of which Miller says, "[t]he narrower and more reasonable definition of fetishism ... [applies when it can be] said that goods are used vicariously.... [when]
instead of engaging in social interaction, people become obsessively concerned with their
individual relation to material goods.... While some goods such as private art collections
or guns may indeed favor antisocial orientations, others such as the telephone and bus do
not" (Miller 1987: 204).

otherwise separated as work and leisure spheres. There are diverse areas which can be selected for emphasis by this kind of productive consumption, often conceived of as small domains or ponds in which one can feel oneself to be a significant fish.

Both my patronage of local crafters and my organizational work with them count as attempts to establish organic solidarity in the Durkheimian sense; I have offered to do what I can do to help them do what they do.

Even more powerful, personally, are efforts that seem, in retrospect, to have been pointed toward the establishment of mechanical solidarity, or true identity in the sense of "oneness" or mathematical equivalence, as in the statement "a = a," which is the mathematical definition of identity. I helped sell etchings with Chris and Denise Morse, wrote up sales slips for Matthew Smith, and even managed to cut myself with an X-acto knife while helping Matthew take down his booth. In one very small way, I was them—or was interchangeable with them—for a couple of hours; I was doing what the artists were doing. My appreciation for the "backstage" parts of the Craftsmen's Fair clearly makes me one of MacCannell's tourists.

Beyond that, however, I had a product on display at the 1993 Craftsmen's Fair: a promotional booklet I had written called *An Introduction to the Work of Matthew Smith*. Thus, in the midst of 160 artists and crafters set up in booths containing their finest work, I, too, could legitimately see myself as a producer, as someone who belonged. I think I only recognized after the fact, in the context of writing this chapter, the mild overdetermination that fueled my desire to spend so much time at the fair. I made sure to give copies of "my" booklet to Matthew's craftmaking colleagues, and almost craved their positive reviews. This little bit of self-promotion undoubtedly represents my own reaction to what Aronowitz (1992: 249) calls "the crisis of leisure—the effort of people to regain their sense of craft, and liberate themselves from their complete dependence on the wage relation for personal and social meaning."

Not only was I able to see myself as a producer while at the Craftsmen's Fair, I enjoyed participating in its "underground" economy. Matthew Smith, who has become a good friend, paid me for my writing with a combination of prints and things he got from other crafters in trade for his prints. Furthermore, I suspect that we were both rather relieved that I kept such poor records of my writing time that we had to abandon our initial agreement, which translated writing into hours, hours into dollars, and dollars into prints. Instead, I'll get what I get. Matthew and I are both confident that what I'll get is what I should get. This is clearly not the economy of the shopping mall.

And Back Again, to the Real World

Up to this point, I have outlined three different ways of relating to the authenticity I think I find at the farm and the Craftsmen's Fair. As MacCannell's tourist, it is enough simply for me to see a true craftsperson, a worker who actually makes something and who appears to be far less alienated from the products of his or her work than I seem to be from the non-products of my post-industrial worklife. In addition, I have attempted to find roles for myself in these worlds of craft. And finally, I have tried to assume the central role in these worlds, the role of producer. I have done everything from going to *see* the potter to trying to *be* the potter, even if trying to be the potter is little more than a nostalgia-driven bourgeois placebo for alienation, as Aronowitz and Miller would probably suggest.

I have devoted a third of this chapter to describing my after-hours farming and crafting because *I am not unique.* A particular combination of time, money, and access, what Alison Wylie has called privilege, has given me the chance to act upon my need to experience authenticity, to regain a sense of craft, and to build an identity. Furthermore, I am admittedly quite fortunate to have a job that allows me to read about and write about my life, to turn life into work, and to turn work into an opportunity to reflect on my own life. From drafting this essay I did, indeed, gain what I take to be useful insights into why I allow virtually nothing to interfere with my Saturday afternoons at the barn.

However, my reading of Aronowitz, MacCannell, and Miller assures me that the needs I satisfy with cows and crafts are common, if not universal, in modern capitalist societies. On that reading, I am not prepared to concede that the identity problems to which I direct my historical archaeological work belong exclusively to the middle class, but even if they do, they still deserve attention, as I have already argued. Furthermore, I am not so naive as to suggest that I have somehow gotten clear of capitalism by milking a few cows or buying a few prints. I have crafted my own provisional, middle-class solution to the problem of identity in contemporary America. By describing what I want from the farm and from the Craftsmen's Fair, I mean to describe two other things: what I, as a contemporary American, want out of historical archaeology, and, more importantly, what I think many of my fellow citizens want—or need—from historical archaeology. What we all need, I believe, is information and interpretation that helps us to understand how our lives have come to be the way they are, that allows (and encourages) us to decide whether this is good or bad, and that helps us figure out how to live our way into the future on our own terms and in our own best interests. The underlying purpose of my work in historical archaeology is to use archaeological artifacts, sites, and research questions to open up spaces for public discussions that take quite a bit less for granted than the ideologically driven, cliche-ridden, ad hominem diatribes that far too often pass for legitimate dialogues in the popular media. In the context of the work reported in this essay, my goal is to help people think more deeply about how they establish local identity, and the consequences of whatever strategies they adopt for dealing with this issue.

THREE GUIDES

In the following section I deal somewhat more conventionally with the work of three scholars to whom I turned for guidance as I set out to conceptualize the historical archaeology of identity. In addition to characterizing the principal ideas of Aronowitz, MacCannell, and Miller, I briefly outline the particular historical archaeologies of identity that could be built on the foundations laid by their scholarship.

Aronowitz: The Archaeology of Work, Labor, and Service

In his recent collection of essays, *The Politics of Identity*, former steelworker and union activist Stanley Aronowitz directly addresses the dismal prospects for establishing meaningful personal and social identities in post-industrial America. He identifies a modern American identity crisis rooted in:

> the declining proportion of Americans producing, transporting, and handling capital and consumer goods and, perhaps more importantly, the dispersal of production sites from cities and large towns dominated by factories to small communities and rural areas [many of them "offshore"] where industrial workers are isolated. (Aronowitz 1992: 51)

This trend is mirrored by declining membership in traditional trade unions and the declining influence of labor as a voting bloc. Furthermore, Aronowitz identifies a number of issues, such as home ownership, suburbia, consumerism, education, and even the representation of labor in popular culture, that are both causes and effects of the dissolution of working-class identity. The allure of home ownership and consumer goods, two "carrots" that inspire the ever accelerating cycle of Fordism, is explained in large measure by the shifts from work (as in craftwork) to labor and from labor to "service jobs ... centered in activities whose social use is open to serious question and ... [which are] largely a form of disguised unemployment" (Aronowitz 1992: 248). Satisfaction and identity, once found in making things, then found in solidarity with others engaged in wage labor, must now be squeezed out of consumption, ownership, tourism, and other supposed leisure activities that are the realms in which most Americans do whatever "work" they do, given Aronowitz's (1992: 249) definition of work as "that human activity which expresses creative achievement and corresponds, therefore, to part of desire, our will to objectivate ourselves individually and collectively by creating objects or social relations." If a craft worker identifies with his or her products, and if an assembly line worker identifies with his or her fellow workers on the shop floor (or, as Chuck Orser suggested in Santa Fe, in the bar next door after work), what about the telephone solicitor who interrupted your dinner last week, trying to sell you vinyl siding? Just what is there for "Mary, the *Time–Life* Operator" to identify with?

As for solutions to America's post-industrial identity problem, Aronowitz is certain that there can be no return to "the era of workers' power" (Aronowitz 1992: 12) and that "the old notion of the social which, after all, depended on an intimate tie between work and morality, can[not] be saved" Aronowitz (1992: 247). This is because "the claim that labor as a form of life should be central to human existence no longer corresponds to the actual development of the productive forces" (Aronowitz 1992: 250). As I was writing the first draft of this chapter, the *Boston Globe* reported that Digital Equipment is building a new $425 million microchip-manufacturing facility that will require the hiring of no additional workers; the 300 people who staff Digital's existing semiconductor plant will be able to run both "factories" (Stein 1993: 77). Rather than a return to the past, Aronowitz (1992: 72) suggests that:

> In the United States, where socialism, anarchism, and laborism have suffered marginal existences for most of this century, we are afflicted with a serious case of social amnesia, the only treatment for which is the emergence of a new radicalism at once sophisticated and militant.

As for the first project of this new radicalism, "the task remains for labor to abolish itself" (Aronowitz 1992: 252), and in its place Aronowitz proposes a new social contract under which income is both guaranteed and disconnected from work.[5]

---

[5]Miller agrees with Aronowitz that we cannot return to the past. He says, "There is little reason to think that a return to craft production on a large scale would produce more than a radical restriction of the availability of goods to elite sections of society" (Miller 1987: 185).

This is, as Aronowitz acknowledges, a radical program. However, the analysis upon which this program rests, the double shift from work to labor and from labor to service (a shift that has left many displaced blue-collar workers alienated from alienation and longing for the good-old-days of ample work, strong unions, and workers' solidarity) is an ideal and important topic for public interpretation based on historical archaeological research and findings. The material record of capitalism (a.k.a., the stuff historical archaeologists dig up) is replete with arti-factual markers of work, labor, and service (see, for example Paynter 1988). Every artifact we recover was subject to one or more of these processes. When rescued from the disciplines of art history and the history of technology (see Miller 1987: 111 on this point), this artifactual evidence can play an important role in helping people to understand the transformations of work into labor and labor into service. Then, per-haps, they may be moved to "audit" their own lives, searching for their work and finding it, perhaps, hidden in the middle of a weekend, that two-day chunk of time that has been misidentified for so long as time off.

MacCannell: The Archaeology of Cannibalism

"Time off" is, of course, a perfect lead-in to Dean MacCannell, author of *The Tourist* (1976) and *Empty Meeting Grounds: The Tourism Papers* (1992). While the essays collected in *Empty Meeting Grounds* are somewhat more entertaining than those in *The Politics of Identity*, MacCannell and Aronowitz agree on the seriousness of the conditions of postindustrial, postmodern life, and both share an activist stance. Says MacCannell (1992: 8–9) in the introduction to *Empty Meeting Grounds*:

> When a subject is manipulated into acting against its own self-interest, it can pretend, even to itself, that it is "disinterested" and "neutral," when in reality it is only neutralized.... This kind of cultural frame-up, that results in people and groups volunteering to be exploited, appears to be replacing visibly vicious forms ... [and] reflects the strength of social engineering: powerful new techniques for the manipulation of symbols ... An aim of *Empty Meeting Grounds* is to expose this engineering to close examination as a first step toward taking it down.

The principal difference between MacCannell and Aronowitz is that while Aronowitz is content to survey western societies, MacCannell's examination is global.

In his leadoff essay, "Cannibalism Today," MacCannell provides the inspiration for an image I used in my introduction, the image of capitalism coming face to face with itself. MacCannell describes many encounters between capitalism and itself, but rather than taking place in downtown America, MacCannell's encounters occur in places like

New Guinea. Furthermore, the meetings between tourists and Sepik River natives that MacCannell chronicles aren't just about capitalism coming face to face with itself, they are also about cannibalism coming face to face with itself. The point of the title "Cannibalism Today" is to highlight MacCannell's belief that capitalism is, for all intents and purposes, cannibalistic.

The central conceit in "Cannibalism Today" is that "there is no *real* difference between moderns and those who act the parts of primitives in the universal drama of modernity" (MacCannell 1992: 34), that tourist encounters in the so-called backcountry are "a collaborative construction of postmodernity by tourists and ex-primitives who represent not absolute differences but mere differentiations of an evolving new cultural subject" (MacCannell 1992: 35), and that "the encounter between tourist and other[6] is the scene of a shared Utopian vision of profit without exploitation, logically the final goal of a kind of cannibal economics shared by ex-primitives and postmoderns alike" (MacCannell 1992: 28). Postmodern tourists may think they head into the bush in order to view preindustrial lives that are very different from their own. The savage they think they see may be either Rousseau's noble savage or some sort of human nightmare from the lower rungs of savagery–barbarism-civilization. But in either case, and especially the later, the savage that tourists do see, MacCannell would argue, embodies much more similarity than difference.

Cannibalism is by no means dead, and it is far livelier on Wall Street than it ever was in the Highlands of New Guinea. Says MacCannell (1992: 66):

> Cannibalism in the political–economic register is the production of social totalities by the literal incorporation of otherness. It deals with human difference in the most direct way, not merely by doing away with it, but by taking it in completely, metabolizing it, transforming it into shit, and eliminating it.

In light of MacCannell's assertion that "Eurocentric culture is based on a denial of its own violent, homoerotic, and cannibalistic impulses" (MacCannell 1992: 36) and his sense that "cannibalism today is a total

---

[6]Toward the end of "Cannibalism Today," MacCannell offers an important critique of this term, "it would be best not to continue to use the term 'the other'.... The use of the term 'other' (small o) promotes the self, ego, the first person singular, by pretending to do the opposite; that is, by bringing up 'the other.' The unmarked, undifferentiated 'other' is nothing other than the self-interested expression of ego masked with sociability: the 'discourse of the other' is the way a cannibal ego manufactures an aura of involvement with the world outside itself while neutralizing it" (MacCannell 1992: 66).

phenomenon; that there is no publicly recognized alternative to the 'inevitable incorporation'" (MacCannell 1992: 68), he finds very little irony in the fact that in a recently reported experiment in gene grafting, a human gene was grafted onto a chromosome of domestic cattle. Reports MacCannell (1992: 68) in the conclusion of his essay:

> If everything goes according to the quoted scenarios of the bio-technologists, agricultural economists, and international food-marketing companies, "billions" of humans will be served human genetic material in their Big Macs. Again, it is the normalizing tone of the news account, the strong sense that there is nothing unusual here, which is symptomatic of the pervasive cannibal unconscious.

In "Cannibalism Today" MacCannell has written what Foucault would recognize as an archaeology of cannibalism.

The task that falls to me in the remainder of this section is to propose a historical archaeology of cannibalism that would be recognized as an archaeological project by archaeologists. As is the case with the double transformation involving work, labor, and service, cannibalism, defined as an almost blind, unquenchable appetite for incorporation, can be read relatively easily from the historical archaeological record. There is, for example, the European appropriation of china from China, as evidenced both by the China trade and by the vigorous attempts to establish European china industries, attempts whose earthenware by-products—especially Josiah Wedgwood's creamware—transformed the dinner tables of the world and the worklives of thousands of Staffordshire pottery workers (McKendrick 1982). The analysis of historical archaeological sites in terms of the histories and patterns of their ownership seems also to be an important avenue for undertaking, and then putting on display, a historical archaeology of cannibalism. Such a historical archaeology would pay attention to who was chewing on whom, and what was getting gobbled up in the dog-eat-dog world of nineteenth-century business and industry. The incorporation of small railroad lines into larger ones, small oil companies into larger ones, small water rights into larger ones, and so many of the great success stories in American business history are undisguised tales of cannibalism; the teeth marks are still to be found on the deeds, census schedules, tax records, and other documents that illustrate patterns of ownership. The "dirt" side of this concern with patterns of ownership is a search for physical markers, both structural and artifactual, that document the process of a big corporate dog chewing and swallowing a smaller one.

Finally, there is a topic that unites the concerns of MacCannell

and Aronowitz, a topic that may be used as a basis for historical archaeological inquiry and for public interpretation. In his discussion of the
restoration of the Statue of Liberty, MacCannell (1992: 147–157) observes that Miss Liberty is a European made to welcome other Europeans in an age when America needed human fodder for its frontiers
and factories (Thompson 1992). Thus, she has relatively little to say
to today's Asian and Latin American immigrants who are washing
ashore on a post-industrial continent that feels pretty full to many of
those already here. (Who could be more desperate than an immigrant
with few skills in a society that no longer needs labor?) During the by-
gone age represented by the Statue of Liberty, America was "a kind of
do-it-yourself, make-over European culture" (MacCannell 1992: 154),
importing the ideas of capitalism (among others), along with an expanding source of labor that was also an expanding market. Furthermore,
until Frederick Jackson Turner closed the frontier in 1892, America had
something to ante up, a wide variety of natural resources just waiting to
be conceptualized as potential value and transformed into commodities
by immigrants who were once counted as "income" but are now seen as
"expense." When Aronowitz points out the weakness of working-class
identity in America in relation to the strength of working-class identity
in Europe, what he may be seeing is the result of identity building in two
very different contexts, one seen as a banquet table of nearly limitless
possibilities, the other something closer to a zero-sum game. Given the
history of American political and economic expansionism (embodied by
concepts such as "manifest destiny"[7]), it is not surprising that it was the
Nixon administration (rather than the first Roosevelt administration)
that "began to recognize that unemployment was no longer cyclical but
had become a structural feature of the economy which could not be
eradicated even by high growth rates" (Aronowitz 1992: 247). Nor is it a
surprise that even in the 1990s, the mantra of "growth, growth, growth"
is intoned by both major parties.[8] The foregoing analysis strongly suggests that contemporary Americans could really use a historical archaeology of expansionism, one that restores contingency to a process that
people take as an article of faith, a faith that is, in turn, used to vilify
other people who are seen as standing in the way of progress.

[7]In *The Cultivation of Hatred* (1993), Peter Gay links manifest destiny to Darwinian
evolution and nationalism, seeing in the late nineteenth-century social application of
each of these ideas a peculiar Victorian genius for moralized aggression and restraint,
which ultimately led, in Gay's eyes, to the carnage of World War I.

[8]Miller, too, speaks of the hollow promise of economic growth as a social cure-all when he
suggests that "With growing ecological constraints future expansion will come increasingly from scientific innovation rather than new physical resources" (Miller 1987: 185).

Miller: The Archaeology of Consumption

Interestingly, Aronowitz, MacCannell, and Miller all agree that work (not necessarily craft or labor) is essential to the establishment of meaningful personal and social identity, and Aronowitz clearly agrees with Miller that "progress cannot be through recapturing something simpler and past, but only through a new mastering of the enormity of the present" (Miller 1987: 192). The principal distinction between Aronowitz and MacCannell, on the one side, and Miller, on the other, is that Aronowitz is concerned by "the change from the ideology of redemption through labor to the redemptive character of the individual possession of non-productive things" (Aronowitz 1992: 241), whereas Miller strongly believes that there is important work to be done (in Aronowitz's sense of the term "work") through the consumption of even the most trivial mass-produced schlock (Miller 1987: 190–192). According to Miller, "[t]he workplace is not, and, indeed, never has been the only site for self-production through work" (Miller 1987: 210).

The process that characterizes consumption-as-work is creative recontextualization, a term I have already defined. Because "goods which are identical at the point of purchase or allocation may be recontextualized by social groups in an infinite number of ways" (Miller 1987: 196), Miller sees consumption as active and sees identity as one of its chief by-products. "Mass goods ... are an integral part of that process of objectification by which we create ourselves as an industrial society: our identities, our social affiliations, our lived everyday practices.... they [mass goods] are directly constitutive of our understanding of ourselves and others" (Miller 1987: 215).

Furthermore, Miller is as much an activist as either Aronowitz or MacCannell:

> the scale of production must make it unlikely that this could ever become again the main arena through which people can identify with self-constructed culture. In turn, the possibility for consumption emerges once goods ... are understood as a major constituent of modern culture. From this, it will be shown that, ironically, it is only through the creative use of the industrial product that we can envisage a supersession of any autonomous interest called capitalism, and that only through the transformation of the state's services can the state also be reabsorbed as an instrument of development. In short, consumption is a major factor in the potential return of culture to human values (Miller 1987: 192).

Miller's (1987: 15) call to arms is a call to reverse the neglect "that consumption has suffered ... in our assessment of history" and to "pay far more attention to the qualities and consequences of ... material culture" (Miller 1987: 217). His avowedly hopeful goal is to achieve "a critical understanding of society ... [that is] founded upon an image based less upon what industrial culture has forced us to become than upon what it might allow us to be" (Miller 1992:18).

While Miller makes a persuasive case for the study of consumption, his book is not bursting with well-developed case studies. Even so, it is not difficult to begin outlining the historical archaeology of consumption. Miller's key move is his rejection of the essentialist idea that the full measure of an object's meaning has been inscribed upon it by the processes of production, and that consumers are simply passive receptors of these inscribed meanings (see Potter 1992: 13–14 on this point). A historical archaeology of consumption, based on Miller, would entail two research strategies: identifying the physical evidences of creative recontextualization and exploring the social contexts of recontextualization. The physical evidence of recontextualization is at least two-fold and would include the postmanufacture modification of individual objects and, more importantly, the spatial dimension of the acquisition, use, and discard of material goods. The key unit of analysis would be the collection, constellation, or configuration of artifacts, and the key question would be "what was it with?" rather than "what is it?" Knowing that eighteenth-century Annapolis printer Jonas Green had some creamware wouldn't be meaningful data, from the standpoint of understanding recontextualization, without a consideration of the particular "ceramic context," "tableware context," "dining-room context," or other context into which Green brought the creamware that he bought. Recontextualization, in turn, can serve as the basis for comparison between sites, which leads directly to the research strategy of examining the social context of recontextualization, which is simply another name for the historical archaeology of identity. Some of the most powerful current work along these lines is being done by Leland Ferguson (1991, 1992) and others who are studying the capacity of enslaved African Americans to fashion a culture, despite the shackles of slavery.

TWO CASE STUDIES

In the first two-thirds of this essay I have attempted to establish the importance of identity as a generally unresolved issue in modern American life. In the preceding section, I briefly outline several generic historical archaeologies of identity. These archaeological programs deal with broad issues that seem to characterize postindustrial life anytime, anywhere. But people don't experience all of capitalism all at once; they experience specific local trends and events that are expressions of capitalism. Local historical archaeologies that address these trends and events are, therefore, simultaneously, commentaries on capitalism in a postindustrial world. That is, there are dozens of historical archaeologies of cannibalism that could, and should, be done across the United States, but in each case and for each audience, it will be necessary to find the face that cannibalism wears locally.

In the following section, I discuss the historical archaeology of identity in Annapolis, Maryland, and New Hampshire. In each example I identify a local identity problem; single out the ideological aspect(s) of that problem; connect the identity issue with its roots in a capitalist economy, society, and culture; and, finally, propose a starting point, based in material culture, for a local discourse that could, potentially, lead to a less ideological solution to the community's identity problem. The principal tie between the case studies in this section and the autobiographical material I presented at the beginning of this essay is that the local identities I have targeted with historical interpretations in both Annapolis and New Hampshire, in need of replacement because they are based on flawed premises, have arisen in the first place as collective responses to the same impulses that push me out to the farm each week and to the Craftsmen's Fair each year. Given that, it is important to note that my use of concepts such as "possessive individualism" and "creative recontextualization" is different from other uses of these terms elsewhere in this book; while I have an appropriate level of concern with what people in Annapolis or New Hampshire did 100, 200, and 300 years ago, I am, in this essay, substantially more concerned with what people are doing today. I have turned to Aronowitz, MacCannell, and Miller as guides to understanding the contemporary audiences for my historical archaeological interpretations, rather than as guides to understanding the historic subjects of those interpretations. I am not uninterested in identifying evidence for creative recontextualism from the eighteenth or nineteenth century, but I am much more interested in catching late-twentieth-century folks in the act of creatively recontextualizing me.

Annapolis: The Archaeology of Tourism

Even before the first trowel full of dirt was excavated by "Archaeology in Annapolis," Mark Leone knew what the archaeology was "about." Leone set out, explicitly, to do a historical archaeology of capitalism in an eighteenth-century city that had been a center for both commerce and government. His main tool for achieving this goal has been the suggestion that whatever else it is, Deetz's (1977) "Georgian order" is the order of merchant capitalism (Leone 1988).

Even with this theoretical position in place, it took several years of work in public for us to identify the specific faces of contemporary capitalism in Annapolis, that is, the local issues to which we needed to direct our archaeological findings. Our first real breakthrough was the tour we wrote for the 1986 field season at the Main Street site (Leone, Potter, and Shackel 1987), which was an archaeologically based tour about tourism, given to tourists. We decided to focus on tourism for several reasons. During the 1980s, the issue of tourism was in the news on an almost weekly basis, as the 32,000 citizens of Annapolis coped with controlling the potentially destructive behavior of more than 1 million visitors each year. As MacCannell and many others have clearly demonstrated, tourism is an important, if not defining, feature of modern, postindustrial capitalism. Tourism is a product of "leisure" time, which is itself a product of the removal of production from the home, the replacement of craft by labor, and the measurement (and valuation) of work by the clock (and management), rather than by the product (and the worker). Finally, tourism has a long history in Annapolis, and that history is intertwined with a local identity problem of even longer standing.

Annapolis' identity problem is that the city has been, almost since its birth in 1649, a "place without placeness." By this I mean that, Annapolis has never had a strong identity based on work in the form of "physical labor transforming the object" (Miller 1987: 191) resulting in "culture physically produced by the appropriation of nature" (Miller 1987: 193). Annapolis has never had a productive relationship with its environment strong enough to serve as a focus for identification. Given this lack of a "dialectic of labor, according to which the relations of humans with nature form the character of social relations" (Aronowitz 1992: 78), much of the history of Annapolis is a chronicle of one small city's struggle with precisely the kinds of identity problems now faced by Akron, Chicago, Detroit, and all the other deindustrialized rust belt "ghost towns that were once bustling communities" (Aronowitz 1992: 3), denatured cities "where we have witnessed a fracturing of traditional working-class identities." The only difference is that Annapolis has never had working-class identities.

To fill this "identity gap," but more explicitly to generate economic benefits, Annapolis has issued a series of invitations to a variety of outsiders, including state government (in the 1690s), the national government (in the 1780s), the fledgling United States Naval Academy (from the 1810s through the 1840s), business and industry (in the 1890s), and wealthy tourists (since the 1960s). While not all of these invitations have been accepted, most have been, and as a result, Annapolis has harvested money, identity, and a steady stream of disputes over local political authority. One solution to the problem of establishing and maintaining control over outsiders has been the development, largely unconsciously, of an ideologically charged history and historiography.

The centerpiece of the version of history that Annapolis uses to keep visitors at bay is a set of stories about George Washington's 20 or more visits to the city. In these stories, facts about Washington's visits are selected or suppressed in a way that gives Washington all the attributes of the "quality tourist" so carefully defined by Annapolitans in editorials and political cartoons, at city council meetings, and in local election campaigns. In short, Washington is portrayed as a tourist, and his deference to local authority is held up as a model for contemporary tourist behavior, despite the fact that tourism, as we know it today, did not even exist until many decades after Washington's death. The ideologically charged historiography of Annapolis is a version of historic preservation with two key attributes. The first is a strongly articulated belief in the intrinsic values of the things that preservationists preserve. The second is a largely unconscious attempt by local preservationists, most of whom are outsiders, to hide the contemporary values that drive preservation (including their desires for local identity) by constructing a claim to identity that involves gently appropriating the artifacts left behind by a previous generation of outsiders, the cultural giants who roamed the narrow cobbled streets during Annapolis' colonial Golden Age (Leone and Potter 1992: 486).

The solution offered by historical archaeology is twofold. First, the artifactual record from any late-eighteenth-century site in Annapolis will contain within it the real roots of modern tourism, which are to be found in the labor practices that produced creamware plates, rather than in the diaries of George Washington. The spiritual ancestors of Annapolis' contemporary tourists are all the pottery workers in Staffordshire who were beginning to learn the time disciplines of wage labor at the same time that Washington was going to the races, visiting his stepson, and dancing the night away in Annapolis. Second, a principal goal of the public interpretive program of "Archaeology in Annapolis" has been to provide a forum for historically grounded local discourse conducted without the distracting buzz of ideology in the background. In the context of the "tourism problem," we hope to contribute to a discussion in which neither tourism nor the roles traditionally associated with tourism are seen as natural, inevitable, or historically "given." Rather, by showing that tourism has a history that includes a beginning, a middle, and us, we have hoped to encourage both visitors and hosts to move toward a redefinition of the tourist situation based on accurate representation and mutual interest, rather than on misrepresentation and one-sided self-interest.

An Interlude: Vulgar Identity

Inspired by Meltzer's use of the term "vulgar ideology" (Meltzer 1991) and by Annapolis' portrayal of George Washington as a tourist, I want to take a break between my two case studies to introduce the term "vulgar identity." Vulgar identity, or spurious identification—vigorous assertions that "a = b" in the face of compelling evidence to the contrary— is precisely the phenomenon targeted by the "history watch" proposed by James Banner in *The Public Historian* (see also Graham 1993). Banner's basic point is that downtown Baghdad would look very different today if "Iraq = Vietnam" had prevailed over "Sadaam = Hitler" in the public debate over American policy in the Middle East (Potter n.d.), and his proposal, only mildly tongue-in-cheek, is for a rapid-response team of "unaffiliated ... historians prepared to assess the use of history by senior national policymakers" (Banner 1993: 49). Vulgar identity is not unique to historians. Its simplest archaeological version may be found in all the analogies we use to explain features of our sites to the public. While most of us know better, we end up calling privies "eighteenth-century bathrooms" and wampum "Indian money," even though these are demonstrably false identities. The problem with using analogy (or metaphor) as an explanatory tool is that it allows us to focus on similarity, to ignore difference, and to fill in what we don't know with data from our own lives, a phenomenon that is extremely common at outdoor history museums (Potter 1994: 155–166).

While there may be relatively little harm in calling a privy an eighteenth-century bathroom, there are other, broader vulgar identities that have the potential to foster serious historical misunderstanding. As an example, take the town of Wolfeboro, New Hampshire, which has for many years called itself "America's First Summer Resort," an identity perpetuated by the title of a recent volume on the archaeology of the town's most important historical archaeological site, the eighteenth-century Governor John Wentworth Plantation (Starbuck 1989). Built between 1768 and 1775, and lost to fire in 1820, the plantation served as the summer home of New Hampshire's last colonial governor, and this is the source of the town's proudly worn label. Today Wolfeboro is an important regional center for lake-related summer tourism.

However, as Starbuck's report clearly demonstrates, John Wentworth had virtually nothing in common with today's tourists, and his plantation was not a resort under any conventional definition of the term. Most historians agree that Wentworth's goal in establishing a summer residence so far inland was to spur the economic development and exploitation of New Hampshire's rich interior. And his ability to physically relocate the seat of government was likely a vestige of the "royal progress" of the European Renaissance. Thus, the frames of reference for understanding the Wentworth Plantation include Henry VIII of England and the (re)Development Authority established several years ago to guide the post-closure conversion of Newington's Pease Air Force Base to peacetime uses, but do not include waterslides, miniature golf courses, steamed hot dogs, or any of the other features that define the summertime cultural landscape of the New Hampshire Lakes Region.

The harm in seeing Wentworth as a summer tourist, rather than as a head of state or as a proponent of economic development, is that this interpretation tends to "naturalize" contemporary tourism in the Lakes Region by giving it a longer history than it actually has. This, in turn, helps to naturalize the social relations of tourism, including the mutually demeaning master/servant relationship between locals and tourists.[9] Rather than the somewhat equal trades identified by both Handler (1988) and MacCannell, i.e., "I'll give you a look at my 'authenticity' in exchange for your money," the transmogrifications of Wentworth's plantation into a resort and Wentworth into a tourist make all the visitors into governors and all the locals into chambermaids who are denied even the limited dignity of Handler's Quebecois, who "put on a show" of being members of a folk culture.

New Hampshire: The Archaeology of "Mass Hysteria"

Like Annapolis, New Hampshire has an identity problem (Potter 1993b). In Annapolis, the key question is basically personal: "What does it take to be a 'true' Annapolitan." In New Hampshire, the question is considerably broader: "What is New Hampshire?" And the real problem is the answer: "Whatever Massachusetts isn't!" Just as Annapolis has spent more than 300 years issuing invitations to outsiders and then dealing with the consequences of various acceptances, New Hampshire has spent more than 300 years fighting a political and economic battle with Massachusetts that we stubbornly insist on discussing in moral terms.

[9]Most tourism, MacCannell argues, "rests on a social relationship between tourists and locals which is fleeting and superficial and subject to a great deal of self-interested manipulation by both parties" (MacCannell 1992: 177). He goes on to suggest that "[a]ny social relationship which is transitory, superficial, and unequal is a primary breeding ground for deceit, exploitation, mistrust, dishonesty, and stereotype formation" (MacCannell 1992: 177).

Initially, the Granite State and the Bay State struggled over territory; New Hampshire has several historic sites that are seventeenth-
century markers of the various boundaries that Massachusetts hoped
to establish between the two colonies; one of these is in Laconia, nearly
60 miles north of the current Massachusetts–New Hampshire border.
Once the political boundary was firmly fixed, various Massachusetts
interests, many of them centered in Boston, set themselves to work
establishing economic hegemony over northern New England, including New Hampshire. This economic domination has been expressed in
many ways, from the control of water rights along New Hampshire
rivers and streams to the establishment of a railroad-based Boston
"milkshed," to the late twentieth-century Boston real estate market
that, despite its ebbs and flows, reaches deep into New Hampshire even
during the worst of slumps. Without intending any disrespect toward
the state that once paid my salary, I would not object too strenuously to a
characterization of New Hampshire as an economic satellite of Massachusetts, both in the past and in the present.

Despite reams of solid historical evidence portraying the relationship between Massachusetts and New Hampshire as primarily economic, contemporary popular discourse in New Hampshire pays scant
attention to the nuts and bolts of economic hegemony, and focuses
instead on the intrinsic moral weaknesses of people from Massachusetts and the inferiority of the Massachusetts—or Taxachusetts—way
of doing things. One example of New Hampshire's rabid anti-Massachu-
setts sentiment is the suggestion, made in a Letter to the Editor of the
Union Leader, that the American flag should have 49 nice white stars
and a black "M" for Massachusetts in the lower left-hand corner of the
blue field. In turn, once everyone down south is defined as a "Masshole,"
it becomes not just acceptable, but almost a moral imperative, to devise
as many ways as we can to take their money so we can use it to run our
state and local governments.[10] We have state-run liquor stores on our
Interstate highways, just north of the border, and both the liquor stores
and a flock of border-hugging shopping malls routinely fill their regis-
ters with Massachusetts cash due to New Hampshire's lack of a sales
tax. Not only do we in New Hampshire work overtime in our efforts to
nickel-and-dime our neighbors to the south, we tend to blame Massachusetts for our social problems, and we reject, out of hand, almost any

---

[10]As an index of the degree to which this "philosophy" is institutionalized, New Hampshire
state law (RSA 175:10) requires the state's liquor commission to spend 80% of its
appropriation for advertising with out-of-state media and only 20% with media in the
state.

new idea that bears the stain of having been tried first in Massachusetts.[11] Sometimes it seems as if the philosophy of the entire state
of New Hampshire is to figure out what Massachusetts is doing and then
do exactly the opposite.

Left unaddressed both here and in my previous discussion of Annapolis is the issue of agency. With respect to the George Washington
stories that serve the interests of contemporary residents worried about
being swamped by visitors, I doubt very much that there is any grand
plot; I agree with Wallace (1986: 137) that many versions of history,
even some that are quite beneficial to certain particular interests at the
expense of others, have been developed more or less unconsciously from
various social positions, rather than consciously as tools of domination.
By the same token, in my analysis of the uses (or non-uses) of history
by the city of Annapolis and the United States Naval Academy reported
elsewhere (Potter 1994: 109–115), I have suggested that both sides have
tacitly agreed not to use history against one another in their ongoing
struggles for land on the Annapolis peninsula, each fearing that the
other might win.

With regard to agency in the creation and propagation of "Mass
hysteria," the issue is somewhat more complex. I cannot yet confirm or
reject, but must certainly entertain, the hypothesis that there are, in
fact, local class interests served by shifting New Hampshire's appraisal
of Massachusetts from economic to moral grounds. Moral grounds are
usually simple, straightforward, black and white, good or bad, us versus
them. Economic grounds, however, are substantially more shady. Despite my characterization of New Hampshire as economically over-
shadowed by Massachusetts, there are many gradients that separate
full sun from total shade, and I suspect that there are some in New
Hampshire who would fear an economically based discussion of the
relationship between the two states because it would show them to have
a good bit more in common with the dominators than with the dominated. A morally based approach to identity that deflects all negative
attention southward also discourages the identification of some of "us"
who share a variety of traits with the "them" against whom "we" are all
united. New Hampshire is not, and was not, without a resident economic elite, an elite that cannot help but benefit from being able to
disguise itself and its interests by pointing to the bigger boogyman

[11]The one exception to this general rule was New Hampshire's quick adoption, several
years ago, of a budgetary "technique" first discovered in Massachusetts. This technique
is actually a loophole that ultimately allowed more than 30 states to augment their
general operating funds and balance their budgets using hundreds of millions of dollars
of money from the federal Medicaid program.

down south. The situation I am hypothesizing here is the same one faced by the American revolutionary leaders who had to inspire enough of a revolution to get rid of the British, but not so much of a revolution that they, too, would be displaced.

As in Annapolis, the goal of a historical archaeology of identity in New Hampshire is to establish a productive public discussion of serious issues, enacted without the burden of an ideology that allows us to know all the answers before we ask any questions. A historical archaeology of the relationship between Massachusetts and New Hampshire could start with some of the explicit "border sites," but far more important is an archaeology that ranges freely across the entire state. Almost any historical archaeological site in New Hampshire will yield evidence of the relationship between the occupants of that site and various powerful economic interests to the south. Individual artifacts and classes of artifacts can be analyzed from the standpoint of their place of manufacture or their point of importation into North America. The histories of land and water rights can be examined to determine patterns of ownership. And finally, there is the issue of the harvesting of raw materials such as lumber and minerals; knowing who called the shots and who made the profits from the exploitation of a particular piece of property can help us refine our understanding of the influence of Massachusetts interests in New Hampshire. The end result of analyses at all of these levels, from the artifact up to the property and beyond, could be some sort of "MQ"—a "Massachusetts Quotient" that measures the strength of Massachusetts' influence on a particular site or group of sites.

The reasons for doing such work parallel the reasons for doing, and interpreting, the archaeology of tourism in Annapolis. I am convinced that everyone involved would benefit from changing the tone of public discourse on the contemporary relationship between Massachusetts and New Hampshire. Nobody wins when one group of people believes that another group deserves to be fleeced. People in New Hampshire, in particular, need to know as much as they can about the history of their relationship with Massachusetts so as to protect themselves from further domination, and keep themselves from trying to get back at people who bear little responsibility for economic conditions they may find both unpleasant and unpleasant to think about.

New Hampshire is a conservative state, committed to capitalism and the wisdom of the free market. For that reason, it may just be that the patina of moral superiority we use to gild our popular discussions of Massachusetts is actually serving to protect us from our own worst fear: the possibility that the most painful aspects of New Hampshire's domination by Massachusetts have come about as a result of capital and capitalists operating precisely as capitalism says they should.

CONCLUSIONS

This chapter is much more a proposal than a report, though I have attempted to incorporate an adequate amount of data to make my basic points. Historical archaeology has long been defined as "the study of the spread of European culture throughout the world since the fifteenth century and its impact on indigenous peoples" (Deetz 1977: 5) and for somewhat less time as the study of worldwide capitalist expansion. Even this second definition is not specific enough, and the goal of this chapter has been to outline two additional levels of specificity: first, the historical archaeology of identity (as identities are formed by capitalism); and second, two specific historical archaeologies of identity, the archaeology of tourism in Annapolis and the archaeology of "Mass hysteria" in New Hampshire. These examples are intended only as mild suggestions for what other historical archaeologies of identity might look like. One size does not fit all, and I am certain that nothing I have outlined here will be especially useful elsewhere until the waist is taken in and the sleeves are let out.

REFERENCES

Abercrombie, N., S. Hill, and B. Turner
    1980   *The Dominant Ideology Thesis.* Allen and Unwin, London.
Aronowitz, Stanley
    1992   *The Politics of Identity: Class, Culture, Social Movements.* Routledge, New York.
Banner, James M.
    1993   The History Watch: A Proposal. *The Public Historian* 15(1):47–54.
Deetz, James
    1977   *In Small Things Forgotten.* Doubleday, Garden City.
Ferguson, Leland
    1991   Struggling with Pots in Colonial South Carolina. In: *The Archaeology of Inequality* edited by Randall H. McGuire and Robert Paynter, pp. 28–39. Basil Blackwell: Oxford.
    1992   *Uncommon Ground: Archaeology and Colonial African–America.* Smithsonian Institution Press, Washington, D.C.
Gay, Peter
    1993   *The Cultivation of Hatred.* W.W. Norton: New York.
Graham, Otis L., Jr.
    1993   Editor's Corner: The History Watch. *The Public Historian* 15(3):7–14.
Handler, Richard
    1988   *Nationalism and the Politics of Culture in Quebec.* University of Wisconsin Press, Madison.
Kottak, Conrad P.
    1994   *Anthropology: The Exploration of Human Diversity.* McGraw-Hill, New York.
Leone, Mark P.
    1988   The Georgian Order as the Order of Merchant Capitalism. In *The Recovery of*

Meaning: Historical Archaeology in the Eastern United States, edited by Mark P. Leone and Parker B. Potter, Jr., pp. 235–261. Smithsonian Institution Press, Washington, D.C.

Leone, Mark P., and Robert Preucel
1992   Archaeology in a Democratic Society: A Critical Theory Perspective. In *Quandaries and Quests: Visions of Archaeology's Future*, edited by LuAnn Wandsnider, pp. 115–135. Center for Archaeological Investigations, Carbondale.

Leone, Mark P., and Parker B. Potter, Jr.
1992   Legitimation and the Classification of Archaeological Sites. *American Antiquity* 57(1):137–145.

Leone, Mark P., Parker B. Potter, Jr., and Paul A. Shackel
1987   Toward a Critical Archaeology. *Current Anthropology* 28(3):283–302.

MacCannell, Dean
1976   *The Tourist: A New Theory of the Leisure Class*. Schocken, New York.
1992   *Empty Meeting Grounds: The Tourist Papers*. Routledge, New York.

Macpherson, C.B.
1962   *The Political Theory of Possessive Individualism: Hobbes to Locke*. Oxford University Press, Oxford.

McKendrick, Neil
1982   Josiah Wedgwood and the Commercialization of the Potteries. In *The Birth of a Consumer Society: The Commercializatin of Eighteenth-Century England*, edited by Neil McKendrick, John Brewer, and J.H. Plumb, pp. 100–145. Indiana University Press, Bloomington.

Meltzer, David
1981   Ideology and Material Culture. In *Modern Material Culture: The Archaeology of Us*, edited by Richard A. Gould and Michael B. Schiffer, pp. 113–125. Academic Press, New York.

Miller, Daniel
1987   *Material Culture and Mass Consumption*. Basil Blackwell, Oxford.

Paynter, Robert
1988   Steps to an Archaeology of Capitalism: Material Change and Class Analysis. In: *The Recovery of Meaning: Historical Archaeology in the Eastern United States*, edited by Mark P. Leone and Parker B. Potter, Jr., pp. 407–433. Smithsonian Institution Press, Washington, D.C.

Potter, Parker B., Jr.
1992   Middle-Range Theory, Ceramics, and Capitalism in 19th-Century Rockbridge County, Virginia. In *Text-Aided Archaeology*, edited by Barbara J. Little, pp. 9–23. CRC Press, Boca Raton.
1993a   *An Introduction to the Work of Matthew Smith*. Town and Country Reprographics, Concord, New Hampshire.
1993b   A Way of Thinking About Historical Archaeology in New Hampshire. *Archaeology of Eastern North America* Vol. 21, 111–136.
1994   *Public Archaeology in Annapolis: A Critical Approach to History in Maryland's Ancient City*. Smithsonian Institution Press, Washington, D.C.
n.d.   The Useful Past and the Used-Up Past. Paper presented at the Conference on New England Archaeology, April, 1992, to be published in *Northeast Anthropology*.

Potter, Parker B., Jr., and Mark P. Leone
1992   Establishing the Roots of Historical Consciousness in Modern Annapolis, Maryland. In *Museums and Communities: The Politics of Public Culture*, edited by Ivan Karp, Christine Mullen Kreamer, and Steven D. Levine, pp. 476–505. Smithsonian Institution Press, Washington, D.C.

Starbuck, David (editor)
   1989   *America's First Summer Resort: John Wentworth's 18th Century Plantation in Wolfeboro, New Hampshire. The New Hampshire Archaeologist* Vol. 30, No. 1. New Hampshire Archaeology Society.
Stein, Charles
   1993   Disappearing Workers: Jobs Lost Forever to Super-automated Plants. *The Boston Sunday Globe*, August 8, pp. 77–78.
Thompson, Meldrim
   1992   In the Beginning We Needed Immigration. Editorial in the *Union Leader*, Manchester.
Tilley, Christopher
   1990   Claude Levi-Strauss: Structuralism and Beyond. In *Reading Material Culture*, edited by Christopher Tilley, pp. 3–81. Basil Blackwell, Oxford.
Wallace, Michael
   1986   Visiting the Past: History Museums in the United States. In *Presenting the Past: Essays on History and the Public*, edited by Susan Porter Benson, Stephen Brier, and Roy Rosenweig, pp. 137–161. Temple University Press, Philadelphia.
Wilson, E.
   1985   *Adorned in Dreams*. Virago, London.

The Contested Commons

Archaeologies of Race, Repression, and Resistance in New York City

4

Terrence W. Epperson

> They hang the man and flog the woman
> Who steals the goose from off the Common;
> But let the greater criminal loose
> Who steals the Common from the goose.
> —(Anonymous Late Medieval Folk Wisdom)

INTRODUCTION: THE COMMONS AND THE AFRICAN BURIAL GROUND

The Commons, the area surrounding and including the present-day location of City Hall in lower Manhattan, has been an intensely contested landscape since the seventeenth century. The non-elite inhabitants of New Amsterdam, and later New York City, claimed this unappropriated land as a Commons in the traditional medieval sense, as an area where subsistence activities such as cattle grazing and firewood collection could be conducted (Thompson 1993). By the end of the seventeenth century, a portion of the Commons was being utilized as an African burial ground and ritual space. By the second quarter of the eighteenth century, the colonial government was attempting (with limited success) to restrict and regulate activities on the Commons, including burials. Reactions to recent excavations within the African Burial Ground and subsequent controversies regarding the project research design demonstrate that the contestation continues unabated. This project provides an ideal opportunity to address several aspects of the archaeology of capitalism, including the social construction of racial

Terrence W. Epperson • Cultural Heritage Research Services, Inc., North Wales, Pennsylvania 19454.

Historical Archaeologies of Capitalism, edited by Mark P. Leone and Parker B. Potter, Jr. Plenum Press, New York, 1999.

categories, the formulation of hegemonic and counter-hegemonic historical consciousness, the essentialist/social constructionist debate, and the role of descendent communities and their allies in archaeological, historical, and bioanthropological research (for general background on the project see Cook 1993; Coughlin 1994; Dunlap 1993; Harrigton 1993; Harris et al. 1993; Howard University and John Milner Associates 1993; Jorde 1993, and Howson and Harris 1992).

After a short historical overview, this paper examines four moments of cultural contestation on the Commons: the 1712 Rising, the 1741 "Great Negro Plot," a 1757 Pinkster Day celebration, and a 1788 petition against the desecration of the African-American graves. In each instance these historical moments are linked with aspects of recent and ongoing struggles over the excavation, analysis, preservation, and commemoration of the African Burial Ground.

In October of 1697, as construction of New York's first Trinity Church was nearing completion at the present-day intersection of Wall Street and Broadway, the following regulation was enacted:

> Ordered, That after the Expiration of four weeks from the date hereof [10/25/1697] no Negroes be buried within the bounds & Limitts of the Church Yard of Trinity Church, that is to say, in the rear of the present burying place & that no person or Negro whatsoever, do presume after the terme above Limitted to break up any ground for the burying of his Negro, as they will answer for it at their perill, & that this order be forthwith published. (Stokes 1915: 403 quoting Trinity Church mss. minutes).

Interments within the 5- to 6-acre portion of the Commons subsequently recognized as the African Burial Ground probably began soon after enactment of this regulation. It is estimated that some 10,000 to 20,000 New Yorkers of African descent were buried in this area during the eighteenth century. At least half of the present African-descent population in the United States probably has at least one ancestor buried in this area (Michael Blakey, personal communication).

The location of the separate burial ground assigned to/appropriated by the enslaved and non-enslaved African community was later described as "unattractive and desolate" (Valentine 1847: 567). The earliest known documentary reference to African burials on the Common was provided in 1713 by the Reverend John Sharp (Chaplain to her Majesties Forts and Forces in the Province of New York in America):

> In Religious respects there is but little regard had to them, their marriages are performed by mutual consent without the blessing of the Church and they are buried in the Common by those of their own country and complexion without the office, on the contrary the Heathenish rites are performed at the grave by their countrymen (Sharpe 1713: 355).

In 1731 the Common Council of New York City passed or reiterated a series of 39 laws, many of which were intended to limit traditional activities on the Commons, including: burning lime (to manufacture mortar and plaster), digging holes and cutting sods, cutting timber by brickmakers and charcoal burners, and cutting hoop sticks (saplings used to make hoops for casks). The Common Council also ordered construction of a gunpowder storage house on the Commons.

The 1731 acts also included "A Law for Regulating the Burial of Slaves." This act included three provisions:

> Ordained ... that all Negro, Mulatto, and Indian slaves ... be buried by Day-Light
>
> Not above twelve slaves Shall Assemble or meet together at the funeral of any Slave
>
> Ordained that no Pawl [pall] be allowed or admitted at the funeral of any slave; [nor shall] any slave presume to hold up a Pawl or be the Pawl Bearer at the Funeral of any Slave (Minutes of the Common Council 11/18/1731)

In 1745 a military palisade was constructed across Manhattan at the northern margin of settlement (Harris et al. 1993: 11; Maerschalck 1755). Most, if not all, of the African Burial Ground was situated north of this palisade, placing it "beyond the pale" in the literal and original sense of the term.

In addition to the Burial Ground, the Commons became the site of several disciplinary institutions. In 1735–1736 New York City's first almshouse was constructed on the Commons immediately south of the burial ground, at the present site of City Hall. This institution marked a profound shift in official attitudes toward poverty and delinquency. Unlike the earlier program of "out-relief," which provided direct subsidies to impoverished individuals while they continued to live in the community, aid was now contingent upon residence in the almshouse (Harris et al. 1993: 9; Gray 1988; Ross 1988). The cost of poorhouse operations was partially offset by petty commodity production by inmates. Recent archaeological investigations have encountered evidence of copper-alloy straight-pin and bone-button manufacturing, and documentary research reveals the sale of garden produce (Baugher et al. 1990; Grossman 1991). Copper-alloy straight pins, used to secure burial shrouds, were the most common grave-related artifacts recovered from the African Burial Ground; it is quite possible that many of these pins were manufactured at the poorhouse.

In the opening chapter of *Wealth of Nations*, first published in 1776, Adam Smith used the manufacturing of straight pins as a case study of the advantages offered by the technical (and implicitly social) division of labor (Smith 1986: 109–111). Smith ends the first chapter by asserting that, because of the division of labor, "the accommodation of [the frugal European peasant] exceeds that of many an African king, the absolute master of the lives and liberties of ten thousand naked savages." (Smith 1986: 117).

Within the poorhouse complex, time and architectural space were carefully controlled to inculcate the disciplines and separations of emergent industrial capitalism, and the decision to have inmates produce straight pins may not have been coincidental. However, the administrators of the poorhouse complex were continually frustrated by their inability to provide the appropriate degree of spacial segregation between diseased and healthy persons and between deserving and undeserving poor. The completion of the New Gaol in 1759 and the Bridewell (an institution for the incarceration of debtors and vagabonds) in 1776 provided more refined spatial differentiation. These three disciplinary institutions were symmetrically aligned on the east–west axis that would later define the orientation of City Hall (constructed in 1803–1811) and the surrounding park.

By the time of the American Revolution, the Commons had also become an important military landscape. Prior to the Revolution, two barracks had been constructed immediately south of the African Burial Ground, and after the British took control of New York City in September of 1776, two additional barracks were built. During the Revolution the Bridewell and the New Gaol housed American prisoners of war, including Ethan Allen. William Cunningham, the provost marshall for British prisons in New York, reported the execution of "275 American prisoners and obnoxious persons" in this area. His account indicates that the executions and burials occurred in or near the southern margin of the African Burial Ground (Harris et al. 1993: 14–15).

After about 1795, the northern portion of the Commons was no longer used as a burial ground. In 1813 David Grim, who at the age of 76 was a leading light in the New-York Historical Society, drafted "A Plan of the City and Environs of New York." The map purportedly depicts Grim's memory of the landscape in 1744, some 69 years earlier, when he was seven years old. Significantly, Grim does not include the African Burial Ground in his remembered landscape, even though the "Negroes Burial Ground" is delineated on maps drafted in 1735 and 1754 (Plan of New York 1735; Maerschalck 1755). Instead, Grim chose to provide graphic depictions of the executions of African-descent insurrectionists on the Commons following the alleged 1741 "Great Negro Plot" (Davis 1985; Grim 1854). This selective memory is not surprising. By the time Grim drafted his map, a radical transformation in official land-scape definition had occurred. With the construction of City Hall, the "Commons" became the "Park." In addition, the Common Council had initiated a massive landscape-alteration program with the filling of the low-lying northern portion of the Commons, including the site of the African Burial Ground. Once the burial ground was safely buried beneath 20 to 30 feet of urban fill, real estate values improved dramatically:

> The lots adjoining, and including the premises, and including the African burying ground, for many years since the American war, were regarded as uninviting suburbs. The streets have since been widened, the face of the ground wholly changed, and it is now covered with a flourishing population, and elegant improvements. [(*Smith, ex. dem. Teller, v. Burtis & Woodward*, 9 Johnson Reports 182 (N.Y. Sup. Ct., 1812), cited in Howson et al. 1992.]

Ironically, although the filling of this area helped erase the African Burial Ground from the dominant historical consciousness, it also protected much of the site from subsequent urban development, setting the stage for its dramatic "rediscovery" by archaeologists in the spring of 1991, during testing conducted prior to construction of a 34-story federal office complex (Wilson and Howson 1997). Archaeological excavations resulted in the disinterment of more than 400 burials before community pressure and congressional intervention resulted in a discontinuation of the excavations in July 1992. In October 1992, President Bush signed Public Law 102-393, an appropriations bill that contained a provision ordering the General Services Administration to scale back its construction plans and permanently halt excavation of human remains at the site. Congress also appropriated $3 million for a permanent memorial on the site and empanelled a Steering Committee to advise GSA regarding commemoration and interpretation of the site (Cook 1993; Harrington 1993). Although the 34-story tower was completed as originally designed, the planned adjacent four-story pavilion was not constructed. The pavilion site contains an undetermined number of unexcavated burials and is slated to become the site of an African Burial Ground Memorial.

Although the original osteological analysis was performed by the Metropolitan Forensic Anthropology Team (MFAT) headquartered at Lehman College in the Bronx, by the end of 1993 the human remains had been transferred to the Cobb Biological Anthropology Laboratory at Howard University, for a six-year multidisciplinary analysis program that could ultimately cost $20 million (Scarupa 1994: 21). By halting the excavations and forcing a reformulation of the research design, the mobilized African American community members and their allies were able to "seize intellectual control" of an extremely important scientific project (LaRoche and Blakey 1997: 100).

The New York City Landmarks Commission officially designated the African Burial Ground and the Commons Historic District on February 25, 1993, and on April 19, 1993 the African Burial Ground was designated a National Historic Landmark.

THE 1712 RISING:
COROMANTEE, CHRISTIAN, AND WHITE IDENTITIES

> Some Cormentine Negroes to the number of 25 or 30 and 2 or 3 Spanish Indians having conspired to murder all the Christians here, and by that means thinking to obtain their freedom, about two a clock this morning put their bloody design in Execution ....
> —*The Boston Weekly News-Letter* April 7–14, 1712

> Some Negro slaves here of the Nations of Carmantee & Pappa plotted to destroy all the Whites in order to obtain their freedom ....
> —the Rev. John Sharpe to the Society for
> the Propagation of the Gospel June 23, 1712

As the moon was setting at about 2:00 A.M. on Sunday, April 6, 1712, some two dozen enslaved African Americans and Native Americans assembled in the East Ward orchard of John Crooke, a New York City cooper, and initiated an insurrection that had been planned since New Year's Day (March 25), 1712. Two of the insurrectionists torched an outbuilding, and as the townsfolk ran from their homes to fight the blaze, nine persons of European descent were killed and seven others were wounded. Upon hearing of the insurrection, Governor Hunter ordered a cannon to be fired as an alarm and immediately mobilized the troops. By the end of the following day, the uprising had been quelled. A total of 47 people were eventually accused of involvement in the attempted uprising; of this number 19 individuals were eventually executed, many of them on the basis of rather questionable evidence (Scott 1961). The convicted insurrectionists were probably executed on the Commons and buried in the African Burial Ground.

While the narrative history of this uprising has been covered elsewhere in considerable detail, several nuances bear directly upon the archaeological analysis of the Commons. The two accounts quoted above concur on one issue and differ significantly on a second issue. The newspaper dispatch places the blame primarily upon "Cormentine Negroes;" similarly, the Rev. Sharpe ascribes responsibility to "Negro slaves ... of the Nations of Carmantee & Pappa." These accounts are corroborated by court records indicating that eight of the accused New York City insurrectionists (including one of the alleged ringleaders) were known by Akan day-names. Two of the accused were named Cuffee, the masculine day name for a child born on Friday; four were named Quaco or Quacko, the masculine name for a child born on Wednesday; and two were named Quashi or Quasi, the masculine name for a child born on Sunday. However, the accused insurrectionists also included seven men named "Tom."

The innate rebelliousness of Akan-speaking "Coromantee" slaves was a theme that immediately resonated with both English and colonial audiences. The hero of Aphra Behn's popular 1688 romantic novel *Oroonoko, or, The Royal Slave* was a wrongfully-enslaved "Coramantien" Prince, and the newspaper that reported the New York City uprising also carried an account of the murder of a Jamaica (West Indies, not Queens) plantation owner's wife by seven "new Cormantine slaves." English slaveholders, particularly in the Caribbean, elaborated complex stereotypes to classify their bound laborers, both African and European. Scottish servants were thought to be "hardworking, loyal, unproblematic, and responsive to patronage," while the Irish were denigrated as "violent, dangerous, untrustworthy, and aggressive." English and Welsh servants fell somewhere in the middle of the continuum (Beckles 1989: 98–99). When referring to their African laborers, the planters generally reserved their highest praise for the Akan-speaking Coromantee (with numerous variations in orthography) from the Gold Coast, who were simultaneously valued and feared. Since planters often assigned workers to segments of the productive process on the basis of these stereotypes, Coromantees were often overseers or held other positions of relative responsibility.

The issue of "ethnic" identity should, however, be approached with extreme caution (Williams 1989). Walter Rodney (1969), in a seminal article entitled "Upper Guinea and the Significance of the Origins of Africans Enslaved in the New World," warned against simplistic analysis of the "tribal identity" of enslaved Africans. Citing the example of the Mandinga, he stressed the importance of pre-enslavement transformations in ethnic identity related to processes of state formation and class conflict. Multilingual Mandinga traders along the Gambia river exercised cultural and political hegemony that dated to the fourteenth-century expansion of the Mali Empire and were, therefore, well placed to become middlemen and interpreters in the developing Atlantic slave trade. Most of the highly-valued "Mandinga" slaves shipped to Spanish America were actually partially assimilated subject peoples from quite disparate groups. In addition, Rodney (1969: 335) suggests that one consequence of Mandinga hegemony was the attempt by enslaved individuals of other groups to pass as Mandinga in order to enhance their status in the eyes of Europeans.

Although all ethnonyms applied to enslaved Africans are problematic, this is particularly true with "Coromantee," which initially denoted individuals taken from any number of quite disparate inland groups, but who happened to be exported through the port of Kormantin. The Coromantee, however, soon became reified as a nation or ethnic group with their own distinctive characteristics. Not surprisingly, Akan culture became a focus and symbol of slave resistance throughout the English colonies. Perhaps the most obvious evidence of this identification was the widespread use of Akan day-names. This practice was adopted by more slaves than the actual number of Akan-speakers warranted, and continued into the third and fourth generation of Creole slaves (Craton 1982: 56–57; Schuler 1970: 29).

The example of the Coromantee reminds us that ethnic identity is not an innate attribute belonging to a particular group of people, but rather an aspect of cultural struggle formulated and reformulated, invented and imposed, within the context of domination and resistance. Initially an invention of slave traders and slave owners, the ethnonym "Coromantee" and the distinctive traits it purportedly represented soon became a basis for resistance.

We turn now to the subtle, yet very important, distinction between the two 1712 accounts. Before the final decades of the seventeenth century, English colonists seldom referred to themselves as "white," choosing instead to self-identify as "Christian" or "English." Note that the newspaper story says the objective of the uprising was "to murder all the Christians," while the Rev. Sharpe says the insurrectionists "plotted dto destroy all the Whites" Rather than being a mere semantic quibble, this discrepancy marks a pivotal moment in the social construction of racial difference in colonial New York. A 1712 census of the counties of New York, Kings, Richmond, Orange, and Westchester listed 10,511 "Christians" and 1775 "slaves." In New York, the terms "slave" and "Negro" were conflated to an extent that would have been unthinkable in the Caribbean, where non-enslaved blacks were more numerous. In any event, the dichotomies of Negro/Christian or slave/Christian were rapidly being undermined by Anglican proselytization, only to be replaced by a new dichotomy: Negro/white. In 1680, Morgan Godwyn, an Anglican cleric who had preached in both Virginia and Barbados, published a booklet entitled *The Negro's and Indians Advocate*. The Reverend Godwyn passionately advocated the baptism of slaves, arguing in part that they would become more loyal and obedient as a result: "For

Insurrections and Revolts, nothing can be imagined a greater security against them, than a sincere inward persuasion of the truths of Christianity, with a thorough knowledge of its Principals." (1680: 130).

With the founding of the Society for the Propagation of the Gospel in Foreign Parts (SPG) in 1701, Godwyn's recommendations became official Anglican policy. In 1704 Elias Neau, a French Huguenot who had previously been given a life sentence as a galley slave because of his religious beliefs, conformed to the Church of England and was given an appointment by the SPG to catechize the "Negros and Indians" in New York City. By October of 1705 Neau's school had enrolled 42 "Negroes" and 4 "Indians" who had been sent by 36 separate slaveholders. In response to the most common criticism expressed regarding his school, Neau secured passage of a 1706 assembly bill specifying that baptism of enslaved persons in no way affected their status as slaves. In 1710 Robert Hunter, a member of the SPG, was appointed Governor of New York, providing additional support for Neau's mission (Cohen 1971: 17–18; Manross 1974: 110).

It came as a severe shock, therefore, when Neau's school, some of its students, and Christianity itself were implicated in the 1712 insurrection. The Reverend John Sharp reported that "The Spanish Indians were at first most suspected as having most understanding to carry on a plot and being Christians." Sharp here refers to two individuals: Hosea or Hosey, "Indian slave of Mary Wenham," and John, "Indian slave of Peter Vantilborough." Hosey and John were presumably Catholic and had apparently been free Spanish subjects until they were captured as prisoners of war by a privateer. Because of their dark complexions, the privateer was able to sell the men in New York, despite their repeated claims that they were free Spanish subjects. Although sentenced to be hanged for participation in the insurrection, Hosey and John eventually received Royal pardons.

Two of Elias Neau's students were implicated in the uprising. Sharp reports that only one baptized student (whose identity cannot be determined from the sources at hand) was implicated. This individual was hanged during the first wave of executions, although he was subsequently "Pitied and proclaimed Innocent by the Generality of the People." The second accused student was Robin, who, for over two years, had unsuccessfully sought his master's permission to be baptized. The fact that Robin was sentenced to be "hung in chains and so to continue without sustenance until dead" indicates that he was thought to be one of the three ringleaders of the insurrection. Despite Sharpe's statements and Governor Hunter's continued support, the slaveowners became increasingly hostile toward Neau's school, believing religious instruction "Would be a means to make the slave more cunning and apter to wickedness" (Cohen 1971: 21)

Therefore, Sharpe's own accounts indicate an insurrection that was much more complex than an attempt by "some Negro slaves of the Nations of Carmantee & Pappa to destroy all the Whites in order to obtain their freedom." When analyzed within a broader context, we can also see the 1712 Rising as an important transitional moment in the social construction of "white" identity. In the aftermath of the uprising, Governor Hunter advocated passage of a stricter slave code as well as a bill "to Encourage the Importation of White Servants (Scott 1961: 71).

The advocacy of slave baptism by the Anglican Church undermined the customary social opposition of Negro versus Christian. Because the SPG and the Anglican Church challenged the Negro/Christian opposition without fundamentally attacking the social and economic relationship upon which it was based (i.e., slavery), they unwittingly necessitated the formulation of a different set of oppositions. Even though it could be argued that their work was non-racist, it ultimately contributed to the "need" for elaboration of explicitly racist assertions of "Negro" inferiority.

The 1712 Rising raises three issues that are relevant to the ongoing analysis of the African Burial Ground. First, the temptation to focus on the presence of "Africanisms," as the basis of cultural resistance should be approached very critically. In a paper entitled "Objectivity and Critical Analysis in Mortuary Studies" Nassaney (1986) argues against the search for literal "cultural survivals" and argues that acculturation and autonomy should not be viewed as elements in a mutually exclusive dichotomy:

> [C]ontinuity and change are not mutually exclusive processes, but rather articulate in a dialectical relationship. In other words, indigenous groups can be acculturated and still retain a sense of ethnic identity. A group need not maintain cultural isolation and biological purity to assert cultural autonomy and ethnic solidarity.

Like all forms of domination, colonial slavery was characterized by a fundamental contradiction, the tension between inclusion and exclusion, between the need to incorporate the oppressed people within a unified system of control, and the need to create distance, difference, and otherness (Sider 1987). Neither tendency could ever be total and they were in constant, shifting opposition. The Reverend Sharpe saw baptism as a mechanism for enhancing the incorporative aspect of domination by improving surveillance, undermining African cultural traditions, inculcating purportedly shared values, and improving control through better knowledge of slaves' behavior and motivations. However, as is the case with all ideological weapons, Christianity was a double-edged sword. Although deployed as a form of control, religion also become a means of challenging the denial of slave humanity, a basis for resistance that transcended African ethnic boundaries, and a mechanism for surreptitiously maintaining and asserting African spiritual values. Despite the Reverend Sharpe's protestations to the contrary, New York slaveholders realized that Christianity could serve as a basis for slave resistance.

The second issue concerns the construction of "white" identity, an issue discussed in greater detail in the following section (Allen 1994, 1997; Ignatiev 1995). As indicated above, the 1712 Rising occurred at a critical moment in the invention of whiteness. Therefore, any analysis that assumes the existence of static biological races will not be attuned to important realms of cultural struggle and contestation. In addition to being a standard element of conventional Euro-centric histories, the "notion of naturally and qualitatively delineated races" is also a limiting characteristic of many schools of Afrocentric analysis (Blakey 1995: 214).

The third issue raised by the 1712 Rising is the analysis of genetic affinity and cultural identity. The original research paradigm for the African Burial Ground osteological analysis was prepared by the Metropolitan Forensic Anthropology Team (MFAT), headed by James V. Taylor. This approach was based upon an essentialist, biogenetic conception of "race." As control of the analysis was shifted to Howard University this approach was displaced by a research paradigm that emphasizes genetic affinity and cultural identity, greatly enhancing the social relevance and scientific importance of the project (Epperson 1996; LaRoche and Blakey 1997). For example, the project will utilize emergent mitochondrial and nuclear DNA studies to examine genetic origins and change in the archaeological population. DNA-based genetics, anatomical structure, chemical signatures for environments, and cultural traits will be used to link individuals from the Burial Ground with specific cultural/regional origins in Africa. (Howard University and John Milner Associates 1993: 68, citing Vigilant 1991).

However, the example of the Coromantee cited above should warn against expecting any literal and direct linkage between geographical origins and cultural identity. For example, the research design proposes:

> Archaeological, ethnohistorical, and ethnological assessments will be made of the cultural origins of individuals with ornamentally filed incisor teeth and any other evidence of African birth. Patterns of bone chemistry showing

reasonable correlation with such cultural data [as well as genetic affinity data] will be considered reliable regional chemical signatures for individuals for whom other sourcing data are unavailable. These identifications will allow African-born adults to be partitioned for comparison with other samples (Howard University and John Milner Associates 1993: 68).

Ornamentally filed incisor teeth have, of course, been documented in several African contexts. Although supported by documentary evidence (Handler 1994, 1997), the correlation between filed incisors and African birth should be treated as a hypothesis subject to testing. American-born slaves could have learned this custom from recent African arrivals and may have adopted the practice as a form of cultural resistance, similar to the use of Akan day names. Fortunately, the research design also offers a mechanism for testing this hypothesis, the examination of C3/C4 (carbon) ratios. It should be possible to distinguish between reliance upon American maize (a C4 plant) and consumption of tubers and other C3 plants common to tropical West Africa (Howard University and John Milner Associates 1993: 67). Similarly, examination of strontium (87Sr/86Sr) ratios has been successfully used in South Western Africa to distinguish between coastal and inland inhabitants (Howard University and John Milner Associates 1993: 67, citing Sealy et al. 1991). However distinguishing between African and American birth cohorts and determining the geographic origins of interred individuals does not necessarily determine their ethnic identity. To the extent that it analyzes ethnicity as a social construct rather than a biogenetic phenomenon, the current research design has the potential to enhance our understanding of ethnogenesis, the active creation and reinvention of cultural identity under conditions of domination (Mintz and Price 1992; Levine 1977; Sider 1987; 1994; Stuckey 1987).

THE "GREAT NEGRO PLOT" OF 1741

During the winter of 1740–1741 a polyglot group of enslaved, indentured, and wage workers gathered at the tavern of John Hughson to plan an insurrection on St. Patrick's Day 1741. The conspirators included Irish, English, Hispanic, African, and Native American men and women. The insurrectionists torched Fort George, the Governor's Mansion, and the Imperial Armory, all important symbols of Royal authority in New York City. In the hysterical aftermath of the attempted uprising, 13 people were burned at the stake, 21 were hanged, and 77 were transported from the colony as servants or slaves (Davis 1985; Horsmanden 1971; Linebaugh and Rediker 1990: 225–226). The exe-

cuted conspirators included four people of European ancestry. Most of
the executions were carried out on the Commons, at or near the location
of the African Burial Ground. As previously noted, this is the event
David Grim chose to depict selectively on his 1813 "Plan of the City and
Environs of New York." These executions and their subsequent depic-
tion are an important component of the ongoing contestation of the
Commons.

According to subsequent coerced testimony, the insurrectionists
included David Johnson, a journeyman hatter of unknown European
origin who "swore, in that room that he came into, in the presence of
the company, that he would help to burn the town, and kill as many
white people as he could" (Horsmanden 1971: 309). John Corry, an Irish
dancing master, and Hughson, the tavern keeper, reportedly made
similar vows. Although the construct of "whiteness" was well established in colonial law by this date, we should not approach this situation
with preconceptions about who was considered white and what this
category meant. As Noel Ignatiev (1995) has shown in *How the Irish
Became White*, membership in the white club is not an automatic consequence of pigmentation. When David Johnson vowed to help "kill as
many white people as he could," "white" clearly referred to the wealthy
and powerful, a category from which he was obviously excluded (Davis
1985: 194).

The first conspirator executed was Caesar, an enslaved African
"owned" by John Varrck, a New York City baker. Caesar was hanged on
May 11, 1741 and his body was hung in chains in a gibbet on a Collect
Pond island near the Commons gunpowder house (Horsmanden 1971:
65–66). Over the coming months many more conspirators were executed on the Commons, both by hanging and burning at the stake. These
events were massively-attended public spectacles. On June 12th John
Hughson, his wife Sarah, and their indentured Irish servant, Margaret
Kerry, were hanged. Caesar had reportedly provided financial support
for Margaret Kerry's child, who was born under suspicious circumstances. John Hughson's body was hung in a gibbet next to Caesar's and
the other conspirators whose crimes were deemed particularly heinous.
When six additional Blacks were executed on July 18th, the bodies of
John Hughson and Caesar were still on display. At that time a "wondrous phenomenon" occurred, which, for white observers, confirmed
Hughson's race treachery. According to the judge and primary reporter
of the case, the corpse of Caesar, who had been "of the darkest complexion," had bleached or turned whitish, while Hughson's complexion
"turned as black as the devil" (Davis 1985: 190–191; Linebaugh and
Rediker 1990: 226).

In the subsequent historiography of the rising there has been a transubstantiation that rivals the "wondrous phenomenon" of Hughson and Caesar's corpses exchanging colors. The initial account of the event, published in 1744, was entitled, *A Journal of the Proceedings in the Detection of the Conspiracy Formed by Some White People, in Conjunction with Negro and Other Slaves for Burning the City of New-York in America*. This account was republished almost verbatim in 1810, but the title was changed to *The New York Conspiracy, or a History of the Negro Plot*. Today, the event is generally recalled, if at all, as the "the Great Negro Plot" (Davis 1985). This shift effectively effaces the multicultural nature of the uprising and, through a process of racialization, marginalizes the threat it posed.

For Linebaugh and Rediker (1990), the events of 1741 represent "a many-sided rising by a diverse urban proletariat—red, white, and black, of many nations, races, ethnicities, and degrees of freedom." They believe that concepts such as nationality, race, and ethnicity have obscured "actual points of contact, overlap, and cooperation" between elements of the early modern working class." They continue by criticizing researchers who "consciously or unconsciously posit static and immutable differences between workers black and white, Irish and English, slave and free," and urge a transAtlantic perspective that examines connections between disparate elements of the working class. This approach is mirrored by Gilroy's (1993: 15) opposition to "absolutist conceptions of cultural difference" and his recommendation in *The Black Atlantic: Modernity and Double Consciousness* that researchers "take the Atlantic as one single, complex unit of analysis in their discussions of the modern world and use it to produce an explicitly transnational and intercultural perspective." In addition to providing important insights into the specific experiences of enslaved and non-enslaved people of African descent in New York City, the African Burial Ground studies also have the potential to force a fundamental reconceptualization of the formation and resistance of the Atlantic working class.

PINKSTER DAY, 1757: THE POLITICS
OF SPECTACLE AND CULTURAL PROPERTY

In his 1845 novel *Satanstoe, or The Littlepage Manuscripts: A Tale of the Colony*, James Fenimore Cooper provided a detailed description of a Pinkster celebration, "the Great Saturnalia of the New York blacks," that purportedly occurred in 1757 (Cooper 1990: 61). Pinkster Day was derived from the Christian holiday Pentecost or Whitsuntide, commemorating the receiving of the holy spirit by Jesus' disciples. This holiday had originally been derived from Shavout, the Jewish festival that celebrates the receiving of the commandments by Moses and the early summer harvest (Harris et al. 1993: 10; Stuckey 1987; 1994; White 1989).

From Cooper's detailed geographical description it is clear that the celebration occurred on the Commons at or very near the site of the African Burial Ground. According to Sterling Stuckey (1994), who has conducted a detailed comparison between this account and the better-documented festivals held in Albany (where the celebration was banned in 1811), Cooper's account is quite credible. Cooper writes that the "Pinkster fields" were located "up near the head of Broadway, on the Common."

> By this time nine-tenths of the blacks of the city, and of the whole country within thirty or forty miles, indeed, were collected in thousands in the fields, beating banjos, singing African songs, drinking, and worst of all, laughing in a way that seemed to set their very hearts rattling within their ribs.... Hundreds of whites were walking through the fields, amused spectators. Among those last were a great many children of the better class, who had come to look at the enjoyments of those who attended them, in their ordinary amusements. (Cooper 1990:).

Because of shifting slave trading patterns, the proportion of African-born (as opposed to Caribbean- or American-born) slaves within the New York City population was increasing (Lydon 1978). Pinkster provided an opportunity for African Americans to become acquainted with African-born slaves and to formulate a collective cultural identity through the celebration of a Judeo-Christian religious holiday. In his account Cooper highlighted the importance of the African connection:

> The features that distinguish a Pinkster frolic from the usual scenes at fairs, and other merry makings, however, were of African origin. It is true, there are not now, nor were there then, many blacks among us of African birth; but the traditions and usages of their original country were so far preserved as to produce a marked difference between this festival, and one of European origin. Among other things, some were making music, by beating on skins drawn over the ends of hollow logs, while others were dancing to it, in a manner to show that they felt infinite delight. This, in particular, was said to be a usage of their African progenitors. (Cooper 1990: 65).

Folklorist James H. Pickering does not question the authenticity of Cooper's account, but challenges the location, suggesting that it occurred in Brooklyn or adjacent Long Island, as such a festival would not be tolerated in Manhattan (Pickering 1966: 17). Stuckey, however, does not question the setting of Cooper's account, but instead offers a compelling explanation of why such celebrations were, indeed, tolerated in New York City and elsewhere. Citing the work of Mikhail Bakhtin (1984:

7), Stuckey (1994: 78) speculates, "No doubt the pathway to tolerance of and fascination with black dance was to some degree smoothed by the presence of laughter, which tended ... to deflect one's attention from the sacred ...." Yet, Pinkster was not a true carnival for the white observers. According to Bakhtin (1984: 79), "Carnival is not a spectacle seen by the people; they live it, and everyone participates because its very nature embraces all the people." Cooper's account (and several others examined by Stuckey) show quite clearly that, for most Euro-Americans, Pinkster was not a carnival in which they participated but rather a spectacle staged for their entertainment. Cooper's own account of the celebrations could be seen as a second appropriation, a retelling of an African festival for a predominantly white audience.

Pinkster is important to the present narrative for two reasons. First, it indicates that the Burial Ground was used by New Yorkers of African descent for rituals other than burials. Second, it raises disconcerting questions about how African and African-American cultural resources are appropriated and transformed into spectacles suitable for mass consumption (Lott 1993), or are put to uses inimical to the interests and desires of the descendant community. In this context the emerging concept of "traditional cultural proprieties" would appear to be extremely relevant (King 1997; Parker and King 1992).

In many ways, this project mirrors issues raised by implementation of the 1990 Native American Graves Protection and Repatriation Act (Public Law 101-601, see Fine-Dare 1997; Merrill et al. 1993; and Zimmerman 1989). As the African Burial Ground excavations proceeded and the extent of the site became increasingly apparent, the mainstream preservation community began to realize that the site was an extremely important cultural resource. However, in terms of National Register significance, the importance of the site was considered almost exclusively under "Criterion D": "[sites] that have yielded, or may be likely to yield, information important in prehistory or history." This is a nice example of what Thomas King calls "archaeo-centricism," a tendency to view cultural resources primarily as sources of archaeological data (King 1997). If a site is significant only for its "information" it becomes a "removable resource," and any adverse effect can be mitigated by scientific study (i.e., excavation):

> [There is no adverse effect when] the property is of value only for its potential contribution to archaeology, historical, or architectural research, and when such value can be substantially preserved through the conduct of appropriate research ... 36 CFR 800.9(C)(1)

An important challenge to this logic was presented in a brief filed by the Minority Environmental Lawyers Association (MELA) (reprinted in GSA 1993: np):

It's ironic that the only identified adverse effect is one which allows unfettered construction after the remains have been studied.... The irony of this conclusion is that it fits very conveniently within the proposed project's aims, specifically it justifies the destruction of the Burial Ground already completed and contemplated destruction of unexcavated Burial Ground.

The MELA brief insisted that the African Burial Ground site also be evaluated under National Register Criterion A: "[sites] that are associated with events that have made a significant contribution to the broad patterns of our history ...." The MELA position has, to a large extent prevailed. The current mitigation measures include preservation in place, a permanent memorial on the site, an extensive program of public participation and education, and eventual reinterment of the remains in accordance with the wishes of the descendant community (Howard University and John Milner Associates 1993: 100–112; LaRoche and Blakey 1997).

Although initially applied to Native-American spiritual sites, the concept of traditional cultural properties has wide applicability. *National Register Bulletin* 38 states that a traditional cultural property can be eligible for inclusion in the National Register of Historic Places "because of its association with cultural practices or beliefs of a living community that (a) are rooted in that community's history, and (b) are important in maintaining the continuing cultural identity of the community" (Parker and King 1992). These criteria provide mechanisms for incorporating spiritual and cultural values, which may not be addressed by conventional archaeology and historic preservation criteria, into National Register assessments. In his professional workshops, Thomas King (1997), coauthor of *National Register Bulletin* 38, uses the African Burial Ground as a paradigmatic example of a traditional cultural property.

Although it has not figured in debates surrounding the African Burial Ground, the concept of traditional cultural properties could be quite applicable in comparable future situations as a mechanism for fostering both community involvement and the participation of professional researchers who are grounded in the cultural context being investigated. For federal undertakings the guidelines require that "culturally sensitive consultation" be conducted by researchers who are thoroughly grounded in the history, culture, and concerns of the community being studied. Diligent application of these criteria could prevent a recurrence of the situation that characterized the initial phases of study at the African Burial Ground, where "anthropologists who had engaged ... in very little study of Africana history and culture" produced a research design that was "culture-less, history-less, and biologically shallow" (LaRoche and Blakey 1997: p. 89).

One excellent example of the necessity of having researchers who are grounded in the history and culture of the community being studied is provided by a multivalent symbol, a pattern of nail heads found on lid of one of the coffins. This elaborate symbol was initially interpreted as a heart, but an African-American researcher recognized a resemblance to *Sankofa*, an Asante *Adinkra* symbol (LaRoche and Blakey 1997; Perry 1997a, 1997b). This recognition was confirmed by an analysis performed by a Ghanian historian of African Art (Ofori-Ansa 1995: 3). The Ghanian connection with the Burial Ground project was solidified in 1995 when a contingent led by Nana Oduro Namapau II, President of the Ghana National House of Chiefs, toured the Cobb Biological Anthropology Laboratory at Howard University and the Burial Ground site in Manhattan (Anonymous 1995a, 1995b; Gaines 1995). This visit was part of a five-city "Fihankra" tour initiated in Ghana in December of 1994 "to perform traditional rituals to atone for the misdeeds of those ancestral rulers who helped sustain the trans-African slave trade" (Anonymous 1995b). At the Burial Ground, the chiefs performed a libation ceremony of atonement and purification, confirming the importance of the property as a sacred ritual space.

Perhaps the most important struggle over the excavation and interpretation of the African Burial Ground has been the determination that the project be accountable to, and address the interests of, the African-American descendant community. In large measure this effort to define and control cultural property has been a success, preventing the project from becoming another Pinkster Day celebration, an event the dominant culture perceives as a spectacle staged for its benefit and amusement.

THE 1788 PETITION AND "DOCTOR'S RIOT"

In 1788 a delegation of enslaved and free African Americans presented a petition to the New York City Common Council in which they complained:

> That it hath lately been the constant practice of a number of young gentlemen in this City who call themselves Students of Physick, to repair to the Burial Ground assigned for the use of your petitioners, and under the cover of the Night, and in the most wanton Sallies of Excess, to dig up the Bodies of the deceased friends and relatives of your Petitioners, carry them away, and without respect to Age or Sex, mangle their flesh out of a wanton Curiosity and then expose it to Beats and Birds. (Heaton 1943: 1862).

Outrage against resurrectionists, people who stole bodies for dissection, resulted in the April, 1788 "Doctors Riots." This disturbance included a multiracial, multiclass assault against the New Gaol, where several doctors were being held in protective custody (Ladenheim 1950). Five rioters and three militia members guarding the jail were killed during the disturbance

For many in the African-American community, the 1991–1992 archaeological excavations at the Burial Ground site were understandably interpreted as the modern-day equivalent of bodysnatching, and their reactions were not dissimilar to those of the 1788 petitioners. By April of 1992 it was becoming increasingly evident that the number of burials excavated would greatly exceed the original estimates of 50 interments (Brown 1992a). In addition, GSA was becoming increasingly intransigent in its position that the construction project would be completed on schedule, regardless of community concerns about the Burial Ground. On April 25 (four days before the acquittal of four Los Angeles policemen who had been videotaped beating Rodney King) Sonny Carson, a well-known activist, was quoted, "This could be a very hot summer if the federal government doesn't yield to our demands." (Browne 1992b). By late June the legendary jazz violinist Noel Pointer was actively organizing the support of artists and collecting signatures on petitions to Congress (Strickland-Abuwi 1992). By late July efforts to halt the excavations had garnered the support of Mayor Dinkins and the Congressional Black Caucus (Browne 1992c). In addition, Congressman Gus Savage (D-Illinois), chair of the Subcommittee on Public Buildings and Grounds, convened hearings in Manhattan in late July in an attempt to force GSA to submit an acceptable research design before proceeding with the excavations (Boyd 1992a). On August 9, a 26-hour vigil was conducted at the site by a wide-ranging coalition of cultural workers, including contingents of Native-American activists (Boyd 1992b). By this date the excavations had been halted and control of the project was being transferred to Howard University and John Milner Associates (JMA).

Although there was strong support for transferring the project to the JMA/Howard University team, the new researchers faced the formidable tasks of garnering support for the reformulated research design while simultaneously assuring that the research was responsive to the needs and concerns of the descendant community (Officer 1993a, 1993b, 1993c). In accordance with the American Anthropological Association's Statement on Ethics and Professional Responsibility and the World Archaeological Congress' First Code of Ethics, Michael Blakey's research team recognized the right of the descendant community to accept, modify, or reject the research design. The pressure to have the osteological analysis performed by Howard University initially arose from two sources: the perception that MFAT was disrespectful and unprofessional in their handling of the human remains, and the desire to have the analysis performed by a historically black institution. However, many of the activists also soon began to apprehend the fundamental differences between the two research paradigms. The original research paradigm was a non-historical approach predicated on an essentialist, biogenetic concept of race (Dibennardo and Taylor 1983) that most members of the descendant community found to be demeaning and scientifically invalid. The Howard University team offered an anti-essentialist approach that foregrounds issues of history and culture; challenges the concept of biological races; and emphasizes genetic affinity, cultural identity, and the physical manifestations of class-based oppression (Blakey 1987, 1996; Brace 1995; Epperson 1996; Goodman and Armelagos 1995; LaRoche and Blakey 1997; Lieberman and Reynolds 1995; Mukhopadhyay and Moses 1997; Sauer 1992).

In an article entitled "Race, Identity, and Political Culture," Manning Marable (1992) distinguished between two conceptions of "Blackness": racial identity, an imposed category of domination that refers only to physical attributes, and cultural identity, a category that also includes African-American history, politics, and religion. As we have seen, the MFAT research paradigm was concerned primarily with identity in the first sense, while the Howard University paradigm represents an important attempt to also encompass identity in the second sense. The most important lesson of the African Burial Ground project is that the act of "seizing intellectual power" (LaRoche and Blakey) by the descendant community has resulted in a research program that is not only more responsive to the needs and concerns of the community, but is also indisputably better science.

CONCLUSION: ESSENTIALISM, IDENTITY POLITICS, AND THE ANTI-RACIST STRUGGLE

One of the important symbolic victories won by the African-American community in New York City was a change in the name of the burial ground site. A 1735 map depicted the area as the "Negro Burying Place" (Stokes I: plate 30) and a 1755 map carried the notation "Negros Burial Ground" (Stokes I: plate 34). During the early phases of the project the site was generally referred to as the "Negro's Burial Ground." However, as awareness of the project increased within the African-American community, pressure grew to avoid use of the word "Negro." It was argued that when they had the opportunity to name their own cultural institutions during the eighteenth century, people of African descent generally preferred the term "African" (e.g., African Methodist Episcopal Church), although this issue subsequently became very controversial (Stuckey 1987: 193–244). In addition, an 1812 New York Superior Court document cited above refers to the area as the "African Burying Ground." For the most part this transformation has been accepted by the mainstream press and cultural institutions. However, two major "gatekeeper" institutions, *The New York Times* (Dunlap 1993) and the New-York Historical Society, continue to resist this name change.

The move from "Negro's Burial Ground" to "African Burial Ground" is indicative of the extent to which the biogenetic category of race has been successfully displaced by the cultural category "African." Nevertheless, although race is, to a large extent, "debiologized" by this maneuver, distinctions such as European and African often remain as essential (in both senses) categories.

The discontinuation of burial excavations and the redirection of the African Burial Ground research design are important victories that attest to the power of identity politics. A mobilized and politicized minority community was able to halt construction of part of a federal complex that *had* to be built and subsequently force a major paradigm shift in an important research project. Nothing presented in this paper is intended to detract from the significance of these remarkable accomplishments. This project, however, also rises important issues that bear upon debates about essentialist and social constructionist theories of identity. In various forms, these debates are ongoing in the gay and lesbian, feminist, and African-American communities (Fuss 1989). For example, a 1994 Princeton University conference that featured presentations by Cornel West, Patricia Williams, Stuart Hall, Toni Morrison, and Angela Yvonne Davis focused on the issue of political essentialism (Winkler 1994).

In this analysis we have seen how identities such as Coromantee could simultaneously serve as both a means of domination and a basis for resistance. Similarly, despite attempts by the Anglican hierarchy to deploy religion as a means of controlling enslaved Africans and African Americans, Christianity could also serve as a basis of resistance. What is required is a "double-strategy" that fights oppression (homophobia, racism, sexism) while simultaneously interrogating and valorizing "difference" (Scott 1988).

LaRoche and Blakey (1997) quite appropriately situate the African Burial Ground research design within the tradition of "vindicationist" studies. However, this placement must be further characterized by a brief examination of current debates within activist African-American scholarship. In his classic essay "Anthropology and the Black Experience," St. Claire Drake discusses the literature of "racial vindication," which can be traced to eighteenth-century attempts "to disprove slander,

answer pejorative allegations, and criticize pseudoscientific generalizations about Africans and people of African descent." A classic example
of this genre is the Reverend Norman B. Wood's *The White Side of a
Black Subject (enlarged and brought down to date), A Vindication of the
Afro-American Race From the Landing of Slaves at St. Augustine, Flor-
ida, in 1565 to the Present Time*, which was published in 1897, one year
after W.E.B. DuBois received a doctorate in History from Harvard
University (Drake 1980: 10). African–American scholars and activists,
including DuBois, assessed disciplines in terms of how favorable or
inimical they were to the "vindication" struggle. Until Franz Boas
began popularizing his work, anthropology was (quite correctly) viewed
as an unequivocal enemy of this struggle, much as African intellectuals
tended to consider the discipline as adjunct to oppressive colonialism.
Although mainstream British and American anthropology remained
undeniably racist, African-American scholar/activists began to realize
the vindicationist potential of anthropology. Although Drake recognizes
the value of this approach, he also discusses its limitations. He closes his
essay by stating, "Anthropology is a tool—certainly—but it should not
be only that; it has always had affiliations with art and literature as
well as with administration and revolutionary action. Beyond the black
experience lies the human experience" (1980: 29).

In his recent book *W.E.B. DuBois and American Political Thought:
Fabianism and the Color Line*, Adolph Reed, Jr. is extremely critical of
the literature of "racial vindicationism," stating that it is a "defensive
psychology" that "often leads to a conceptual narrowness and atheoreti-
cism" (1997: 5). In place of the vindicationist paradigm, Reed advocates
what he calls a generativist approach, "which resolves the tensions
between the scholarly and hortatory imperatives in Afro-American intellectual life. Its objectives are probing and tough-minded academically
and, simultaneously, directly linked to civic concerns" (1997: 183). Although it is not discussed in these terms, the research program for the
African Burial Ground has, in many important respects, already transcended the limits of its vindicationist origins and incorporates elements of the generativist approach advocated by Reed. The descendant community and the researchers are interacting in a dialectical
relationship. While the research design must (and does) address vindicationist concerns, the researchers also demonstrate how the project
can transcend the defensive posture of countering racist mythologies
and adopt an assertive posture that poses new questions and offers
findings that will force a major rethinking of American and trans-
Atlantic history that transcends the immediate initial concerns of the
descendant community.

Whether we like it or not, there is no such thing as non-political anthropology (Harrison 1991; 1995), and those of us who are not members of minority communities should be as clear as possible about the implications of our work. For example, an effort to deconstruct categories such as "race" could have the unintended effect of undermining very powerful identity-based political action, an approach characterized by some critical race theorists as "vulgar anti-essentialism" (Crenshaw et al. 1995: xxvi). One approach is to join in the anti-racist struggle by interrogating the category of "whiteness:"

> One change in direction that would be real cool would be the production of a discourse on race that interrogates whiteness.... [O]nly a persistent, rigorous, and informed critique of whiteness could really determine what forces of denial, fear, and competition are responsible for creating fundamental gaps between professed political commitment to eradicating racism and the participation in the construction of a discourse on race that perpetuates racial domination. (Hooks 1989, see also Epperson 1997; Hartigan 1997; Marable 1995; Page and Thomas 1994).

Although it is seldom expressed in these terms, the struggle against the essentialist concept of race is also an aspect of the struggle against capitalism itself. Race has been—and continues to be—"essential" for the development of capitalism in two senses. Racism was, and continues to be, essential in the philosophical sense, "one of the most blatant and potentially evil forms of essentialist thought" (Crapanzano 1986: 20). Racism has also been essential within the political economy of capitalism as a mechanism for creating discipline, distinctions, and divisiveness within the working classes (McGuire and Payner 1991; Robinson 1983: 51)

Race is not an innate attribute of the human condition. Rather it is an ideology, a social construct that is being constantly reinvented and reritualized (Fields 1990; Goldberg 1993). Race is not a thing or an attribute that explains behavior or historical events. Race was not the *a priori* explanation for Trinity Church's 1697 decision to ban persons of African descent from their burial ground. Rather, the essentialist conception of race and the attendant racism emerged from, and is nurtured by, countless moments of class-based oppression. Today, we are faced with a decision: we can either continue to recreate and re-enact "race," or we can join in the anti-racist struggle.

Acknowledgments

Over the course of several years many individuals have offered assistance for this analysis. First and foremost, the principal researchers on the African Burial Ground project have been unfailingly friendly and receptive, including Michael Blakey, Mark Mack, Warren Perry, and Sherrill Wilson. Cheryl LaRoche kindly shared a prepublication copy of "Seizing Intellectual Power: The Dialogue at the New York African Burial Ground" the excellent paper she coauthored with Michael Blakey. Additional assistance was provided by Betsey Bradley, Len Bianchi, Jean Howson, Peggy King Jorde, and Michael Parrington. I would also like to thank the co-participants at the Santa Fe seminar for a delightfully challenging and invigorating week in the desert. In particular, Alison Wylie understood what I was trying to say better than I did. In the process of explicating my paper she helped me clarify and focus my presentation.

REFERENCES

Allen, T. W.
  1994 *The Invention of the White Race: Volume One, Racial Oppression and Social Control.* Verso, London.
Allen, T. W.
  1994 *The Invention of the White Race: Volume Two, The Origin of Racial Oppression in Anglo America.* Verso, London.
Anonymous
  1995a [photo caption] To Atone for the Misdeeds of the Past. *New York Times,* August 5, 1995.
  1995b Royal African Delegation Plans to Visit African Burial Ground. *New York Amsterdam News,* August 5, 1995, p. 30.
Bakhtin, M.
  1984 *Rabelais and His World.* University of Indiana Press, Bloomington.
Baugher, S., E. J. Lenik, T. Amorosi, D. Dallal, J. Guston, D. A. Plotts, and R. Venables.
  1990 The Archaeological Investigation of the City Hall Park Site, Manhattan. Report prepared by the New York City Landmarks Preservation Commission for the New York City Department of General Services.
Beckles, H. McD.
  1989 *White Servitude and Black Slavery in Barbados, 1627–1715.* University of Tennessee Press, Knoxville.
Behn, A.
  1987 *Oroonoko, or, The Royal Slave.* [1688] (a critical edition edited by Adelaide P. Amore). University Press of America, Lanham, Maryland.
Blakey, M. L.
  1987 Skull Doctors: Intrinsic Social and Political Bias in the History of American Physical Anthropology. *Critique of Anthropology* 7(2):7–35.
  1995 Race, Nationalism, and the Afrocentric Past. *Making Alternative Histories: The Practice of Archaeology and History in Non-western Settings,* edited by P. R. Schmidt and T. C. Patterson, pp. 213–228. School of American Research Press, Santa Fe.
  1996 Skull Doctors Revisited: Intrinsic Social and Political Bias in the History of American Physical Anthropology, With Special Reference to the Works of Ales

Hrdlicka, In *Race and Other Misadventures: Essays in Honor of Ashley Montague in His Ninetieth Year*, edited by L. T. Reynolds and L. Leiberman, pp. 64–95. General Hall, Inc., Dix Hills, New York.

Boyd, H.
1992a   Dinkins, Prof. Clarke, Others Testify at Burial Ground Hearings. *New York Amsterdam News*, August 1, 1992, p. 3.
1992b   Hundreds Pay Respects at Burial Ground Vigil. *New York Amsterdam News*, August 15, 1992, pp. 3, 35.

Brace, C. L.
1995   A Four-Letter Word Called "Race." In *Race and Other Misadventures: Essays in Honor of Ashley Montague in His Ninetieth Year*, edited by L. T. Reynolds and L. Leiberman, pp. 106–141. General Hall, Inc., Dix Hills, New York.

Browne, J. Z.
1992a   500 More Bodies Found at Negro Burial Site. *New York Amsterdam News*, April 18, 1992, pp. 1, 34.s
1992b   Pols Demand Burial Ground be Made an Historic Site. *New York Amsterdam News*, April 25, 1992, pp. 2.
1992c   Dinkins Demands Halt to Digging at Burial Ground. *New York Amsterdam News*, July 25, 1992, pp. 1, 14.

Cohen, S. S.
1971   Elias Neau, Instructor to New York's Slaves. *New-York Historical Society Quarterly* 55:7–27.

Cook, K.
1993   Black Bones, White Science: The Battle over New York's African Burial Ground. *The Village Voice*, May 4, 1993.

Cooper, J. F.
1990   *Satanstoe, or The Littlepage Manuscripts: A Tale of the Colony* [1845], with an Historical Introduction by K. S. House. State University of New York, Albany.

Crapazano, V.
1986   *Waiting: The Whites of South Africa*. Random House, New York.

Crenshaw, K., N. Gotanda, G. Peller, and K. Thomas.
1995   Introduction. In *Critical Race Theory: The Key Writings that Formed the Movement*, pp. xiii–xxxii. New Press, New York.

Craton, M.
1982   *Testing the Chains: Resistance to Slavery in the British West Indies*. Cornell University Press, Ithaca.

Cray, R. E.
1988   Poverty and Poor Relief: New York City and its Rural Environs, 1700–1790, in *Authority and Resistance in Early New York*, edited by William Pencak and Conrad Edick Wright, pp. 173–201. New-York Historical Society, New York.

Davis, T. J.
1985   *A Rumor of Revolt: The "Great Negro Plot" in Colonial New York*. The Free Press, New York.

Dibennardo, R., and J. V. Taylor
1983   Multiple Discriminant Function Analysis of Sex and Race in the Postcranial Skeleton. *American Journal of Physical Anthropology* 61:305–314.

Drake, St. C.
1980   Anthropology and the Black Experience. *The Black Scholar* 11(7):2–31.

Dunlap, D. W.
1993   A Black Cemetery Takes its Place in History. *New York Times*, February 28, 1993, p. E5.

Epperson, T. W.
  1996 The Politics of "Race" and Cultural Identity at the African Burial Ground Excavations, New York City. *World Archaeological Bulletin* 7:108–117.
  1997 Whiteness in Early Virginia. *Race Traitor* 7:9–20.
Fields, B. J.
  1990 Slavery and Ideology in the United States of America. *New Left Review* 181:95–118.
Fine-Dare, K. S.
  1997 Disciplinary Renewal Out Of National Disgrace: Native American Graves Protection and Repatriation Act Compliance in the Academy. *Radical History Review* 68:25–53.
Fuss, D.
  1989 *Essentially Speaking: Feminism, Nature and Difference*. Routledge, New York.
Gaines, P.
  1995 Bones of Forebears: Howard U. Study Stirs Ghanian Chiefs to Honor Ages-Old Link to U.S. Blacks. *Washington Post*, August 3, 1995.
Gilroy, P.
  1993 *The Black Atlantic: Modernity and Double Consciousness*. Harvard University Press, Cambridge.
Godwyn, M.
  1680 *The Negro's & Indians Advocate, Suing for the Admission into the Church: or A Persuasive to the Instructing and Baptizing of the Negro's and Indians in our Plantations.... To Which is added, A brief Account of Religion in Virginia*. London.
Goldberg, D. T.
  1993 *Racist Culture: Philosophy and the Politics of Meaning*. Blackwell, Oxford.
Goodman, A. H., and G. J. Armelagos
  1996 The Resurrection of Race: The Concept of Race in Physical Anthropology in the 1990s. In *Race and Other Misadventures: Essays in Honor of Ashley Montague in His Ninetieth Year*, edited by L. T. Reynolds and L. Leiberman, pp. 174–186. General Hall, Inc., Dix Hills, New York.
Grim, D.
  1854 *A Plan of the City and Environs of New York*. Drawn in 1813, depicting 1744. (Lithograph by G. Gayward for *Valentine's Manual*, 1854). David T. Valentine. Valentine Co., New York.
Grossman, J. W.
  1991 The Buried History of City Hall Park: The Initial Archaeological Identification, Definition, and Documentation of Well-preserved 18th-Century Deposits and Possible Structural Remains of NYC's First Almshouse. Report prepared by Grossman and Associates, Inc., for the New York City Department of General Services.
GSA (General Services Administration, Region 2, Complier)
  1993 Comments on the Draft Research Design for Archaeological, Historical, and Bioanthropological Investigations of the African Burial Ground and Five Points Area, New York, New York. General Services Administration, Region 2, New York.
Handler, J. S.
  1994 Determining African Birth from Skeletal Remains: A Note on Tooth Mutilation. *Historical Archaeology* 28:113–119.
  1997 An African-Type Healer/Diviner and His Grave Goods: A Burial from a Plantation Slave Cemetery in Barbados, West Indies. *International Journal of Historical Archaeology* 1:91–130.
Harris, G., J. Howson, and B. Bradley
  1993 African Burial Ground and the Commons Historic District: Designation Report. New York City Landmarks Preservation Commission, New York.

Harrison, F. V.
    1991   Anthropology as an Agent of Transformation: Introductory Comments and
    Queries, In *Decolonizing Anthropology: Moving Further Toward an Anthropology for
    Liberation*, edited by Faye V. Harrison, pp. 1–14. American Anthropological Asso-
    ciation, Washington, D.C.
    1995   The Persistent Power of "Race" in the Cultural and Political Economy of Rac-
    ism. *Annual Review of Anthropology* 24:47–74.
Hartigan, J., Jr.
    1997   Establishing the Fact of Whiteness. *American Anthropologist* 99:495–505.
Heaton, C.
    1943   Body Snatching in New York City. *New York State Journal of Medicine* 43:1861–
    1865.
hooks, b. [Gloria Watkins]
    1990   Critical Interrogation: Talking Race, Resisting Racism. In *Yearning: Race, Gen-
    der, and Cultural Politics*, pp. 51–56. South End Press, Boston.
Horsmanden, D.
    1971   *The New York Conspiracy*. Edited with an Introduction by T. J. Davis. Beacon
    Press, Boston.
Howard University and John Milner Associates
    1993   Foley Square Federal Courthouse and Office Building, New York, New York:
    Research Design for Archaeological, Historical, and Bioanthropological Investiga-
    tions of the African Burial Ground (Broadway Block) New York, New York (December
    14, 1993). Prepared for General Services Administration, Region 2, New York.
Howson, J., and G. Harris
    1992   African Burial Ground: National Register of Historic Places Registration Form.
    NYC Landmarks Preservation Commission, on file.
Ignatiev, N.
    1995   *How the Irish Became White*. Routledge, New York.
Jorde, P. K. (compiler)
    1993   Final Recommendations to the Administrator, General Services Administra-
    tion and the United States Congress on the Memorialization of the African Burial
    Ground.
King, T. F.
    1997   Identification and Management of Traditional Cultural Places. (a short course
    at the annual meeting of the American Cultural Resources Association, St. Louis,
    Missouri, September 19, 1997.)
Ladenheim, J. C.
    1950   The "Doctors Mob" of 1788. *Journal of the History of Medicine* 5:23–43.
LaRoche, C. J., and M. L. Blakey
    1997   Seizing Intellectual Power: The Dialogue at the New York African Burial
    Ground. *Historical Archaeology* 31(3):84–106.
Levine, L. W.
    1977   *Black Culture and Black Consciousness: Afro-American Thought from Slavery to
    Freedom*. Oxford University Press, New York.
Lieberman, L., and L. T. Reynolds
    1995   Race: The Deconstruction of a Scientific Concept, In *Race and Other Misadven-
    tures: Essays in Honor of Ashley Montague in His Ninetieth Year*, edited by L. T.
    Reynolds and L. Leiberman, pp. 142–173. General Hall, Inc., Dix Hills, New York.
Linebaugh, P., and M. Rediker
    1990   The Many-Headed Hydra: Sailors, Slaves, and the Atlantic Working Class in the
    Eighteenth Century. *Journal of Historical Sociology* 3(3):225–252.

Lott, E.
1993   *Love and Theft: Blackface Minstrely and the American Working Class.* Oxford University Press, New York.
Lydon, J. G.
1978   New York and the Slave Trade, 1700 to 1774. *William and Mary Quarterly* 35:375–394.
Maerschalck, F.
1755   *A Plan of the City of New York from an Actual Survey Anno Domini M,DDC,LV.*
Manross, W. W. (editor)
1974   *S.P.G. Papers in the Lambeth Palace Library: Calendar and Indexes.* Clarendon Press, Oxford.
Marable, M.
1992   Race, Identity, and Political Culture, In *Black Popular Culture: A Project by Michele Wallace,* edited by Gina Dent, pp. 292–302. Bay Press, Seattle.
1995   Beyond Racial Identity Politics: Toward a Liberation Theory for Multicultural Democracy, In *Beyond Black and White: Transforming African–American Politics,* pp. 185–202. Verso, London.
MCC (Minutes of the Common Council, cited in text by date of entry)
1905   *Minutes of the Common Council, 1675–1776.* Dodd, Mead, New York.
1917   *Minutes of the Common Council, 1784–1831.* Dodd, Mead, New York.
McGuire, R. H., and R. Payner (editors)
1991   *The Archaeology of Inequality.* Blackwell, Oxford.
Merrill, W. L., E. J. Ladd, and T. J. Ferguson
1993   The Return of the *Ahayuda*: Lessons for Repatriation from Zuni Pueblo and the Smithsonian Institution. *Current Anthropology* 34:523–568.
Mintz, S. W., and R. Price
1992   *The Birth of African–American Culture: An Anthropological Perspective.* Beacon Press, Boston.
Mukhopadhyay, C. C., and Y. T. Moses
1997   Reestablishing "Race" in Anthropological Discourse. *American Anthropologist* 99:517–533.
Nassaney, M.
1986   Objectivity and Critical Analysis in Mortuary Studies: A North American Case Study. Paper presented at the World Archaeological Congress, Southhampton, England.
Officer, D.
1993a   Scientists Probe African Burial Ground for Answers to Puzzles. *New York Amsterdam News,* August 21, 1993, pp. 2, 30.
1993b   Part II: Artifacts Tell Stories of the Dead in Slave Burials. *New York Amsterdam News,* August 28, 1993, pp. 2, 30.
1993c   Part III: New Technology Puts "Life" to Old Bones. *New York Amsterdam News,* August 28, 1993, pp. 2, 48.
Ofori-Ansa, K.
1995   Identification and Validation of the Sanfoka Symbol. *Update: Newsletter of the African Burial Ground & Five Points Archaeological Projects* 1(8):3. Sherrill D. Wilson, Newsletter Editor. New York.
Page, H. E., and R. B. Thomas
1994   White Public Space and the Construction of White Privilege in U.S. Health Care: Fresh Concepts and a New Model of Analysis. *Medical Anthropology Quarterly* 8: 109–116.
Parker, P. L., and T. F. King
1992   Guidelines for Evaluating and Documenting Traditional Cultural Properties.

National Register Bulletin 38. U.S. Department of the Interior, National Park Service, Washington, D.C.

Perry, W. R.
1997a   Analysis of the African Burial Ground Archaeological Materials. *Update, Newsletter of the African Burial Ground & Five Points Archaeological Projects* 2(2):1, 3–5, 14.
1997b   Archaeology as Community Service. *Society for the Anthropology of North America Newsletter*, pp. 1–3.

Pickering, J. H.
1966   Fenimore Cooper and Pinkster. *New York Folklore Quarterly* 22(1):15–19.

Plan of New York
1735   Plan of the City of New York in the Year 1735. Cartographer unknown. 1735, depicting 1732–35. (Stokes, Vol. 1, Pl 30).

Reed, A. L., Jr.
1997   *W. E. B. DuBois and American Political Thought: Fabianism and the Color Line.* Oxford University Press, New York.

Roedigger, D.
1991   *The Wages of Whiteness: Race and the Making of the American Working Class.* Verso, New York.

Rodney, W.
1969   Upper Guinea and the significance of the Origins of Africans Enslaved in the New World. *Journal of Negro History* 54:327–345.

Ross, S. J.
1988   Objects of Charity: Poor Relief, Poverty, and the Rise of the Almshouse in Early Eighteenth-Century New York City, In *Authority and Resistance in Early New York*, edited by W. Pencak and C. E. Wright, pp. 138–172. New-York Historical Society, New York.

Sauer, N. J.
1992   Forensic Anthropology and the Concept of Race: If Races Don't Exist, Why are Forensic Anthropologists so Good at Identifying Them? *Social Science and Medicine* 34:107–112.

Scarupa, H. J.
1994   Learning from Ancestral Bones: New York's Exhumed African Past. *American Visions* February/March, 1994:19–21.

Schuler, M.
1970   Akan Slave Rebellions in the British Caribbean. *Savacou: A Journal of the Caribbean Artists Movement* 1(1):8–32.

Scott, J. W.
1988   Deconstructing Equality-Versus-Difference: Or, the Uses of Post-structuralist Theory for Feminism. *Feminist Studies* 14:33–50.

Scott, K.
1961   The Slave Insurrection in New York in 1712. *New-York Historical Society Quarterly* 45:43–74.

Sealy, J. C., N. J. van der Merwe, A. Sillen, J. F. Kruger, and H. W. Krueger
1991   87SR/86SR as a Dietary Indicator in Modern Archaeological Bone. *Journal of Archaeological Science* 18:399–416.

Sharpe, J.
1712   [Letter written 6/23/1712 to the secretary of the Propagation of the Gospel in Foreign Parts.] reprinted in the *New York Genealogical and Biographical Record* (1890) 21:162–163.
1713   Proposals for Erecting a School, Library and Chapel at New York. (MSS. 841,

Lambeth Palace Library, London). Reprinted in *Collections of the New-York Historical Society for the year 1880*, pp. 341–363. Printed for the Society by Trow & Smith Book Manufacturing Co., New York, NY.

Sider, G.

  1987   When Parrots Learn to Talk, and Why They Can't: Domination, Deception, and Self-Deception in Indian–White Relations. *Comparative Studies in Society and History* 29:3–23.

  1994   Identity as History: Ethnohistory, Ethnogenesis and Ethoncide in the Southeastern United States. *Identities: Global Studies in Culture and Power* 1(1):109–122.

Smith, A.

  1986   *The Wealth of Nations*, Books I–III [1776], Introduction by A. Skinner. Penguin Books, London.

Stokes, I. N. P.

  1915   *The Iconography of Manhattan Island, 1498–1909.* Robert H. Dodd, New York.

Strickland-Abuwi, L.

  1992   Jazz Great Noel Pointer Fights to Save 18th-Century Black Cemetery. *New York Amsterdam News*, June 27, 1992, pp. 3, 23.

Stuckey, S.

  1987   *Slave Culture: Nationalist Theory and the Foundations of Black America*. Oxford University Press, Oxford.

  1994   *Going Through the Storm: The Influence of African American Art in History.* Oxford University Press, New York.

Thompson, E. P.

  1993   *Customs in Common: Studies in Traditional Popular Culture.* The New Press, New York.

Valentine, D. T.

  1827–1866   *Manual of the Corporation of New York*. David T. Valentine, New York.

Vigilant, L. A.

  1991   African Populations and the Evolution of Human Mitochondrial DNA. *Science* 253:1503–1507.

White, S.

  1989   Pinkster: Afro-Dutch Syncretization in New York City and the Hudson Valley. *Journal of American Folklore* 102:68–75.

Williams, B.

  1989   A Class Act: Anthropology and the Race to Nation across Ethnic Terrain. *Annual Review of Anthropology* 18:401–444.

Wilson, S. D., and J. Howson

  1997   Modern Myths of the African Burial Ground. *Update, Newsletter of the African Burial Ground & Five Points Archaeological Projects* 2(2):8–9.

Winkler, K. J.

  1994   The Significance of Race. *The Chronicle of Higher Education* May 11, 1994, pp. A10, A14.

Zimmerman, L. J.

  1989   Made Radical by My Own: An Archaeologist Learns to Accept Reburial, In *Conflict in the Archaeology of Living Traditions*, edited by R. Layton, pp. 60–67. Routledge, London.

Integration into Capitalism and Impoverishment | III

Capitalism lives on profit and poverty. The ways this occurs as described here include farm tenancy, and the deliberate withdrawal of capital from a locale, racism, and ideology. These are ways that see that people are paid very poor wages, are charged a great deal for basic resources, or become so encompassed by ideology that profit goes to others nonviolently.

Our authors do not subscribe to the argument that when some people are making money, everyone benefits. They deny the argument that as a society produces wealth, everyone gets some of it. All boats do not rise with the rising tide of prosperity. This is not an ideology found behind the work of the authors in this section.

Orser, Purser, Mullins, and Leone describe in detail, through archaeology, the methods by which maximum wealth is extracted from whole groups of people, representing millions of individuals. These means are not foreign to anyone, but are widely known and practiced. For the most part they are tolerated and defended. But when condemned, like racism, they are often practiced anyway. We have in this section the antidote to the milder kind of historical archaeology that seeks to describe those who are marginalized, underrepresented, or hidden. We see here that those without history are deliberately dispossessed, cursed, and cheated, which is both why they have no history and what their history needs to include.

Charles Orser describes farm tenancy as a long-term, widespread form of agricultural productivity effecting millions of U.S. farmers on hundreds of thousands of farms. It affects more white people than black people; is disregarded by historical archaeologists, who normally operate without a sense of either problem or social potential; and is a significant way of studying poverty, class, and cross-regional comparisons. Tenancy is a form of labor that yields a predetermined split of the crop between capitalist and worker that always puts the farmer at the disadvantage.

Orser compares ceramic assemblages between several sites on one plantation and then at sites between two plantations, one in Georgia and another in Texas. While the results within one plantation show stratified access to purchasing power, and thus to income, the cross-regional comparison is inconclusive. Orser is looking for a way to study the effect on wealth produced by farm tenancy. He was not able to find an absolute measure through use of Miller's price index of English ceramics, but he did find a uniform settlement pattern and architecture.

Margaret Purser solves Orser's problem of identifying a uniform pattern for characterizing impoverishment by examining reuse of metal objects she found throughout sites in Paradise Valley, Nevada. Reuse, mending, and adapting one thing to another produces multiple uses for objects. Prehistorians may remember that the Binfords found stone tools with multiple edges for multiple cutting purposes at the end of the Mousterian, a period of fast change in habitat and subsistence. Paradise Valley dried up and was mined out simultaneously, and those people who stayed attempted several ways of making a living at once. Their strategy shows in the metal artifacts—many unrecognizably changed from more easily identifiable initial uses. Regional impoverishment also shows in their archaeological deposits. While deposits often represent many owners or renters, the remains have been so changed, so continuously, that anything organic has been eaten; anything made of metal reused or sold; and all containers recycled.

Paul Mullins achieves many goals in his paper. One goal is tied to Charles Orser's effort, and describes reuse of domestic ceramics, as well as people who show no commitment to use matched sets in the conventional Victorian way. Mullins deals with African Americans whose social and economic place was defined by racism. The archaeology of their homes showed that they bought what was available, and used older and unmatched dishes. These two characteristics, reuse and episodic buying of what was available, mark the kinds of comparative indices Orser sought in order to discover tenancy.

Mullins, however, deals with impoverishment from within. People may know their circumstances are poor and may know that they and their neighbors, locality, and brothers and sisters are exploited. But most such individuals never accept the marginalized and despised lot given to them when they are called "poor." They use the material world to their advantage. They used mail-order catalogues and locally available national brands to escape the local cheat.

The most important contribution Mullins makes is to show that, despite the racism that marginalized them, African Americans used goods to circumvent exploitation in two ways. One way was through avoiding local adulterated products often sold at usurious prices. Such avoidance provides a context in which to understand the use of national brands of bottled and canned goods. The other was to create a visual environment that served to convince whites that they were the model for emulation. Thus, the common items of Victorian America served to contradict racist accusations that black skin was a sign of inherent inferiority. Thus, Purser's glass lampshade and parlor dish, and the Maynard's porcelain birds, were not emulation at all, they were negations aimed at ethnic and racist slurs. Orser will find the same among his tenants, who refused to believe that they could be "poor white trash."

Leone's concern is integration into a capitalist market. Integration always leads to a position in a class, including self-identity. It might also lead to poverty. He attempts to identify a change in ideology, the mask for capitalism's exploitation. The masks are the practice of individualism, rationalism, mechanical time, and measured space. He argues that individualism was made possible through disciplines, or the little and ever-present technical maneuvers done all day, everyday, by anyone. Such routines teach time and work disciplines. Thus, Leone is arguing that ceramic change can measure level of a household's integration into capitalism.

Leone's work on eighteenth and nineteenth century ceramics from Annapolis builds on his earlier work with Paul Shackel. They both attempt to create an index for the degree of participation in a modern way of conceptualizing time, cause, and individuality. Leone's question is: How do you tell degree of integration into capitalism? He offers an index that compares the variation in ceramic styles and ceramic forms from a stratum at a site. The more that people ate from matched sets, the more modern they were; the more forms of vessel types, the more segmented, and thus, modern, their behavior. The higher the index value, the more integrated into the market, with small numbers of vessels and little variation in decoration producing small index values. Thus, the scale is open ended.

5

Ex Occidente Lux?
An Archaeology of Later Capitalism in the Nineteenth-Century West

Margaret Purser

Babbitt (bab'it): 1. any of various alloys of tin with smaller amounts of anti-mony and copper, used as an antifriction lining for bearings. 2. a self-satisfied person who conforms readily to conventional, middle-class ideas and ideals, esp. of business and material success: from the main character in the novel (1922) [by Sinclair Lewis].
> —*Random House Dictionary of the English Language*,
> Unabridged Edition, 1971, p. 106.

INTRODUCTION: OLD BEARINGS, NEW DIRECTIONS, AND SINCLAIR LEWIS

In the summer of 1985 I was cataloguing a sparse trash scatter out in the sagebrush behind a ranch at the northeast end of Paradise Valley, Nevada. For the most part, the dump had yielded a disappointingly meager and conventional list of items: early machine-made sauce bot-tles, some generic white ironstone, bits of kerosene-lamp chimney glass, and some fragments of shoe leather inexplicably overlooked by the local coyotes. The dates ranged in the first two decades of the twentieth century, a full 40 years too late for the homesteading period I had been hoping to find. But they did mesh reassuringly with the dates of ranch tenancy by a local Basque family, the Mendiolas. Nothing in the trash dump was particularly redolent of Basque ethnicity, but I was getting used to that. At least there were some family descendants still living in the Valley. Maybe I could interview them about when they'd lived on the Reinhart Ranch.

Margaret Purser • Department of Anthropology, Sonoma State University, Rohnert Park, California 94928.

Historical Archaeologies of Capitalism, edited by Mark P. Leone and Parker B. Potter, Jr. Plenum Press, New York, 1999.

In amongst the other debris were one or two objects I could not identify. One piece particularly intrigued me: a cast-metal bearing, obviously part of some larger piece of ranch equipment, with a residue of silvery metal dribbled around the bottom of the cup. Robert Humphrey, the Reinhart's current owner and a retired Nevada sheriff who'd grown up on ranches in the eastern part of the state in the 1930s, kindly explained the mysteries of babbitt to me, and the specific use of the soft tin alloy to mend and refit old, worn bearings. I remember thinking what a delicious irony this brought to the name of Sinclair Lewis's protagonist of his 1922 novel, *Babbitt*; that it honestly did not occur to me that Lewis might have noticed the same irony can be attributed to that sublime hubris characteristic of early graduate school years.

It is equally telling that I found the babbitt bearing to be an insignificant artifact from too recent a period. The significant events in the Valley's history had occurred in the early years of settlement, and in the subsequent decades of the silver-mining boom and commercial grain and cattle production. By the 1920s, it was all over; the "bust" had begun. Besides, the bearing itself represented the modern technology of internal combustion engines, of John Deere and Henry Ford. These were the known, contemporary aspects of the Valley's material culture, as opposed to those of the unknown past that I was there to explore. I did not even photograph it.

Trapped in a frontier mythology that owed as much to Zane Grey and Lorne Green as it did to Frederick Jackson Turner, it never occurred to me to treat the bust as an event at least as significant as the boom had been. I did not see the quality of Basque ethnicity in the Mendiola family's tenancy of the ranch, as opposed to direct ownership. And I read babbitt bearings as one of those quaintly self-reliant practices prized by the local ranchers, venerated in their stories about making a living in the Nevada desert. The bearing represented an idiosyncratic modification of a mainstream technology not substantively different from the one familiar to me. I failed to recognize it for what it was: an integral component of an altogether *different* technology, and one that, for that time and place, had been very much in the mainstream. People had even written novels about it.

This paper makes two basic points. First, the vantage point of the American West during the late nineteenth and early twentieth century is an important one from which to contemplate an archaeology of later capitalism because of the relatively later dates involved and the ambiguously peripheral position the region has occupied in the nation's social and economic history. Second, any such archaeology, regardless of regional focus, must initiate a much broader and more thoroughgoing understanding of the material culture of capitalism than historical archaeologists have been willing to undertake thus far.

Capitalism may be a global process, but it goes on in small places, and as a result varies distinctly over relatively small scales of space and time. The quality of the material culture thus produced is equally variable and complex, and needs to be seen as such. It was a material culture that was inherently ambivalent and ambiguous, open to strategic manipulation on many levels, and not always used in the manner suggested by the "package label."

But all this ambiguity does not mean that its deeper logic is inaccessible to archaeologists. The near-constant reworking of physical and ideological reality, and the fundamentally contested nature of the resulting material world, did leave identifiable patterns, at a minimum of two levels. Materially, as the babbitt bearing indicates, this was a complex, highly variable world of objects in which superficial, mass-produced homogeneity masked consumer goods that were curated, mended, and recycled; buildings and other structures that took various forms over time; and systems of land use that overlaid and interpenetrated one another.

Ideologically, it was a world in which material culture itself served as a form of social babbitt. The increased availability of mass-produced goods and a consumer-oriented popular culture functioned superficially to ease the appearances of social tension. And yet, like the babbitt in the bearing, this mending left a mark in the increasing status orientation of consumer culture as a whole, and in the subtle reorganization of consumption itself to craft a workforce suitable to the needs of industrial capitalism (cf. Ewen 1976, 1982, 1996; Lears 1983, 1994; Miller 1987, 1995; Nye and Pedersen, 1991).

The central archaeological question for all this is: How do we define, identify, and interpret all this ambiguity, pluralism, and strategic manipulation? It is the assertion of this paper that these patterns can only be identified by archaeologists working back and forth across the range of scales at which capitalism was, and is, relevant, from the smallest local household to the vast sweep of global economic cycles. Only then do the human actions that produced such material patterning emerge. These actions cannot be explained fully as either the economically determined automata of an encroaching world system, or as idiosyncratic, and ultimately circumscribed, resistance to such a system. Rather they constitute inherently, necessarily ambiguous material and ideological strategies for surviving the economic vicissitudes of later capitalism, and translating that survival into success.

The ability to simultaneously explore the particularistic detail of local social dynamics and the more generalized regional and national context into which these minutiae fit is the lure of an expanded model of capitalist material culture. The difficulties of such an undertaking include determining the extent to which archaeology can escape a simplistic equation between individual and artifact, or the equally superficial equation of smaller- and larger-scale phenomena.

Some brief examples are provided to support these points, based on research on the small community of Paradise Valley, Nevada from the 1860s to the 1920s. Along with much of the intermountain west, Paradise Valley experienced an extensive period of deindustrialization between the late 1880s and World War I. The changes in material culture seen in the community over the same period do not merely reflect the means used to survive the economic and social dislocation of the time. These changes in consumption patterns, built environment, and technology also constituted a clever bit of ideological babbittry: a means of translating this process of decline into a form of success. The questions become: whose success, in what terms, and to whose benefit? Furthermore, did this locally focused manipulation of material culture constitute "resistance" to the ravages of later industrial capitalism? If so, resistance on whose part, in a community split fundamentally along lines of landowners and tenants, employers and laborers, merchants and customers, residents and migrants?

CAPITALISM FROM THE WEST

As Don Hardesty and Alison Wylie suggested at the time, there are many similarities between the debates that emerged in western American history in the late 1980s, and historical archaeology during the same period (Hardesty 1991; Wylie 1992). In particular, the efforts to recast a single, homogenized, and inevitable American frontier epic into many "longer, grimmer, but more interesting" histories closely parallels the struggle of many historical archaeologists to incorporate broader, more complex, and more critical approaches in their own work (West 1990, 1991).

These parallels are particularly significant for those who would do an archaeology of capitalism. The renewal of interest in the American West as a capitalist enterprise has been sponsored by far-reaching critiques both by and of the "New Western Historians" (Limerick 1991, Robbins 1991, West 1991; for recent critiques and responses see Etulain 1996a&b; Klein 1997). This issue of regional variation is one that cannot be avoided in any discussion of the development of capitalism as

an undeniably global phenomenon. Equally significant is the opportunity to examine capitalism in its later, industrialized phases, when
overt European territorial expansion had been replaced by a more
economically manifested encroachment, which Walter Nugent has described as a global contest between frontiers and empires (Nugent 1989,
1991).

Perhaps even more to the point for contemporary historical archaeology is a central tenet of much of the new western history: the processes of capitalist exploitation seen in the nineteenth-century West did
not end in 1900, any more than a Turnerian frontier closed. The environmental degradation; dependence on government subsidies; subjugation
of ethnic and racial minorities; and highly unstable, mobile labor structure that characterize today's west began with the industrial exploitation of the lands between the Rockies and the Sierras in the 1840s. If
there is any place where an archaeology of capitalism can confront its
unavoidably critical, self-reflexive nature, it is here.

What kind of capitalism are we dealing with in the industrial West
of the mid-nineteenth through early twentieth centuries? Apparently
straightforward categories such as "mercantile" versus "industrial" capitalism, as these characterized relations between "colonies" and "nation–
states", take on added complexity in what Richard White has described
as the extractive economy of the American West: the high-tech, capital-
intensive industries designed to extract precious metals and bulk commodities from regions that bore the more ambivalent label of "territo-
ries" (White 1991: 236–269. Even the region's idealized agribusinesses,
such as the western cattle industry, could be described quite easily as
the mass production and marketing of a basic commodity, and the
concomitant creation of an industrialized, wage-labor class structure,
replete with its own contested ideologies imbedded in a romantic cowboy
mythology (cf. Robbins 1991: 196; Montejano 1987; Schwantes 1987).

The American West also saw some of the earliest manifestations
of later capitalism, particularly the phenomenon some have called "deindustrialization." The term remains problematic and highly debated as
a component of contemporary capitalist economics. However, there is no
question that the wholesale removal of capital from the industrial West
that followed the initial collapse of precious-metal mining and speculative agriculture at the turn of the century, and the resulting widespread depopulation, social dislocation, and economic decline, pro-
foundly marked the history of the region and its integration into
national and international economies.

One final parallel between writing archaeologies of capitalism and
histories of the West is the constant tension between spatial and temporal phenomena that resonates through the interpretations of both

groups of scholars. Western historians speak frequently of the analytical problems inherent in dealing with a West that is both place and process; historical archaeologists struggle to integrate their inexorably physical, bounded sites with global-scale processes that span centuries. This struggle to understand phenomena that literally "take place" both spatially and historically is at the heart of much current debate in social theory in general, and is particularly crucial to an archaeology of capitalism.

Many historians reflect this material plurality in their descriptions of the American West as a place characterized by the simultaneous juxtapositioning of various forms and phases of capitalism: deindustrialization and underdevelopment; resource extraction and commodity consumption on a vast scale; and dizzying, incessant swings between cash gluts and capital extraction, labor shortages and labor surplus (Limerick 1987, Paul 1988, Malone 1991, 1996; Robbins 1991, 1994; White 1991, 1995). It was a place and time where fundamental material processes worked across grand scales and in often paradoxical fashion. Two central factors unify this otherwise kaleidoscopic array—one economic and one ecological.

The West's extractive economy rendered it extremely sensitive to national and international market fluctuations. This was particularly true for market trends that affected the availability of foreign investment capital, upon which Western development has always been singularly dependent. And yet the West developed very few productive industries of its own, outside a few clusters of factories in urban California. The region remained remarkably distant from both the markets for its own extracted mineral and agricultural resources and the production centers on which it depended for goods and services, until well into the twentieth century (White 1991: 236–297; Limerick 1987: 78–96; Nash 1973). Indeed, these material paradoxes were part of what defined the West as a region. As Richard White has stated so succinctly, "what westerners produced they did not consume, and what they consumed they did not produce", (1991: 242).

Ecologically, the American intermountain West is one of several regions around the globe characterized by relatively marginal environments into which European migration expanded during the nineteenth century. As was the case with the Argentine pampas, the Siberian steppe, the southern African veldt, and the Australian interior, the "Great American Desert" was opened to agricultural exploitation during a period of relatively higher rainfalls and cooler temperatures sometimes referred to as a "mini-Ice Age." As this climatic cycle began to close during the 1880s, rainfall levels and water tables dropped. Over-exploited grasslands became dust bowls, and regions that had participated in massive speculative agricultural booms based on grain and livestock production saw economic collapses as total and devastating as any mining bust. Lands that had always been marginal became overtly hostile to permanent human settlement unless massively irrigated. Water, always a valuable commodity in the arid west, became a fundamentally political element (Blouet and Luebke 1977; Meinig 1962, 1968; Reisner 1986; Worster 1985, 1992, 1994).

The events unfolding between the early 1890s and World War I typify this conjunction of economic and ecological factors. The British banking failures of 1890 rapidly drained away investment capital from mining districts on both sides of the Sierras and the Rockies, as well as from the corporate grain and cattle ventures of Texas and the Great Plains. The ensuing financial crisis triggered in eastern industrial cities by the same banking failures lowered the demand for western metals, as did the monetary crisis brought on by the fight over silver-backed currency during the elections of 1892 and 1896. At the same time, technological innovations in agricultural production, driven in part by the chronic labor shortages on huge western farms and ranches, combined with the growing national depression and international competition to collapse the prices for western agricultural products.

All these trends collided head-on with the climatic fluctuations that western ranchers still call the "killing winters" of the mid- to late-1890s, when millions of head of livestock died on winter ranges. Meanwhile, declining rainfall and water tables severely restricted grain cultivation everywhere outside the increasingly well-irrigated Central Valley of California, and the lush, rain-shed valleys of eastern Oregon and Washington.

In response to these events, corporate entities who held control of western capital, largely railroad and banking firms located in New York, Chicago, and San Francisco, as well as London and Berlin, began to systematically remove or restructure their investments. It was a time of massive labor strikes and their violent suppression, widespread foreclosure and bankruptcy, depopulation, and consolidation. It is this process of stripping capital from the region, both in terms of investment and actual production, that constituted a form of deindustrialization.

What did the material culture of this kind of capitalism look like? It was the stuff of conundrum. More and more mass-produced goods were available, but real access to them was increasingly restricted for large sectors of the population. People were scattered far less evenly across the landscape than in earlier, less "settled" times. They lived in built environments that seemed to literally sheer apart into building traditions of spare vernacular expediency which might or might not vary from region to region, and opulent corporate homogeneity, which made the streets of San Francisco mirror those of Sydney, Vancouver, and Vladivostok. The world of people's daily lives simultaneously collapsed into the surviving towns and cities, and expanded outward through increasingly accessible (and heavily subsidized) mass communication and transportation networks. Across the scale, from consumer goods to houses to settlement patterns, objects, spaces, and technologies simultaneously became more functionally specialized and restricted, and yet more formally varied and multiply exploited.

MATERIAL CULTURE OF LATER CAPITALISM

The material culture of the past two centuries generates significant methodological problems for historical archaeologists grappling with questions about the development of capitalism as an economy and a culture, irrespective of regional context. The first of these is what to do with mass-produced artifacts. The ubiquitous bottles, plates, and tin cans that compose our data remain largely intractable to substantive analysis, if only due to their sheer volume. This numerical saturation is compounded by the frustrating barriers to comparing these items across any broader archaeological contexts, and a persistent difficulty in determining precisely *whose* ideology, mindset, or behavior they express. In particular, it has proved difficult to wean ourselves from the prehistorian's emphasis on production and manufacture as direct manifestations of essentially individual behavior, and to come to terms with the much more collective, indirect kinds of information represented by consumption, use, and display.

The second factor becomes increasingly significant as one moves closer to the present. This is the greatest survivability of larger-scale material elements from the more recent past: buildings and other standing structures, landscapes, and technological systems. It is not possible in such situations to leave off the archaeological analysis at the bottom of the test pit. Aside from the intellectual turf wars this foray into the world of larger objects unavoidably triggers among architectural historians and geographers, there is the very real problem that historical archaeology has had with integrating analysis across varying scales of material culture. We tend to hold one or the other end of the scale as a sort of constant, where it serves as either a passive stage set or evidentiary window dressing to the "real" data we are using. This analytical awkwardness imposes a false consistency on the material world generated by the people of the immediate past. It also reinforces an unfortunate polarity in much of our work that limits archaeological interpretation to either locally focused particularism or grand-scale generalization, leaving little available for bridging the two.

Part of the solution to these problems lies in defining what could be called the "material culture of capitalism" in a much broader and more comprehensive way than has been done to date in archaeology. At least three aspects of this material culture must be acknowledged and incorporated into archaeological interpretation. First, it was increasingly a material culture made by one group of people to be lived in and used by others. This was true across a wide range of material phenomena, from mass-produced foodstuffs and other consumer goods to tenement and pattern-book housing, federally mandated grid-plan settlement patterns, and mass transportation and communication technologies. A series of questions thus focus on the consequences of separating such fundamental material processes, and on determining how great was this perceived distance between consumption and production.

Secondly, in this industrially produced material world, people increasingly exchanged much of their direct knowledge of production for a culturally and commercially mediated, highly manipulable knowledge of consumption. This shift is directly related to forms of both social control and resistance. Consumption is the language of Pierre Bourdieu's differentially competitive French bourgeoisie; it provides the structure to Arjun Appadurai's "regimes of value" (Bourdieu 1984; Appadurai 1986; see also Douglas and Isherwood 1978). In the ranked classes of capitalist society, differential fluency in the many conflicting languages of consumption helps mark class identity both internally and externally.

Because they operate on so many levels, consumption practices can both substantiate and subvert the ideological hegemonies of the day. Sorting out the archaeological ramifications of such contextual plurality has filled the pages of books and journals since the mid-1980s (cf. Spencer-Wood 1987; Klein et al. 1991; Little and Shackel 1992). Once again, the issue of scale, of *who* is exchanging what messages with *whom*, becomes critical: Is it a face-to-face competition between neighboring households, or a class-structured boundary exercise between factions in a community? In what ways do these smaller scale (and more archaeologically accessible) exchanges invoke and manipulate broader ideological themes that have currency across the society at large? How often do such exchanges depend on partial (and selectively incomplete) translations across social categories like gender, ethnicity, race, or class? And how extensively are such inherently ideological systems of communication manipulated by structures of profit-making and social control?

Finally, there is the debate over the special nature of material culture in a capitalist world. While attempting to avoid a simple redefinition of commodity fetishism, is it possible to define a "modern materialism", as Chandra Mukerji has done, that describes and explains the culturally privileged role capitalist societies have assigned to material phenomena since the fifteenth century (Mukerji 1983; see also Thompson 1979; Miller 1987; Brewer and Porter 1993; Schuurman and Walsh 1994; Bermingham and Brewer 1995)? More importantly, is it possible to analyze the highly variable, inherently contextual, strategic nature of this materialism without resorting to a *deus ex machina* of technological innovation, an overly rigid opposition of dominance and resistance, or a reduction of human diversity to degrees of variance from some assumed set of "norms" regulating gender roles, ethnic identity, or class conflict (for discussion see Beaudry et al. 1991; Paynter and McGuire 1991; Praetzellis, Praetzellis, and Brown 1988)?

In sum, it has proved much easier to categorize the material culture of capitalism than to analyze it. Current social theory has begun to supply complex and creative ways to analyze consumption patterns as simultaneously economic, social, and cultural phenomena. Indeed, the 1990s have seen a flurry of publications on the subject from both historical and contemporary perspectives, and across a wide range of disciplinary venues, specifically geared to material culture and its role in consumption practices (cf. Adshead 1997; Cross 1993; de Grazia and Furlough 1996; Horowitz 1992; Melling and Barry 1992; Miller 1995a, 1995b, 1997; Mort 1996; Nye and Pedersen 1991; Slater 1997). These works provide an incredibly valuable source of substantive frameworks for archaeological analysis. However, in our research we continue to have difficulty placing all this consumption in a context that is sufficiently global in scale to encompass the expansion of western capitalism, and yet sufficiently sensitive to the face-to-face human interactions that gave these consumption acts any meaning.

The crucial factor is to develop ways to investigate the local meanings of globally available goods, materials, and technologies that neither vitiate the power relationships that structure these data, or stall out any sense of the dynamic change constantly transforming *all* the contexts in which these data were (and are) relevant. This ability to integrate analyses across broader scales of both space and time does not mean simply expanding the scale of analysis, jumping from fine-grained artifact analysis or particularistic local history to spatial analysis and global process. Rather it requires some set of analytical techniques that identify what it is that connects phenomena *across* the different scales of human activity. It is into this analytical locus between various scales of space and time that the material culture of later capitalism fits. It answers questions, not in spite of its ambiguous, contested, and constantly mediated qualities, but precisely because of them.

SOME ASSEMBLY REQUIRED: MATERIAL PATTERNING IN PARADISE VALLEY

The material culture of Paradise Valley, Nevada proves a case in point. Settled in the early 1860s by agriculturalists expecting to profit from marketing their crops to the mining districts of the Humboldt ranges some 80 miles to the south, this well-watered valley between the Owyhee and Black Rock deserts experienced a small boom of its own. Grain agriculture proved commercially profitable on a much greater scale than anticipated when the Central Pacific Railroad went through Winnemucca, just 40 miles south of the Valley, in 1868.

By the early 1870s, silver had been discovered in the Santa Rosa mountains that ringed the northern end of the Valley, and sparked a local mining rush capitalized almost entirely (and highly uncharacteristically) by local merchants and ranchers. But by the close of the century, the same economic trends affecting the rest of the West had seriously undermined the economic autonomy of the local community. At the same time, declining water tables made grain agriculture less reliable in the western side of the Valley, and totally impossible on the eastern side.

While much of their county's economy was dismantled around them, the propertied families of the Valley struggled to maintain their customers, control their labor pool, and protect and expand their landholdings. Immigrant families from Italy and the Basque country, who made up a large number of these customers and laborers, employed a wide range of strategies designed to generate household income and maintain financial and social support along kinship lines that extended throughout the rest of Nevada and into Utah, Idaho, and California, as well as back to the old country. And large numbers of Northern Plains Paiutes, as well as Chinese immigrants and Euro-Americans from a wide range of ethnic backgrounds, found themselves relegated to unalterably peripheral roles in the community as members of a vast pool of migratory labor. These skilled and unskilled workers were driven from agricultural season to season, and from mining boom to mining boom, throughout a highly volatile employment network that encompassed the western United States and Canada, and episodically ran as widely as the entire Pacific Rim (White 1991: 279–280).

All this effort generated a material culture that, at first glance, reflects an utterly predictable encroachment of mass-produced, nationally marketed consumer goods, building styles, and communication and transportation technologies into an essentially rural, environmentally marginal sector of the United States. Yet when the different categories of material culture are compared internally, it is clear, and equally predictable, that houses do not change like bottles and tin cans. Landscapes encoded ongoing tensions between local and nonlocal control over property, as well as much more immediate conflicts between local landowners and those who actually used their land, especially tenants. Consumption patterns expressed face-to-face competition between households along overlapping lines of ethnicity, gender, and class by invoking and reinterpreting nationally popular status markers. An archaeologically demonstrated increase in the local consumption of mass-produced goods and styles stands in ironic contrast to the social history of a community that faced far greater economic isolation and social fragmentation by the end of World War I than it ever did in the "frontier" days of the 1860s and 1870s.

Three general phenomena shaped this material culture of deindustrialization in Paradise: the intertwined histories of composite artifacts and maintenance relations, an increasingly restricted land ownership and the resultant practice of strategic tenancy, and a complex reorganization of social life created by, and expressed through, the closing of open space. In each case, change took place in a struggle between landowners and tenants, employers and laborers, and merchants and customers over how to refit a central myth of interchangeable parts. Like the marketing of babbitt to private households with the express purpose of domestically mending that which was meant to be industrially replaced, a tacit acknowledgment of increasing social tension and economic decline was coupled with surface appearances marked by middle-class conformity and convention.

What follows are examples of each of these three material phenomena, and some discussion of how they illustrate the nature of the material culture of later capitalism in the West. The research from which these examples are drawn encompassed 6 years of fieldwork, and included methodologies drawn from vernacular architecture, geography, folklore, and oral history, as well as archaeological survey and site analysis. Intended to generate a broad research design capable of incorporating any scale of material data, and applicable to any time between initial European settlement and the present, the project was necessarily broad in scope. Substantive discussions of the results are found elsewhere, and will be dealt with in a much more summary fashion here (cf. Purser 1987, 1989, 1992a, 1992b, and 1997).

The most immediately accessible aspects of Paradise Valley's material culture initially lay in its familiar consumer goods: the bottles, tin cans, plates, and machine parts documented in trash dumps and store bills. Trends in these records show a predictable, well-documented relationship between the overall availability of goods and the improving structures for supply and distribution that evolved through the later nineteenth century.

For instance, Charles Kemler was still hauling freight through the Valley in 1863 when he purchased a small quantity of goods from a Sacramento general wholesaling firm. The list of goods matches closely the wholesale bills that survive for Chesley Lamance's mid-1860s general store in the Valley, and the purchases that rancher and miller Russell Furman made at that store between 1867 and his death in 1871. The goods were primarily foodstuffs, mostly staples in bulk units. Some were apparent luxuries, judging by their quantity or price relative to other items: oysters, prunes, and possibly lobster. Tobacco and whiskey were relatively expensive items bought more regularly and in larger quantities than other nonfood consumables. In contrast, coffee and tea were relatively cheap, even at retail. Bottled patent medicine purchases recorded Furman's declining health.

Manufactured goods were equally limited and basic, and related largely to cooking and eating: tin cups, knives and forks, a camp kettle, a coffee pot, and a Dutch oven. Furman had purchased bulk grain for his flour-milling business, garden seeds for cultivation, and powder and shot for hunting and self-defense. Kemler and his teamsters needed axle grease and tar. Neither Kemler nor Lamance had troubled much over the selection of goods to make available to customers; each used a few generalized wholesalers or jobbers operating out of the railroad centers of Winnemucca or Sacramento. The lists thus reflected the daily labor, maintenance activities, and sustenance predictable for a rancher or freighter making a living in the sparsely settled Nevada of the 1860s.

Archaeological deposits dating to this early period of settlement could not be located during this project, partially because of the relatively ephemeral nature of both settlement and refuse volume produced before about 1875. Artifacts inventoried in the surface trash scatter at the site of a homestead dating to the late 1870s and early 1880s clearly demonstrate that the site occupants had moved beyond the materially limited times of early Valley settlement.

Nonetheless, the artifacts do not present a startlingly different world in terms of the kinds of goods used. Johnny and Ida Merchant had moved to the eastern rim of the Valley to farm after Johnny had worked a stint as clerk in Kemler's new Paradise general store. In spite of their efforts, the homestead failed in a few years, primarily due to lack of water. Merchant's former employer (and likely creditor) Kemler took up the land to graze cattle.

Surface debris at the old foundations of the Merchant cabin, and refuse scattered in the sagebrush to the south, indicated a relatively comfortable standard of living. There were wine, whiskey, and gin bottles, as well as those that might have contained beer or soda water. Someone in the house had a taste for sardines, and cooked with Worcestershire sauce. Small quantities of canned goods would have been used fairly regularly, at least on a seasonal basis. And in the household ceramics and furniture there are hints at higher aspirations: The good china was hand painted, the pressed glass parlor dish was good quality, the big iron cookstove had been shipped in from Chicago. Except for fragments of two cast-iron cookstoves and one broken pitchfork, there is almost no non-can metal of any size left of the site. The most noticeable use of brand names is on the patent medicine and sauce bottles: Paine's Celery Tonic and Lea and Perrins' Worcestershire.

For the sheer volume of merchandise they represent, the books from J.B. Case's 1919 store belonged to another world. They listed over 100 specialized wholesale suppliers who shipped goods to Paradise from 10 different states. Case's customers bought ready-made suits from New York tailors, car tires from Chicago, and Coleman lamps from Dallas. Their children's toy marbles came from San Francisco, as did shoes, peanut butter, oysters, and sardines. Local customers could buy Heinz spaghetti and tomato soup, Kellogg's Corn Flakes and castor oil, Cuticura soap, Levi–Strauss overalls, and John Deere plows.

In like manner, the household trash scatter behind the Reinhart Ranch testifies, at least to some extent, to an increase in the overall range of goods available. There are wine, whiskey, and soda-water bottles, as well as Curtice Brothers sauce bottles and a Tonneau mustard jar. Ceramics, though less decorated, were more numerous and diverse in form: cups, plates, bowls, and covered dishes, most in plain white ironstone. There was a painted milk-glass shade from a kerosene lamp, some polychrome printed china, tongues from women's leather shoes with fancy stitching, and part of a child's brightly colored rubber ball. Wooden paint buckets with residues of dark red and white pigments clinging to the slats, and a broken marbled-ceramic doorknob indicate some occasional household maintenance. Tin cans are much more numerous and diverse in size than at the Merchant homestead. And the amount of metal at the site is considerable, particularly small scraps and bits reworked by hand to serve small, expedient tasks around the ranch.

If anything, the Reinhart consumer goods seemed a bit limited in number and diversity, given the relative abundance of goods Case's store bills would indicate. Initially this appeared to be the effect of the site's character: It was a surface dump, exposed to scavenging and other disturbance, and hardly provided a secure provenience. It is also possible that it was a simple matter of income—tenant ranchers and new immigrants limiting unnecessary expenditures. But it was puzzling objects like babbitt bearings that first hinted that the familiarity of these items belied a very unfamiliar quality.

These intimations were borne out dramatically in subsequent examinations around the Valley of larger farm equipment, vehicles, household furniture, and even certain categories of foodstuffs in use from the 1870s through the 1920s. Much of the consumer goods of early Paradise Valley (1860s to 1880s) were composite items, made of mass-produced parts that were assembled or more fully processed locally. Furthermore, they frequently were assembled or processed, not by their ultimate consumer, but by intermediate specialists; the blacksmiths, carpenters, saddlers, brewers, bakers, and dressmakers who operated small shops and stores in the local town. What these tradespeople assembled, they also mended or restocked in a complex web of social and economic interdependencies that historian Robert Blair St. George has called "maintenance relations" (St. George 1983; Purser 1992).

These locally focused structures linking producers, consumers, and mediating specialists were highly sensitive to shifts in technology that originated well outside local contexts. What the archaeological and documentary records of Paradise Valley actually track is the gradual replacement of locally assembled, processed, and maintained consumer goods with goods either more fully processed at distant production centers (like the increasingly processed brand-name foodstuffs of the early twentieth century), or composed of replaceable parts not intended to be either assembled or mended locally (like the vehicles and farm equipment made increasingly of cast- or stamped-metal components following the 1890s).

These Paradise Valley consumption practices are not a story of simple technological determinism. Purchase patterns of these items also reflect the changing dynamic of the Valley's economy that involved the seasonal availability of cash, the escalating competition between Paradise merchants and their Winnemucca rivals, and the dual character of later Paradise households. This latter paired a household's increasing social and economic isolation within the local community with a near inundation by brand-name consumer goods and the national-scale popular culture through which they were marketed.

Cash flow, commercial competition, and the replacement of locally maintained material culture were all closely connected phenomena. When the miller Russell Furman periodically applied credit to his account at Lamance's store between 1869 and 1871, he had the option of paying cash, but he seldom did so. More often he exchanged flour from his mill, or labor, or, on one occasion, "19 lbs. of fish," all in an effort to reduce his growing bill. That bill never dropped below $200 and went as high as $458.

Furman may be an unusual example; he was embroiled in a lengthy lawsuit over the title to his mill, which he eventually lost. But his accounts do give a clear picture of the degree to which the early Paradise economy relied on barter exchange, with seasonal influxes of cash based on the agricultural cycle. To a certain extent, a barter economy continued in Paradise well after the turn of the century. Store accounts of the 1890s and 1900s still showed customers "buying" small amounts of cash from merchants as though from a bank, in addition to exchanging farm goods, labor, and services for store goods.

Extended credit was a powerful competitive tool for Paradise storekeepers. Part of the reason Paradise residents chose to order suits or plows through Case's store, rather than order it themselves through catalogues, may have been the cash payment policy of most catalogue houses. At Case's they could run credit. Case was also willing to go to considerable lengths for customers. He even filled individual orders with Winnemucca pharmacists during his regular freight runs to the railroad depot, as in the case of the "three tubes of strychnine tabs for Mr. Johnson" that appear on a 1919 wholesale invoice from the Eagle Drug Company. It is not known whether Winnemucca merchants would run credit accounts for Paradise customers with the same flexibility as their local stores, but it seems unlikely. As a result, the majority of Paradise residents remained largely dependent on Valley merchants for their more lenient credit and barter arrangements, even as late as the 1920s.

The significance of this fact becomes more clear when the ties between the declining number of local services and the increasingly diverse sources of mail-order goods provided by Paradise stores are examined. Case's 1919 customers *had* to send out to Winnemucca to fill their prescriptions because Dr. Powell had closed his Bridge Street pharmacy and moved to Oregon several years before.

The loss of smaller businesses and specialized trades was one of the more dramatic effects of the regional economic downscaling that occurred during the last decade of the nineteenth century and the first decades of the twentieth. To every extent possible, Paradise merchants tried to step into the market gap left by the declining number of tradespeople who had occupied the mediating nodes of maintenance relations in the community's past. However, they did so by replacing blacksmiths, carpenters, and tailors with ready-made, catalogue-order goods whose maintenance was either a matter of reordering replacement parts from the same distant supplier, or melting a little babbitt on the cookstove to do the job at home.

For this reason, the relative paucity of consumer goods at the Reinhart dump cannot be attributed to any lack in the availability of goods. It may be related to the changing character of the consumer goods themselves, which displaced the logic of local material culture from the community, in any integrative sense, to increasingly isolated individual households. In spite of increased availability, actual purchasing power had not increased. For a newly immigrated Basque family leasing a ranch, what cash was available went into agricultural equipment, whose careful curation and maintenance absorbed an increasing amount of the family's labor.

The changing economic climate in which Paradise residents lived thus reorganized many of the consumption patterns that characterized the smaller-scale material culture of the Valley by reducing the economic diversity of the local community and by isolating individual households on the basis of income, occupation, and, to some extent, ethnicity. In like manner, and through much the same mechanisms, the organization of property in the Valley shifted from the relatively numerous smaller landholdings and generalized agriculture of the homesteading period, prior to about 1885, to an ever-increasing restriction of property ownership and an overwhelming dominance of livestock production as the sole economic activity of the Valley. As water and silver disappeared almost simultaneously from the Valley, ranchers with sufficient capital shifted to cattle or sheep as a way to produce on drier, poorer-quality lands.

The shift also required vastly greater amounts of land to run profitable herds. Some of the expansion took the form of access to federally owned grazing lands. Within the Valley proper, smaller property owners were displaced by the economic expansion of their wealthier neighbors' losing the lands to debts accumulated at the town stores, or through foreclosure in the many neighbor-to-neighbor mortgages that had provided much of the small-scale capitalization of early Valley settlement.

This trend was demonstrated most dramatically in the ownership of agricultural lands. In the 1880 tax records, three-quarters of the 64 Valley landowners held 1000 acres or less; 65 percent owned one section (640 acres) or less. No holdings exceeded 3000 acres. In 1890 over 60 percent of the landowners still owned a section or less, but three individual ranchers owned 46 percent of all taxed Valley land. By 1910, although the number of landholders remained roughly the same, two ranchers Wilhelmina Stock and Louis Godchaux owned 43 percent of the total Valley acreage. Godchaux alone held over 18,000 of the roughly 86,000 acres taxed (Purser 1987: 26–28).

The shift to livestock raising and larger landholdings also saw the beginning of large absentee landholdings in the Valley. Tax records of 1890 listed Brandenstein and Company and Louis Godchaux as major property owners. Both were partners in a San Francisco butchering plant and shipped cattle from the Paradise ranch, as well as from several others in Nevada, to stockyards in California. In the following decades, they were joined by other California operations, including Evans and Curtner, (later the Milpitas Land and Livestock Company) and G.W. Grayson, partner in a Sacramento butchering firm (Purser 1987: 28).

But the real story of land use, as opposed to direct ownership, is told in the strategic tenancies of many Valley households. Much harder to document in the written record because of the more *ad hoc* nature of leasing and rental arrangements, these practices did indeed manifest themselves in the settlement patterns and built environment of turn-of-the-century Paradise.

In the increasingly stringent economic climate of the later nineteenth century, large-scale property accumulation opened up at least two strategies for non-propertied Valley families. The first has already been mentioned in connection with the Mendiola family, who lived at the Reinhart Ranch in the 1910s and discarded a babbitt bearing in their household trash. The larger corporate ranchers, particularly those who were absentee owners, needed employees to staff and manage their vast holdings. Families would lease parcels or entire ranches for several years, then move to another tenancy elsewhere in the Valley; a practice recorded now only in the oral histories of people who lived on a succession of Valley ranches during their childhoods.

The second, more common practice was to actually purchase a small parcel of land, often just a few lots in the centrally located town, and then to lease several parcels of land in different parts of the Valley specialized for grazing range, hay production, grain crops, and so on. These agricultural townspeople then opportunistically combined the partial and often seasonal incomes produced by hauling freight, running small herds of sheep or cattle, or raising hay on the outlying parcels with the equally sporadic cash income to be made by working as day laborers on the larger ranches, or by practicing crafts such as stonemasonry, carpentry, or blacksmithing.

Often these household-level enterprises were expanded through kin-based partnerships. For example, in 1905 the brother-in-law partnership of Carter and Stewart owned 480 acres that produced hay, and were also "running sheep on shares with B.W. Stewart" (Bragg 1905: 116). In 1910 Stephen Ferraro and a cousin named Mendiete could run 1200 sheep on an unimproved 240-acre parcel of state contract land, in addition to holding Ferraro's small ranch. The Ferraro–Mendiette partnership was a rarity; relatively few of the smaller operations could actually compete directly with the corporate ranches. Of the 23 local landowners holding one section or less in 1910, only 5 were taxed for cattle. Quite often the primary customers for these smaller operations were the larger corporate ranchers themselves, who purchased the grain and hay produced on the smaller holdings.

The material culture of these two forms of tenancy is characterized by an expedient mix of intensive curation and modification of what was owned outright, and an expedient consumerism directed toward what was leased or rented. The result is a pattern that combined frequently anachronistic, but either more mendable or more portable technologies, with extremely contemporary items geared either to direct household production or, sometimes, to status display. This could result in patterns like those found in the metal artifacts of the Reinhart ranch dump, for example, where strips and bars of wrought iron, representing an older, craft-maintained technology, had been carefully curated and reused right alongside what were then the latest babbitt bearings. Likewise, the few items of relatively high-quality in the dump relate to either personal adornment, as in the women's shoes, or to household decoration, as in the painted milk glass lamp and the printed china. Yet in an area renowned for its patterns of vernacular architectural modification, the Reinhart ranch house remained almost pristine in its late-1880s form until well into the twentieth century. No one was willing to invest in building onto the leased structure.

In the case of town-based, patchwork lease-holding, modification of the house was not only more common, it was apparently nearly continual. For town households employing this strategy, the greatly expanded use of town lots sponsored a total reorganization of their domestic environment. Many residents significantly enlarged their town properties at this time by buying up not only a house and lot, but two or three adjacent 50-foot by 100-foot lots as well. The expanded lots and the modified structures on them became centers of operation for such diverse enterprises as providing storage and maintenance facilities, stabling draft animals and other livestock, and housing production and transportation equipment.

This more intensified, transitional land-use pattern produced both considerably expanded lot sizes and general increases in the number and size of outbuildings over the earlier, more traditionally "urban" land-use patterns seen in the more prosperous Paradise of the early 1870s and 1880s. Sheep barns, wagon sheds, and large working garages replaced smaller wood and coal sheds, privies, and wash sheds.

These practices simultaneously redesigned the houses of many town residents, who began to add or enlarge kitchens, back porches, bathrooms, and attached semi-subterranean cellars, in large part to accommodate within the house the types of more narrowly "domestic" activities that had once taken place in the back yard (Purser 1997). Houses in town, even those owned only briefly by individual families, thus became heavily modified over the first decades of the twentieth century. In these modifications, the same mix of curation and currency, of expedient reworking and some amount of socially conscious display, marks every house to some degree.

In many ways, the increasing use of mass-produced goods with their (almost) interchangeable component parts, and the creation of opportunistically assembled, sequentially tenanted, absentee-owned ranches are both analogous to the increasing fragmentation and specialization of space that characterized much of the Paradise Valley built environment over the turn of the century. In spatial terms, specialization is a form of restriction, and people in Paradise Valley were increasingly restricted in how they could use public places in particular. At the broadest scale, the local community saw its control of Valley road systems, land divisions, and land-transfer practices steadily eroded by county authorities bent on centralizing both policy and profits in the county seat and railroad depot of Winnemucca, forty miles to the south (Purser 1989).

More locally, town elites in particular asserted their growing economic dominance by fencing off access to what had been informal gathering areas on empty (but owned) lots, and in the yards of hotels, boarding houses, and large general stores. Commercial structures themselves grew more formally and functionally specialized, and part of their interiors that had been designed to attract public aggregation, like the stoves and counters of the general stores or the barrooms of the large hotels, were increasingly restricted to the use of paying customers.

The subsequent impact on the informal social life of the town was profound. Much of the public gathering and social interaction that had taken place in these more public spaces was displaced into private houses. There, in addition to reorganizing their yards, back porches, and kitchens to accommodate the new economic enterprises of tenant ranching, people redefined parlors and porches at the front of the house to host family gatherings and social visits. It is worth pointing out that such rooms had become stylistically anachronistic by 1900, while in Paradise Valley this date marked the beginning of a new boom in their construction. Furthermore, their appearance marked a parallel decline in the community's reputation for hosting large public celebrations like those on the fourth of July. Instead, oral histories of the first two decades of the twentieth century overwhelmingly stress family holidays such as Christmas. This shift had the effect of neatly sorting celebrations by family, ethnicity, and social status, once again segregating the community into individual households (Purser 1997).

DISCUSSION

At the local scale, then, the ubiquitous consumer goods of later nineteenth- and early twentieth-century industrial capitalism mended, but did not nearly mask, the increasing fragmentation, isolation, and alienation that characterized life in the Paradise community that time period. The Valley's material culture of the earlier period, from the 1860s to the 1880s, exhibited all the hallmarks of immediate post-Civil War industrialism and western frontier settlement. Working from smaller to larger scales, a slender assortment of railroad-transported, mass-produced goods, bearing a small number of early brand names, passed through the doors of the ubiquitous boxlike stores and shops (with their false fronts) into an ever-increasing number of two- or three-room frame cottages. These, in turn, were set in a landscape of small, isolated homesteads connected to a cluster of crossroads towns by way of wandering, doorstep-to-doorstep roads and pathways that linked places with multiple, usually seasonal, routes. While the objects, structures, and technologies of national-scale processes like industrialism or western expansion were thus clearly present, they were embedded in and articulated through an explicitly localized materialism that literally took shape in the forges of local blacksmiths, behind the needles of local dressmakers, or under the hammers of local carpenters.

This localism is not to be romanticized into the quaint, egalitarian frontier pastiche of myth and legend. It certainly did not mask either the considerable degree of social difference among the local residents, or the grinding, often ruthless competition and economic aggression engendered between neighbors by the boom-and-bust cycles that wracked the community. But it did ground an increasingly mass-produced material culture in a local frame of reference that required repeated local modification in order to function and, as such, it retained at the local scale a degree of collective control over the material world that is displayed again and again across social groups and economic swings.

By the late 1880s or early 1890s, much of this localized frame of reference had been displaced, submerged, or abandoned altogether, as the critically necessary babbittry of a later, deindustrializing West took hold. There were more mass-produced goods, but fewer stores selling them, and the blacksmith had moved to Winnemucca and opened a garage. The fancy new three-story hotel had a display room on the first floor, where the traveling salesmen displayed their wares. Homesteads lay abandoned on the landscape outside town, and the buckaroos who rode over the old foundations, looking for lost cattle, owned no land at all. Instead, they lived several miles away in a new bunkhouse, built by absentee landowners to house essentially migrant labor. Meanwhile, houses in town sprouted new kitchens, new parlors, and big new barns in which to keep the new farm equipment. Most of the old roads had grass growing over the wagon ruts, and the few new, county-maintained ones that had replaced them run ruler-straight along the section lines, setting ranch houses adrift two or three miles from the passing traffic.

It is relatively easy, in this context, to trace in the Valley's later material culture the ever greater social distances between the landed and the propertyless in the Valley, and to translate that polarity across the differences in settlement, housing, occupation, and lifestyle that characterized the lives of successive waves of German, Italian, and Basque immigrants, or the perpetual community outsiders of migrant laborers, Native Americans, and Chinese immigrants. It is also possible to read resistance in the strategies of tenancy, income diversification, kinship-bond reinforcement, and home-centered social lives of the community's non-elites.

At the same time, there is at least a surface conformity to an image of early 20th-century middle-class prosperity, in the increasingly careful separation of public and private spaces, the "modernized" reorganization of domestic environments, and the redefinition of gender roles that characterized the community as a whole. Epitomizing the difficulty of determining who dominated or resisted whom in this ambiguous version of material and social "success," one can even chart the eventual cross-marriages that saw Catholic Italians having newly earned ranchland courting (in those oddly anachronistic parlors) the Protestant-Anglo daughters of former town elites, whose commercially based fortunes were declining.

Yet in this multiply divided, diminished place, the interpretive issue of who was resisting whom eventually gives way to an analysis of how both dominance and resistance were directed both inside and outside the Valley proper through the uses of differing scales of material culture, and across differing modes of control over the material world. It is not just a matter of identifying whose resistance, and to whom, but of defining the relevant scales at which such analysis should take place, as well as how archaeological analysis can inform it.

The answer would seem to lie in developing a sense of material culture that is as pluralistic, as nonlinear, and as contested as we have always acknowledged the social and ideological realms of modern capitalism to be. Many archaeologists of the last decade have acknowledged this goal explicitly in their work. But for each period, for each region, and perhaps for each site analysis, the question persists of how to convert abstract goals to explicit method. In Paradise Valley, the material culture lends itself to an archaeology of later capitalism, and of deindustrialization in particular, that is unmistakably marked by its western setting.

Grappling with these dilemmas raises significant questions about the extent to which larger answers are possible in an archaeology of capitalism, and what those answers might look like as they emerge. If any clue is to be read in the work of those who have come to be known as new western historians, it is that no single theory is likely to emerge to satisfy all the questions. Just as we will probably not see a single, unifying replacement for Turner's frontier thesis, we in historical archaeology are not likely to write "an" archaeology of capitalism. This is no plea for a passively relativist stance on what is quite likely the most important project our field faces. But in like manner, the sheer breadth and complexity of the topic demands a methodological creativity and interpretive flexibility we have yet to give ourselves the permission or authority to pursue.

REFERENCES

Adshead, Samuel Adrian M.
　　1997　*Material Culture in Europe and China, 1400–1800: The Rise of Consumerism.* St. Martin's Press, New York.
Appadurai, Arjun
　　1986　Introduction: Commodities and the Politics of Value. In *The Social Life of Things: Commodities in Cultural Perspective*, edited by Arjun Appadurai, pp. 3–63. Cambridge University Press, Cambridge.
Beaudry, Mary C., Lauren J. Cook, and Stephen A. Mrozowski
　　1991　Artifacts and Active Voices: Material Culture as Social Discourse. In *The Archaeology of Inequality*, edited by Randall McGuire and Robert Paynter, pp. 150–191. Basil Blackwell, Oxford.
Bermingham, Ann, and John Brewer, eds.
　　1995　*The Consumption of Culture, 1600–1800: Image, Object, Text.* Routledge, London.

Blouet, Brian W., and Frederick J. Luebke
   1979   *The Great Plains: Environment and Culture.* University of Nebraska Press, Lincoln.
Bourdieu, Pierre
   1984   *Distinction: a Social Critique of the Judgement of Taste,* translated by Richard Nice. Harvard University Press, Cambridge.
Bragg, Allen
   1984   *Humboldt County 1905.* North Central Nevada Historical Society, Winnemucca, Nevada.
Brewer, John, and Roy Porter (editors)
   1993   *Consumption and the World of Goods.* Routledge, London.
Cosgrove, Denis
   1985   *Social Formation and Symbolic Landscape.* Barnes and Noble, New York.
Cross, Gary S.
   1993   *Time and Money: The Making of Consumer Culture.* Routledge, London.
De Grazia, Victoria (editor)
   1996   *The Sex of Things: Gender and Consumption in Historical Perspective.* University of California Press, Berkeley.
Douglas, Mary, and Baron Isherwood
   1978   *The World of Goods: Towards and Anthropology of Consumption.* Allen Lane, New York.
Etulain, Richard W. (compiler)
   1996a   *The American West, Comparative Perspectives: A Bibliography.* Center for the American West, Department of History, University of New Mexico, Albuquerque.
   1996b   *Re-imagining the Modern American West: A century of Fiction, History, and Art.* University of Arizona Press, Tucson.
Ewen, Stuart
   1976   *Captains of Consciousness: Advertising and the Social Roots of the Consumer Culture.* McGraw-Hill, New York.
   1996   *PR! A Social History of Spin.* Basic Books, New York.
Ewen, Stuart, and Elizabeth Ewen
   1982   *Channels of Desire: Mass Images and the Shaping of American Consciousness.* McGraw-Hill, New York.
Hardesty, Donald L.
   1991   Historical Archaeology in the American West. *Historical Archaeology* 25(3):3–6.
Hodder, Ian
   1985   Postprocessual Archaeology. In *Advances in Archaeological Method and Theory, Vol. 8,* pp. 1–25. Academic Press, New York.
Horowitz, Daniel
   1986   *Reading the Past: Current Approaches to Interpretation in Archaeology.* Cambridge University Press, Cambridge.
   1992   *The Morality of Spending: Attitudes Towards the Consumer Society in America, 1875–1940.* I.R. Dee, Chicago.
Klein, Kerwin Lee
   1997   *Frontiers of Historical Imagination: Narrating the European Conquest of Native America, 1890–1990.* University of California Press, Berkeley.
Klein, Terry H., and Charles H. LeeDecker
   1991   Models for the Study of Consumer Behavior. *Historical Archaeology* 25(2):1–2.
Lears, T.J. Jackson
   1994   *Fables of Abundance: A Cultural History of Advertising in America.* Basic Books, New York.
Leone, Mark P.

1988   The Relationship Between Archaeological Data and the Documentary Record: 18th Century Gardens in Annapolis, Maryland. *Historical Archaeology* 22(1):29–35.

1988   The Georgian Order as the Order of Merchant Capitalism in Annapolis, Maryland. In *The Recovery of Meaning: Historical Archaeology in the Eastern United States*, edited by Mark P. Leone and Parker B. Potter, Jr., pp. 235–261. Smithsonian Institution Press, Washington, D.C.

Little, Barbara J., and Paul Shackel (editors)
1992   Meanings and Uses of Material Culture. *Historical Archaeology* 26(3).

Limerick, Patricia Nelson
1987   *The Legacy of Conquest: The Unbroken Past of the American West*. W.W. Norton, New York.

1991   The Trail to Santa Fe: The Unleashing of the Western Public Intellectual; What on Earth is the New Western History? In *Trails: Toward a New Western History*, edited by Patricia Nelson Limerick et al., pp. 59–77, 81–88. University of Kansas Press, Lawrence.

Limerick, Patricia Nelson, Clyde A. Milner II, and Charles E. Rankin (editors)
1991   *Trails: Towards a New Western History*. University of Kansas Press, Lawrence.

Lowenthal, David
1985   *The Past is a Foreign Country*. Cambridge University Press, London.

Malone, Michael P.
1991   'The New Western History,' an Assessment. In *Trails: Toward a New Western History*, edited by Patricia Nelson Limerick et al., pp. 97–102. University of Kansas Press, Lawrence.

1996   *James J. Hill: Empire Builder of the Northwest*. University of Oklahoma Press, Norman.

Meinig, D.W.
1962   *On the Margins of the Good Earth: The South Australian Wheat Frontier, 1869–1884*. Rand McNally & Company, Chicago.

1968   *The Great Columbia Plain: A Historical Geography, 1805–1910*. University of Washington Press, Seattle.

Melling, Joseph, and Jonathan Barry (editors)
1992   *Culture in History: Production, Consumption, and Values in Historical Perspective*. University of Exeter, Exeter.

Miller, Daniel
1987   *Material Culture and Mass Consumption*. Basil Blackwell, Oxford.
(editor)
1993   *Worlds Apart: Modernity Through the Prism of the Local*. Routledge, London.
(editor)
1995   *Acknowledging Consumption: A Review of New Studies*. Routledge, London.

1997   *Capitalism: An Ethnographic Approach*. Berg, Oxford.

Montejano, David
1987   *Anglos and Mexicans in the Making of Texas, 1836–1986* . University of Texas Press, Austin.

Mort, Frank
1996   *Cultures of Consumption: Commerce, Masculinities, and Social Space*. Routledge, London.

Mukerji, Chandra
1983   *From Graven Images: Patterns in Modern Materialism*. Columbia University Press, New York.

Nash, Gerald
1973   *The American West in the Twentieth Century: A Short History of an Urban Oasis*. University of New Mexico Press, Albuquerque.

Nugent, Walter
1989   The People of the West since 1890. In *The Twentieth-Century West: Historical Interpretations*, edited by Gerald D. Nash and Richard W. Etulain, pp. 35–70. University of New Mexico Press, Albuquerque.
1991   Frontiers and Empires in the Late Nineteenth Century. In *Trails: Toward a New Western History*, edited by Patricia Nelson Limerick et al., pp. 161–181. University of Kansas Press, Lawrence.
Nye, David E., and Carl Pedersen (editors)
1991   *Consumption and American Culture. VU University Press, Amsterdam.*
Paul, Rodman
1988   *The Far West and the Great Plains in Transition: 1859–1900.* Harper and Row, New York.
Paynter, Robert, and Randall H. McGuire
1991   The Archaeology of Inequality: Material Culture, Domination, and Resistance. In *The Archaeology of Inequality*, edited by Randall McGuire and Robert Paynter, pp. 1–27 . Basil Blackwell, Oxford.
Praetzellis, Mary, Adrian Praetzellis, and Marley R. Brown III
1988   What Ever Happened to the Silent Majority: Research Strategies for Studying Dominant Groups in Late Nineteenth Century California. In *Documentary Archaeology in the New World*, edited by Mary C. Beaudry, pp. 192–202. Cambridge University Press, Cambridge.
Purser, Margaret
1987   Community and Material Culture in Nineteenth Century Paradise Valley, Nevada. Unpublished PhD dissertation, Department of Anthropology, University of California, Berkeley.
1989   All Roads Lead to Winnemucca: Local Road Systems and Community Material Culture in Nineteenth-century Nevada. In *Perspectives in Vernacular Architecture, III*, edited by Thomas Carter and Bernard L. Herman, pp. 120–134. University of Missouri Press, Columbia.
1991   'Several Paradise Ladies Are Visiting in town': Gender Strategies in the Early Industrial West. In *Gender in Historical Archaeology*, edited by Donna J. Seifert, *Historical Archaeology* 25(4):6–16.
1992   Consumption as Communication in Nineteenth Century Paradise Valley, Nevada. In Meanings and Uses of Material Culture, edited by Barbara J. Little and Paul Shackel, *Historical Archaeology* 26(3):105–116.
1997   Keeping House: Women, 'Domesticity', and the Use of Domestic Space in Nineteenth Century Nevada. In *Images of an American Land*, edited by Thomas Carter, pp. 173–198. University of New Mexico Press, Albuquerque.
Robbins, William G.
1991   Laying Siege to Western History: The Emergence of New Paradigms. In *Trails: Toward a New Western History*, edited by Patricia Nelson Limerick et al., pp. 182–214. University of Kansas Press, Lawrence.
1994   *Colony and Empire: the Capitalist Transformation of the American West.* University Press of Kansas, Lawrence.
Schuurman, Anton J., and Lorena S. Walsh (editors)
1994   *Material Culture: Consumption, Lifestyle, Standard of Living, 1500–1900.* Universita Bocconi, Milan.
Schwantes, Carlos A.
1987   The Concept of the Wageworkers' Frontier: a Framework for Future Research. *Western Historical Quarterly* 18 (January):39–55.
Slater, Don
1997   *Consumer Culture and Modernity.* Polity Press, Oxford, U.K.

Spencer-Wood, Suzanne (editor)
1987   *Consumer Choice in Historical Archaeology.* Plenum, New York.
St. George, Robert Blair
1983   Maintenance Relations and the Erotics of Property. Paper presented at the annual meeting of the American Historical Association, San Francisco.
Thompson, Michael
1979   *Rubbish Theory: The Creation and Destruction of Value.* Oxford University Press, New York.
West, Elliott
1991   A Longer, Grimmer, but More Interesting Story. In *Trails: Toward a New Western History*, edited by Patricia Nelson Limerick et al., pp. 103–111. University of Kansas Press, Lawrence. First published in *Montana*, Summer 1990.)
White, Richard
1991   *Its Your Misfortune and None of My Own: A New History of the American West.* University of Oklahoma, Norman.
1995   *The Organic Machine.* Wang and Hill, New York.
Worster, Donald
1985   *Rivers of Empire: Water, Aridity, and the Growth of the American West.* Pantheon Books, New York.
1992   *Under Western Skies: Nature and History in the American West.* Oxford University Press, New York.
(editor)
1994   *An Unsettled Country: Changing Landscapes of the American West.* University of New Mexico Press, Albuquerque.
Wylie, Alison
1993   Invented Lands/Discovered Pasts: The Westward Expansion of Myth and History. *Historical Archaeology* 27(4):1–19.

Archaeology and the Challenges of Capitalist Farm Tenancy in America

6

Charles E. Orser, Jr.

INTRODUCTION

Historical archaeologists today give the study of plantations a prominent place in their field. Within recent years, plantation archaeology has had a growing presence at several well-established archaeological conferences, and archaeologists are beginning to write more about the subject for a wider audience (see, for example, Ferguson 1992). Archaeologists have shed much-needed light on plantation life, with a great deal of focus on the slave quarters (for overviews, see Orser 1990, 1994a; Singleton 1991).

An archaeological focus on plantation America seems natural. After all, plantations form part of our national psyche. Promoted by novelists, portrayed in movies, and dramatized on television, most Americans have some perception of life on a southern, antebellum plantation. Even with this attention, however, we should not be surprised that plantation life is often inadequately treated by the popular media. Popularists often ignore, downplay, or trivialize the horrors of bondage, the daily hardships experienced by plantation men and women, and the ongoing struggles between plantation workers and owners.

As part of their image of the plantation South, many Americans hold firm to the idea that southern plantation owners were crushed by the War of Rebellion. Many believe that after 1865 the plantation passed from view, as archaic as the spinning wheel. The stately mansions sur-

Charles E. Orser, Jr. • Anthropology Program, Illinois State University, Normal, Illinois 61790-4640.

Historical Archaeologies of Capitalism, edited by Mark P. Leone and Parker B. Potter, Jr. Plenum Press, New York, 1999.

rounded by brown and white fields of cotton, and tall, swaying forests of dark-green sugar cane remained only as tourist curiosities, places for northern journalists to visit after the war. Most Americans believe that plantations, as working estates, were erased from the landscape after 1865.

In accordance with their understanding of the death of the southern plantation, many people believe that farm tenancy was an outgrowth of the plantation's demise, and that the lowly tenant farms dotting the South after 1865 are the logical legacy of the plantation. In truth, tenancy was especially widespread in the South after the American Civil War, truly being "a by-product of the old antebellum plantation system and the efforts at agricultural reconstruction following the war between the states" (Taylor 1938: 146).

Though tenancy's roots extend back in time to hundreds of years before the American Civil War (Mendenhall 1937), it was not until well after 1865 that farm tenancy entered the national consciousness. During the early decades of the twentieth century, several dedicated rural sociologists pushed the details of this system of farming before the nation's citizens and politicians, demanding that it be recognized as the blight that it had become. At that time, most of the farmers in the South—both black and white—were tenants. By 1910, 63 percent of the farmers in South Carolina were tenants; in Georgia and Mississippi, the figure was as high as 66 percent (White and Leonard 1915: 12). With tenants locked into seemingly inescapable cycles of poverty and despair, tenancy had become a major embarrassment to capitalism. The social conditions of tenancy meant that by the early twentieth century it could be truly said that "the greatest single economic and social problem ... throughout the South is farm tenancy" (Hobbs 1930: 119). As late as 1950, tenants still worked 27 percent of the farms in the United States (Batschelet 1953: 24). Astute observers likened America's tenant farmers to a peasantry, men and women who "like the peasantry of other countries ... own no land, or vested values, but subsist on their own daily labor" (Burwell 1880: 6).

Within the past two decades, an increasing number of archaeologists has shown an interest in antebellum plantations, and this number seems to grow every year. But even as more archaeologists are drawn to the important study of the antebellum plantation regime and the system of human bondage it fostered, fewer archaeologists have shown any interest in tenant farming. This lack of interest seems to remain, even after tenancy is identified as both antecedent to, and contemporaneous with, its more glamorous plantation relative. Only a small number of archaeologists has focused on southern farm tenancy (see, for example, Anderson and Muse 1982; Holland 1990; Joseph et al. 1991; Orser 1988a,

1988b, 1991; Smith 1991). There have been even fewer studies of northern tenancy (but see Catts and Custer 1990; Orser 1994b), although tenants were widely scattered throughout the American North (see Atack and Bateman 1987; A. Bogue 1963; M. Bogue 1959; Gates 1941, 1945).

Given that farm tenancy had no geographical limits, the lack of intensive study by archaeologists is puzzling. Perhaps the myth of the tenant farm as strictly southern and postbellum permits many historical archaeologists working outside the South to ignore what some would view as a rather unpleasant episode in American social history. Outside the South, archaeologists find it easy to ignore tenancy, even in well-known "farming states." For example, in 1860, tenants worked 93,000 farms in the Corn Belt alone (Orser 1994b). In Illinois alone, one absentee landlord, William Scully, bought almost 30,000 acres for tenant farms in 1850 and 1851 (Socolofsky 1979: 26). The American press often lampooned Scully as a ruthless exploiter of the poor, and Scully— also a reviled absentee landlord in Ireland—was said to have operated the "most forlorn-looking estate in Illinois" with "miserable tenants" living in unpainted "sheds" (Gates 1941: 76). In spite of this remarkable history, Illinois archaeologists have mostly ignored tenancy. In the past, state-agency archaeologists have not simply been ambivalent about the archaeology of tenancy, many have been openly dismissive about the archaeology of a subject they regard as "unimportant." I know anecdotally that similar attitudes exist in other states as well. In light of what appears to be a conscious decision to ignore a valuable piece of American history, perhaps we can conclude that many people, and even most archaeologists, must prefer the image of the lone farming family standing tall against the challenges of nature, rather than seeing them pitted against the injustices of a profit-seeking landlord in a capitalistic system of agriculture.

As social scientists engaged in examining the entirety of human history, we must ask ourselves why this attitude exists in archaeology. Must we as a discipline continue to seek the approbations of our colleagues through the study of early colonial sites—those contact-period expressions of colonialism—or sites inhabited by the wealthy and the famous? We should not have to ask this question in the late 1990s. Historical archaeologists addressed this very issue many years ago, and many decided that their field provides one of the best ways to study the dispossessed, the downtrodden, and the disenfranchised (see, for example, Ascher 1974: 10–12). Yet, most historical archaeologists have chosen to look away from tenant farmers.

This paper is about the archaeology of farm tenancy. Though fully acknowledging the existence of tenancy in the agricultural North, I focus here on southern tenancy, for two practical reasons. First, I have direct research experience with tenant farm sites in the South, which I concentrated on from 1981 to 1988. During much of this time, I focused on the archaeological implications of tenancy as an exploitative system contained within capitalist agriculture. Second, though inaccurate, the image of tenancy as a "southern problem" persists. Perhaps in light of this faulty perception, it may be said that tenancy can be best interpreted in a familiar setting. For these two reasons, it makes sense for me to concentrate on southern tenancy, even though larger, perhaps even nationwide, studies remain to be completed. Using data collected from tenant sites in South Carolina and Texas, my goal is to demonstrate the importance of the archaeological study of farm tenancy within our larger examination of American capitalism, and to illustrate some of the challenges inherent in such a study.

FARM TENANCY AS A POST-WAR, SOUTHERN REALITY

On April 23, 1866, Karl Marx, long-time critic of capitalism and close observer of the American Civil War, wrote to his friend and colleague Frederick Engels, saying that "After the Civil War phase, the United States are really only now entering the revolutionary phase" (Marx and Engels 1937: 277). Marx's statement seems decidedly odd, especially since the United States had just come through its costliest and deadliest war ever, with over 600,000 soldiers dying from wounds or disease. Over 44,000 casualties had come from Gettysburg alone. In addition to the devastating mortality, several other factors merged to create decisive changes throughout the South. Once powerful senators and judges had lost their voice in the affairs of the nation, and thousands of former property owners had been uprooted, having already seen much of their property become destroyed, damaged, or confiscated. Men and women once held in bondage for life now walked free, looking for work and a decent place to live. All of these nationwide changes were transforming America, making the post-war period even more revolutionary than the war itself. As probably the most perceptive student of capitalism of his day, and arguably of all time, Marx understood the supreme challenge southern capitalists faced with the death of slavery and the social and economic upheaval that would surely follow.

The demise of the Confederate States of America threw the South's plantation system into confusion. The Army of Northern Virginia had surrendered on April 9, 1865, nearly one year before Marx wrote to Engels. Four million African Americans, who shortly before could foresee lifetimes of bondage and resistance, were now ostensibly free to find their own jobs, resettle their families, and live as they chose. Emancipation terrified southern planters, who grew convinced that they would lose their workforce and that their fields would lie fallow. For their part, small-scale, non-African-American farmers and laborers convinced themselves that they would face unfair competition from ex-slaves, who would be willing to work for low wages. A writer in *DeBow's Review*, the leading voice for the cause of the South, proclaimed that "every Negro now cherishes ... the confident expectation ... of 'getting his share of the lands'" (Anonymous 1866a: 440). Another southerner expressed perhaps a deeper fear: "[Our] Lands will be deserted and left to grow up in forests, as hunting grounds for savage tribes of negroes" (Anonymous 1867: 353). Such alarmist views stood in marked contrast to the idyllic image of the antebellum plantation, as succinctly expressed by John Calhoun (1855: 716) prior to the war: "No more beautiful picture of human society can be drawn than a well organized plantation." Thus, planters feared that the beautiful, peaceful, ordered landscapes they imagined they had created would be turned into wild, unkempt forests populated by roving, predatory bands of freed slaves. These freed men and women would carry with them mayhem and destruction beyond anything the planters had experienced during the war.

In addition to their sometimes almost uncontrollable fear of a dark future, southern planters faced a more immediate problem: how to retain their agricultural power and wealth with no work force. As one correspondent to the *Southern Cultivator* wrote: "As soon as the emancipation of our negroes became a fixed fact, the important question forced itself upon my mind, how are we to manage and prosecute our business?" (A Northern Man 1866: 5). It was not an overstatement when, in 1864, Joseph Kennedy (1864: x), the compiler of the 1860 federal census, wrote that "American agriculture is in a transition state." This transition was but one part of the revolution Marx foresaw for the United States.

For many southern planters, the course through the transition seemed easy. They could simply ignore the freed men and women who once cultivated their cotton, sugar, and rice, and hire non-African-American workers. For some, the importation of "Coolies" from India provided the answer to their labor problem (Anonymous 1866b). Others looked to China (Merrill 1869), Europe, and the northern United States (Bell 1867) for replacement farmers. To attract a new workforce, planters held public meetings and wrote inspired pamphlets extolling the climatic and cultural virtues of the South. In 1867, G. A. N. (1867) summarized the situation well when he wrote simply: "Laborers Wanted."

Planters badly needed workers, and they had to devise some way to obtain them. Before long, they came to accept what was for many a terrible realization: Former slaves provided the only real solution to their agricultural woes. Freed men and women were not only available, they also had the agricultural knowledge and experience planters so desperately needed. So, as "S" (1867: 40) from Alabama wrote, "Many planters were forced against their wills to undertake the business [of cooperating with former slaves]. They gave the negroes a part of the crop, and entrusted the management to them." Thus began the period of widespread southern tenant farming, the period that Marx saw as "revolutionary."

FARM TENANCY IN AMERICA

Farm tenancy, or cultivating ground owned by a landlord for an agreed-upon rent, did not begin in 1865 simply because southern planters needed a mechanism to maintain their wealth and control. On the contrary, tenancy has medieval, European roots. Tenancy was common, for example, in late-medieval England, where landlords often required many of their tenants to spend a certain number of days working directly for them. Medieval landowners instituted this "service-tenancy system" as slaves became less available to work newly cleared, manorial fields (Kerridge 1973: 40–42).

The earliest European colonists brought the idea of tenancy with them to the New World. In 1689, Virginia planter William Fitzhugh complained that only three of his tenants could "pay their Rent in money" because they were such "poor needy men" (Virginia Historical Society 1895: 274). The remainder must have paid Fitzhugh in some other currency, perhaps crops or labor. Fitzhugh's problem of receiving rent payments was not unusual, for only six years later, the South Carolina legislature passed an act specifying precisely which "commodities" could be used to pay rent (Cooper 1837: 93–102). Tenancy was not strictly an English institution. For example, the Sieur de Bienville, colonial governor of French Louisiana, had tenants on his property by 1723 (Cruzat 1918: 123). Thus, tenancy was so widespread that it even crosscut national boundaries, and by the 1840s, landlords throughout America commonly hired tenants to work their fields. In the South, antebellum tenants often worked alongside African–American slaves on the same plantations (Mendenhall 1937: 112–113).

By 1865, American tenancy had developed into a complex, hierarchical system. A landlord could make one of several different arrangements with his or her tenants, depending on local conditions, economic realities, and what planters widely called the "custom of the country" (Herndon 1969: 100–101).

Sharecropping and renting were the most common forms of farm tenure. Under both arrangements, farmers had to rent land in order to produce a crop, but the precise details differed. Under sharecropping, landlords required tenants to pay a portion of their crop as rent; in renting, landlords only required tenants to pay an agreed-upon, fixed rent. In a legal sense, however, the distinction between sharecropping and renting was dramatic and important. American courts ruled that the sharecroppers' crops were never really theirs. All sharecropped produce belonged to the landlord, and sharecroppers had absolutely no legal claim to what they had toiled so diligently to produce. As the North Carolina Supreme Court decreed in 1874, although the sharecropper "has, in some sense, the possession of the crop, it is only the possession of a servant, and it is in law that of the landlord" (Hargrave 1905: 9). Other state court judges agreed with this ruling and, by repeating it across the United States, the courts further cemented the sharecropper's lowly social and economic position relative to other farmers. The Supreme Court of Georgia simply and clearly stated the courts' position: "There is an obvious distinction between a cropper and a tenant [i.e., renter]" (Jackson 1912: 584).

Several minor variations in tenancy made it a complex system. Sharecropping was fairly straightforward. Because sharecroppers typically expected to receive one-half of the crop they produced, many southerners referred to them as "half croppers," "half tenants," or "half hands" (Langsford and Thibodeaux 1939: 15, 30). Sharecroppers usually received the necessary fertilizer, seed, tools, and animals directly from their landlords. The sharecropper's job was to supply the labor. Renting was usually more flexible than sharecropping, and several varieties existed. In "share renting," the tenant and the landlord each received a portion of the crop equal to the amount of fertilizer each had supplied. In "third and fourth" share renting, the landlord received one-quarter of the cotton and one-third of all other crops grown by the tenant. In "straight-third" share renting, the landlord received one-third of all the crops grown, but in the "straight-fourth" arrangement, the landlord received one-fourth of only the cotton and the corn. "Half-share tenants" were not technically sharecroppers because they had to provide their own animals, feed, tools, and fertilizer. "Cash renters" paid a monetary rent to their landlords from the funds they earned from the sale of their crops. "Standing renters," however, paid rent in the form of staple crops.

These forms of farm tenancy were arranged hierarchically in what has been termed "the agricultural ladder" (Spillman 1919: 29). The "rungs" of this social and economic "ladder" extended from wage hands on the bottom to independent owner-operators on the top. Landlords were not actually on the ladder, but hovered over it. The hierarchy of the ladder was based purely on the capitalist notion of ownership. Standing renters and cash renters—highest on the ladder directly beneath owner-operators—held estate rights over their crops and either sold or divided them to make their rent. The landlords divided the crops of the lowly ranked sharecroppers. Landlords would hope for good harvests from their most powerless tenants—those "on shares"—because the higher the yield, the greater the landlord's share. Sharecroppers, and sometime even share renters, were powerless because they had no legal right to divide their own crops, and they had to hope that their landlords would not cheat them out of their hard-earned share. One Georgia sharecropper complained that because his landlord refused to show him the receipts from the cotton warehouse, he never really knew his proper share. One year his landlord even "took his share and all of mine and claim I owe him twenty-four dollars in addition" (Maguire 1975: 72). Landlords could perpetrate such overt crimes on those occupying the lowest rungs of the agricultural ladder without fear of legal redress. The sharecroppers' poverty and lack of social standing precluded any serious legal challenge to the landlords' authority and power.

Climbing the ladder required capital and land. Historical statistics suggest that African-American farmers were not provided the same opportunities as their European-American counterparts when it came to the agricultural ladder (Orser 1988a: 106–111). Nonetheless, tenancy was not a racially based system, at least not in theory. Tenancy was rooted in economics and profit, and the structured set of hierarchically arranged social relations embedded within it was the glue that held the system together. Of course, skin color was often a major factor in the daily conduct of tenancy as racism was usually present every time an African-American farmer was denied access to good fields, made to accept an unjust tenure arrangement, or cheated by a landlord. Tenancy did not have to rely on racism to be profitable for landlords, but they could be adept at using racism as a tool for making tenancy even more advantageous for them.

HISTORICAL ARCHAEOLOGY
AND AMERICAN FARM TENANCY

Statistics clearly show that thousands of American men and women labored as farm tenants after 1865, with the greatest numbers being in the South. I have argued elsewhere that tenancy has significant implications for historical archaeology and that tenancy can no longer be ignored in the archaeology of rural America (Orser 1988b, 1991; Orser and Holland 1984). Because little has changed in the 10 years since I first voiced this opinion, I wish to reiterate and reinforce my stance by stating that any broadly conceived archaeological examination of American capitalism must include tenant farming in some way. The sheer magnitude of tenancy was simply too great, and the impact of tenant farmers on the social and cultural fabric of the nation was too strong, for us to designate them simply as "farmers" and then to ignore them.

The hierarchical nature of tenancy, with its obvious economic implications, suggests that the social distinctions between tenure classes will have material dimensions that can be investigated and interpreted by archaeologists. For example, the differences between cash renters and sharecroppers involved more than simply the legal issue of who divided the harvested crop. The important social inequalities engendered by the process of crop division undoubtedly translated into material distinctions as well.

During the 1920s and 1930s, social scientists traversed all corners of the rural South to document the material conditions of families living on tenant farms. Insightful observers such as Margaret Jarman Hagood (1939), Rupert Vance (1929), James Agee and Walker Evans (1941), Thomas Woofter and other (1936), and Arthur Raper (1936) wrote many of today's classic studies of southern tenant farmers. In addition to constructing compelling pictures of tenant life, these writers' careful images are invaluable to archaeologists because each of them presented a vivid personal view of the material conditions of tenancy. Archaeologists can learn much from these observers. For instance, in one of Agee's memorable, verbal tours through a tenant's home, we learn that the family had placed a wooden trunk against one wall and a cast-iron sewing machine in a corner. We see that they used a nail as a coat hanger and that they slept on a thin, lumpy, cornshuck mattress that was "morbid with bedbugs, with fleas, and I believe with lice" (Agee and Evans 1941: 174). In one of his visits to rural Georgia, Raper (1936: 65–66) discovered that of the African-American tenant families he visited, 55 percent owned sewing machines, 23 percent owned pianos and organs, and 19 percent owned phonographs.

The homes of the South's tenants came to represent the visible symbol of the inherent problems contained within farm tenancy, in the same way, perhaps, that the slave cabin had earlier signified the horrors of bondage. Hagood (1939: 97) says that the tenant homes she visited were "usually characterized by a lack of color and by drabness." Vance's (1936) magnificently evocative *How the Other Half is Housed* presents powerful images that reinforce Hagood's view. If the images Vance presented were compiled into a single picture, the typical tenant house in the South would indeed appear as "a dilapidated, unpainted, weather-beaten frame cabin leaning out of plumb on rock or brick pilings—unceiled, unscreened, covered with a leaky roof" (Tindall 1967: 411).

Houses evoke the realities of daily, lived experience. As human-built features on the landscape, houses generally have great visibility, and archaeologists, geographers, folklorists, rural sociologists, and historians of vernacular architecture have long been drawn to these domestic spaces (see, for example, Jurney and Moir 1987; Worthy 1983). After the houses themselves, the physical objects used inside the home may reveal the most about the social standing of southern tenants. Unfortunately, one of the most socially charged objects, the common mattress, does not have archaeological visibility. Tenant farmer Ed Brown clearly and succinctly stated the importance of mattresses when he said: "every time you come up in the world you got a better mattress" (Maguire 1975: 48). The mattress was thus a highly meaningful artifact that reflected one's access to capital and, in turn, one's place on the agricultural ladder. Brown said that wage hands stuffed their mattresses with straw or crabgrass, and that sharecroppers filled theirs with unginned cotton. Cash renters stuffed their mattresses with ginned cotton, free of painful seeds. The remarkable material distinction encapsulated in the common mattress probably has no archaeological correlate, because even mattress buttons, provided they can be identified as such, will reveal nothing about how the tenant had stuffed the mattress. As Brown's testimony suggests, some of the most subtle material differences between tenure classes may be revealed only by living men and women who can remember having been tenants. Such subtleties mean, then, that archaeologists not also using oral information will face real difficulties when it comes to interpreting the material distinctions of tenant families.

With our current knowledge, the best archaeological measures for interpreting the material inequalities between tenant farming classes seems to reside in settlement patterns and houses (Orser 1988a: 245). Archaeologists can easily identify the differences in house types and location and, once identified, they can often use these bits of information to understand something about tenure-class distinction. Often, however, the differences may not be readily apparent, even in settlement patterns and house style and layout (Orser and Nekola 1985). Given the problems inherent in analyzing what appears to be the most useful category of material, it therefore seems abundantly clear that archaeologists will face substantial obstacles when seeking to observe tenure-class differences in the portable objects tenant farming men and women bought and used.

Perhaps the biggest impediment to the archaeological understanding of tenure-class distinctions derives from the tenants' practice of "shifting," or moving from one farm to another. Regardless of skin color, tenant farmers shifted often because it provided a means of obtaining a better tenure arrangement from a new landlord in an environment with a high demand for labor. Thus, shifting was a form of resistance and rebellion. An unhappy tenant could simply run away to a new farm, leaving old debts and obligations behind for the former landlord to sort out. Statistics show, unsurprisingly perhaps, that tenants on the lowest rungs of the agricultural ladder generally occupied farms for the shortest periods of time. In other words, legally insecure tenants shifted more often than tenants who had better agricultural arrangements. In fact, the length of farm occupation generally increased as one moved up the ladder (Raper 1935: 59–61; Schuler 1983: 183). Landlords usually found it pointless to sue tenants for breach of contract because the tenants had nothing the landlords wanted. As a result, landlords were practically powerless to stop shifting unless they resorted to threats, intimidation, and violence.

The practice of shifting represents a significant practical problem for archaeologists. The soil deposits of the tenants' short occupations are usually thin, and one- or two-year occupation levels often can be mixed together by the activities of subsequent inhabitants. At any one homesite, archaeologists would have virtually no way to distinguish between the occupations of a sharecropper in 1875, a share renter in 1876, and a standing renter in 1877. A sequence of this kind was not unknown in the rural South. Raper (1936: facing 61), for example, illustrated a house that six unrelated families occupied in 10 years: one white owner family, three black tenant families, and two white tenant families.

In Raper's example, we may reasonably assume that each tenant family occupied a different place on the agricultural ladder. In light of the many different tenure arrangements that ideally could have been made between a landlord and his or her tenants, and taking into account the effects of shifting on archaeological deposits, it seems unlikely that historical archaeologists will ever be able to make definite statements about tenant-farmer social distinctions strictly from artifacts alone. Farm tenancy was simply too complex in its individualities to permit such fine-grained interpretations. But is such apparent pessimism warranted, particularly in the light of the fact that every social institution archaeologists study is potentially complex and difficult to interpret?

To demonstrate some of the complexities inherent in the archaeological examination of farm-tenant classes using artifacts alone, I use materials collected from two archaeological excavations in the American South. I use these two examples because the principal archaeologist of each project focused specifically on tenancy as a primary goal of the research, rather than as a by-product. The first data set derives from my work in the early 1980s at Millwood Plantation in South Carolina. The second project took place in northeastern Texas as part of the Richland/Chambers Reservoir construction project, located about 60 miles south of Dallas.

A BRIEF NOTE ON THE DATA SETS

The Millwood and Richland/Chambers projects provide excellent data for the investigation of tenant-farmer classes. James Calhoun, eccentric scholar and well-connected member of South Carolina's planter aristocracy, built Millwood Plantation in the 1830s as a slave plantation. After the Civil War, many of his former slaves stayed on the estate as tenant farmers, some remaining until the mid-1920s (Orser 1988a; Orser et al. 1987). In this essay, I use data collected from Calhoun's final residence (Structure 1) dating from the 1860s to the 1890s; a postbellum wage hand's home (Structure 11) dating from 1880 to 1900; and the home of African-American tenants, Mose and Minnie Walker (Structure 17), dating from 1890 to around 1900. Each structure was physically discrete and easily identifiable in the site's deposits. We identified the inhabitants of Structures 1 and 17 using both historical documents and oral information collected from former Millwood tenants (for complete information see Orser et al. 1987).

In the Richland/Chambers Reservoir, archaeologists from Southern Methodist University investigated several dwelling sites once inhabited by black and white tenants and owners (Jurney and Moir 1987). I selected five sites from their sample for my analysis. The Southern Methodist archaeologists concretely identified the residents of three of the sites using written records. For the other two sites, they could only establish that the residents were tenant farmers. White owners, Jonas and Nancy Baker, lived at site 41NV145 from 1859 until the late 1870s. Joseph and Mary Burleson, another family of white owners, lived at site 41NV235 from about 1855 to about 1905. African-American owners and former slaves, Mingo and Nancy Burleson, lived at 41NV267 from about 1873 until 1900. Unnamed tenant farmers inhabited site 41NV305 from the late 1870s until the early twentieth century as well as site 41NV306 from the late 1870s until the late 1890s (Moir and Jurney

1987). All of the sites I selected for analysis are contemporaneous, having been occupied in the late nineteenth and early twentieth centuries. A couple of simple comparisons of these sites illustrate the difficulty of tenant analysis.

Using what has become common procedure in historical archaeology, I attempted to discern differences in the artifact assemblages between the landlord, the tenant, and the wage-hand samples at Millwood Plantation and between the owners and tenants in the Richland/ Chambers Reservoir. I examined the artifact percentages from each site using Robinson's Index of Agreement (Brainerd 1951; Doran and Hodson 1975: 139; Robinson 1951). In this well-worn but useful statistic, the largest percentage of artifacts in one class from one site is subtracted from that of the same class from a second site. This procedure is completed for all artifact classes, the differences are added together, and the sum is subtracted from 200.0. The result is termed the Index of Agreement. Maximum similarity between two samples produces a value of 200.0.

My initial assumption was that, as a class, landlords would have had greater buying power than tenants, and certainly much more than wage hands. Given the hierarchical realities of the agricultural ladder, the wage-hand sample should be most unlike that of the landlord. Further, I also expected that the landlord samples would have greatest similarity to other landlord samples. Collectively, they should have been most unlike the wage-hand or tenant samples.

I investigated the similarities of the samples from Millwood Plantation and from the Richland/Chambers Reservoir by creating five functional categories of artifacts—foodways, clothing, household/structural, personal, and labor—as in the original Millwood analysis (Orser et al. 1987: 39–46). The use of this typology is justified in this particular analysis because I originally designed it specifically to isolate material distinctions among tenure classes. The strength of the typology lies in its segregation of labor-related artifacts, which are significant because, as noted above, assignment to a tenure class carried with it certain requirements about supplying the tools and hardware necessary for producing a crop.

The similarity analysis does not provide clear and unambiguous results as might reasonably be expected (Table 1). The greatest similarity between the samples occurs between the two white owners in Texas (196.6), but the landlord sample is not particularly similar to either owner (141.4, 144.2). The similarities between the Millwood tenant and the Richland/Chambers Reservoir tenants is extremely weak (90.6, 95.5), as is the similarity between the Millwood wage-hand and the Texas tenants (61.4, 66.9). The similarity between the Texas tenants

Table 1. Similarity Matrix for All Artifacts

Tenure class (structure/site number)	Structure/site number							
	1	17	11	145	235	267	305	306
Landlord (St. 1)	200.0							
Tenant (St. 17)	175.4	200.0						
Wage hand (St. 11)	169.4	168.4	200.0					
White owner (145)	141.4	161.8	130.2	200.0				
White owner (235)	144.2	164.6	83.2	196.6	200.0			
Black owner (267)	108.8	126.2	97.6	163.0	159.6	200.0		
Tenant (305)	79.1	95.5	66.9	132.2	129.1	169.3	200.0	
Tenant (306)	72.6	90.6	61.4	127.6	124.6	163.8	193.3	200.0

alone, however, is strong (193.3). Interestingly, the black-owner sample has no particularly strong similarities with any sample. It is, however, more like the white-owner samples in Texas (163.0, 159.6) than the landlord sample in South Carolina (108.8), though still weak.

To extend the analysis, I examined the ceramic vessel forms at the eight sites. Ceramic vessel-form analysis is now a staple of a great deal of historical archaeology, and my decision to investigate it is not revolutionary. My assumption, again, was that the different classes of farm tenants would have had unequal access to purchasing ceramic dishes.

In this simple analysis, I compared the percentages of fine earthenware vessel forms by dividing the sherds into "flat" pieces (plates and platters) and "deep" pieces (bowls and cups). My general assumption was that landlords had greater opportunities to use plates and platters than did the poorer members of tenant society. Thus, I imagined that landlord samples, when compared with non-landlord samples, would contain a disproportionate representation of these kinds of vessels. I further expected similarities between the landlords and similarities between the tenants (Table 2).

The greatest similarity does indeed occur between the white landlord at Millwood Plantation (Calhoun) and the white owners at Texas site 235 (Joseph and Mary Burleson). In fact, the match between the two sites is almost perfect (199.8). This high similarity fits my expectation about the material aspects of the agricultural ladder. Though this particular test is simplistic and based on few sites, it does support the idea that landlords, no matter where they lived, had similar opportunities and buying power. These advantages should translate into material distinctions and, in these samples at least, they appear to have done so. This straightforward interpretation, however, becomes more problematic when we realize that the Millwood tenant sample is also

Table 2. Similarity Matrix for Fine Earthenware Vessel Forms

Tenure class (structure/site number)	Structure/site number							
	1	17	11	145	235	267	305	306
Landlord (St. 1)	200.0							
Tenant (St. 17)	195.6	200.0						
Wage hand (St. 11)	176.8	172.4	200.0					
White owner (145)	152.2	147.8	175.4	200.0				
White owner (235)	199.8	195.8	176.6	152.0	200.0			
Black owner (267)	180.2	175.8	196.6	172.0	180.0	200.0		
Tenant (305)	164.2	159.8	187.4	188.0	164.0	184.0	200.0	
Tenant (306)	193.1	181.8	190.6	166.0	186.0	194.0	178.0	200.0

similar to that of the Texas owner at site 235 (195.8). Further confusion
is introduced by the high index produced by the Millwood landlord-to-
tenant comparison (195.6) and by the high similarity between the Millwood wage-hand sample and the Texas black-owner sample (196.6).

   This simple analysis could be extended in many ways. In one approach, qualitative differences between the sites can refine the information presented in the similarity matrices. Such an analysis is quite
telling. For example, if we examine the three sites at Millwood Plantation, we find that the landlord had four artifacts that we can associate
with "labor" (barbed wire, a horseshoe or muleshoe, a pulley wheel, and
a counterweight). The wage-hand site yielded three "labor" artifacts (a
file, three chain links, and a hammer). The tenant sample, however,
contained several "labor" artifacts, grouped into sixteen separate categories, and including artifacts found at the other two sites (chain links,
a file, three horseshoes, one muleshoe, and barbed wire). From the
artifacts alone, we thus may be tempted to conclude that the residents of
Structure 17 were deeply involved in "labor" activities, whereas the
residents of the other two sites were not as involved. This conclusion
is probably accurate. The landlord at Structure 1 was not a laborer,
and the wage hand probably owned few tools. The residents of Structure 17—who according to oral informants were renters rather than
sharecroppers—undoubtedly owned their own tools and equipment, as
renting required.

CONCLUSIONS

   The above analysis, even though it is recognizably simplistic, allows
me to postulate at least two conclusions. The analysis shows, as we

would expect, that the material dimensions of tenure-class membership were complex. Because American farm tenancy contained so many variations, some of which were even regional, archaeologists will have difficulty interpreting these distinctions. And, though tenant ranking was not inherently based on skin color, racism adds a complication because it played a role in creating deep-seated social and material inequalities among tenants. Archaeologists have yet to examine the precise material nature of these disparities, and the task of discovering them will be long and difficult. My all-too-brief analysis provides only ambiguous results. Future researchers may find that the material aspects of farm tenancy are relatively equal within tenure classes, regardless of skin color. Some evidence for this position already exists. The archaeologists of the Richland/Chambers Reservoir project concluded from their ceramic analysis that the differences they observed in the ceramic samples "were more pronounced across landownership than ethnic associations" (Jurney and Moir 1987: 120). This conclusion is significant, and hopefully will provide one direction for future research.

My analysis also implies that the material aspects of the agricultural ladder may have been regionally based. Regionality was apparent in the Richland/Chambers Reservoir (Jurney and Moir 1987: 120), and we may perhaps tentatively conclude from this that the tenants and landlords in one region may have been more like one another than they were to tenants and landlords in other regions. Such differences may relate to a site's place in regional and national market networks. By the same token, each region of the United States may have had its own agricultural ladder, based on factors deemed locally significant. We know that farm tenancy did indeed have regional characteristics. For example, the agricultural North had a smaller percentage of tenants than the South, and northern tenants generally were better off materially than their southern counterparts (Orser 1988a: 97–98). Even within the South, some places had greater percentages of tenants than others. The precise material aspects of these differences are still unknown. We can imagine that the material distinctions that did exist probably had something to do with the intertwined economic and social elements of rural, tenant life. The realities of farm tenancy, as an economic system alone, were simply too materially based to be otherwise. Landlords had purchasing power and controlled little or nothing. In addition, we cannot diminish the importance of racism and other measures of inequality that could have been promoted across the rural United States.

Statistics compiled by the federal government between 1870 and 1930 may indeed support the conclusion of tenant regionality. But, even if such regional differences are found to be present, why is it so difficult for archaeologists to demonstrate the material differences between tenure classes within a particular region? If we assume that a hierarchical agricultural ladder relegated tenants to certain well-controlled, vertical social positions, then we can also imagine that the members of each tenure class would have roughly the same access to portable commodities, the things archaeologists find every day.

It will undoubtedly take years of research before archaeologists can identify precise material distinctions between tenure classes. Future researchers must look both within individual regions and beyond them. Substantial analytical difficulties will be encountered along the way because of historical realities like tenant shifting. In addition, tenants' activities at their homes undoubtedly mixed and confused the fragile archaeological deposits left by earlier tenants. Many of the sites studied in the Richland/Chambers Reservoir appeared as simple, amorphous sheet middens. The archaeologists were expert in determining the dates of these middens from the artifacts they contained (Jurney and Moir 1987; Moir and Jurney 1987), but they were considerably less successful in discerning tenure-class distinctions in the deposits. In most cases, they could only say that a tenant, of unknown labor arrangement, once lived at a particular site. The effects of shifting probably had much to do with the analytical difficulties faced by the Richland/Chambers Reservoir team. Archaeologists will face significant problems at any archaeological site where shifting has occurred. Problems will occur even in cases where the site consists of much more than simply a sheet midden.

Shifting introduces significant complexity into the archaeological analysis of farm tenancy, but a second, equally challenging difficulty must be laid at the feet of archaeologists themselves. Even when farm tenancy has been the subject of inquiry, some investigators have failed to see individual tenants as members of distinct tenure classes differentiated by the social and economic conditions of a capitalistic system of agriculture. Some archaeologists, though acknowledging the harsh realities of tenancy, have failed to grasp its class-based roots. Their inability or unwillingness to acknowledge the capitalist underpinnings of tenancy has caused severe interpretive problems.

William Adams' (1980) otherwise pioneering research at Waverly Plantation in Mississippi provides a useful example. Adams argues that "the planters and their tenants formed the *Waverly Community*" (Adams 1980: 2; emphasis in original). This community perspective allows Adams and his research team to focus on horizontal relations of community interaction, while ignoring the hierarchical social relations of labor. In the context of farm tenancy their analysis appears unrealistic, as they fail to acknowledge the daily tensions and anger that were inherent in the hierarchically arranged system put into place at Waverly.

At the same time, we also cannot ignore that the material distinctions between tenure classes may be almost imperceptible to archaeologists. As noted above, differences between tenants can be identified in housing and settlement patterns (Orser 1988b; Orser and Nekola 1985), but differences in material culture do not seem especially clear-cut. Our present knowledge of tenancy suggests that the occurrence of labor-related artifacts could represent a potentially useful, though still complex, way in which to perceive tenure distinctions. Interpreting these artifact occurrences, however, is not entirely without problems. Most tenants had to supply their own tools, with the exception of sharecroppers, who received their tools from the landlords (Boeger and Goldenweiser 1916: 7). Should an archaeologist conclude, then, that historically undocumented sites where no tools were found were once inhabited either by sharecroppers (who, theoretically, had no tools) or by owners (who had loaned their tools to sharecroppers)? The Richland/Chambers Reservoir archaeologists did not find any tools at sites 41NV145 or 41NV235, where white owners, Jonas and Nancy Baker, and Joseph and Mary Burleson, respectively, once lived. What can we conclude from the lack of labor-related artifacts about their tenure status or about the kinds of arrangements they made with their tenants? By the same token, should we assume that the tenants at sites 41NV305 and 41NV306 were renters rather than sharecroppers because the artifact samples from these sites include labor-related artifacts? Finally, we cannot rule out the possibility that idiosyncratic behavior played an important role in structuring specific social relations between tenants and landlords. Landlords are known to have exercised great latitude of behavior within the larger, profit-driven system of farm tenancy. For example, Ed Brown's landlord once paid him two dollars to get a marriage license (Maguire 1975: 34), but when Nate Shaw's family sorely needed a well, his landlord would not dig one (Rosengarten 1984: 495). That Shaw's landlord was an African American shows the often non-racist character of hierarchically designed farm tenancy. James Calhoun, the landlord at Millwood Plantation, knew seventeen languages and read ethnographies (Orser 1988a: 26). He is not known, however, to have used his obviously active mind to educate his tenants or to provide outside educational opportunities for them. When interviewed as part of the field research, former tenants generally reported that Calhoun was a cruel master. One elderly former tenant reported that he did not feed slave children who were too young to work, and another said that he fed his slaves and then ignored them and their needs. Another former Millwood tenant stated that Calhoun often obtained land by putting people in debt and then foreclosing on them (Orser et al. 1987: 222–223). This information does not give one confidence that Calhoun or his estate agents were particular mindful of their tenants' needs. Given that tenancy was, at its very foundation, an economic agreement between a landlord and a tenant, we may well imagine that individual attitudes, goals, and prejudices played some part in structuring specific tenant–landlord arrangements. This potential for idiosyncracy, however, does not excuse the unwillingness of some historical archaeologists to study farm tenancy, or once studied, to ignore its capitalistic heart and soul.

The general failure of historical archaeology as a discipline to accept the study of farm tenancy within its wider examination of modern life rests on the tacit acceptance of two related fallacies. I have already addressed the first fallacy—namely, that tenancy existed only in the postbellum American South. The proposition following from this mistake is at least logical: Since tenancy was only a characteristic of the American South, archaeologists working elsewhere in the United States can completely ignore it. This position is particularly unfortunate because many issues that can be examined at tenant sites have wide applicability throughout historical archaeology. The location and identification of tenant sites can be seen as but one part of a larger archaeology of impoverishment. I have argued elsewhere that one of the noblest causes of historical archaeology is the study of the poor and the disenfranchised (Orser 1996: 161; Orser and Fagan 1995: 202–204). Nonetheless, most historical archaeologists have ignored the significance of the controversy once sparked over the archaeology of farm tenancy (Anderson and Muse 1983; Orser and Holland 1984; Trinkley 1983a, 1983b).

The second fallacy is one that I first identified many years ago (Orser 1981: 15). At that time, I argued that historical archaeology as a whole suffered from "temporal bigotry." What I meant was that historical archaeology was not being accorded the respect it rightly deserved in American archaeology. Historic-period sites were being ignored, and even destroyed, by otherwise competent, well-meaning prehistorians. In the intervening years, historical archaeology has truly come of age, and the field has gained a measure of respect both among archaeologists and much of the public at large. Still, the specter of temporal bigotry has not been completely exorcised. The aversion to the archaeology of the most recent past continues as a dearly held tenet in many quarters. Some historical archaeologists still hold on to the cherished idea that "old is better," and most archaeologists would still probably prefer to concentrate on subjects that have greater, rather than less, antiquity. The public generally shows more interest in ancient topics, and funding is usually easier to obtain for such research. In historical archaeology, "antiquity" usually refers to the period of initial European colonialism. The archaeological study of the first days of European expansion is important and should be vigorously continued. The story of capitalism, however, did not end in 1600, 1700, or even 1800. Its history is still being written today, and in our own way, each of us is its coauthor.

Historical archaeologists who ignore capitalism or who figure that the study of its most recent expressions is not really "archaeology," miss the full potential of their field. Undoubtedly, we must continue to be leaders in documenting the daily lives of African-American slaves, Chinese laborers, Irish canal diggers, and the flood of European immigrants who came to America seeking something better than what they knew in their ancestral homelands. Part of what many of these immigrants knew, however, was farm tenancy. Many Europeans came to America only to find the same agricultural system they thought they had left behind. The failure of historical archaeology as a discipline to grapple with understanding the material means by which these peoples became enslaved, discriminated against, hated, impoverished, and even by which they occasionally starved to death, is unfortunate. Without question, the relentless, capitalist drive for profit underlies much of the reason for the inequality between different tenure classes.

In this chapter, I have demonstrated that the study of American farm tenancy, as part of a larger capitalist expression, is fraught with pitfalls. Tenant sites are difficult to interpret because of the hierarchical but fluid nature of the tenant system. Nonetheless, the archaeological study of farm tenancy, though not glamorous, is central to our understanding of rural America. If we can accept that "American history was launched from the countryside" (Hahn and Prude 1985: 3) then we must consider tenancy to be centrally important to that history. This essay is but another attempt to show the significance of farm tenancy in the archaeology of American capitalism.

The search to understand the material aspects of tenancy clearly will take many years and much thoughtful reflection. Despite its complexities and lack of glamour, the study of farm tenancy will push historical archaeology further towards the leading edge of understanding American capitalism. If nothing else, the archaeological study of American farm tenancy demonstrates that the past defies easy interpretation and that it constantly challenges us. The important question now is simple: Are we ready for the challenge?

REFERENCES

Adams, W. H. (editor)
    1980   *Waverly Plantation: Ethnoarchaeology of a Tenant Farming Community.* Heritage Conservation and Recreation Service, Atlanta.
Agee, J., and W. Evans
    1941   *Let Us Now Praise Famous Men: Three Tenant Families.* Houghton Mifflin, Boston.
Anderson, D. G., and J. Muse
    1982   The Archaeology of Tenancy: An Example from the South Carolina Low Country. *South Carolina Antiquities* 14:71–85.
    1983   The Archaeology of Tenancy (2): A Reply to Trinkley. *Southeastern Archaeology* 2:65–68.
Anonymous
    1866a   The Freedmen on the Sea Islands of South Carolina. *DeBow's Review* 1(n.s.):440.
    1866b   Coolies as a Substitute for Negroes. *DeBow's Review* 2(n.s.):215–217.
    1867   Exodus from the South. *DeBow's Review* 3(n.s.):352–356.
A Northern Man
    1866   Farming in the Future. *Southern Cultivator* 24(1):5–6.
Ascher, R.
    1974   Tin*Can Archaeology. *Historical Archaeology* 8:7–16.
Atack, J., and F. Bateman
    1987   *To Their Own Soil: Agriculture in the Antebellum North.* Iowa State University, Ames.
Batschelet, C. E. (supervisor)
    1953   *Portfolio of United States Census Maps, 1950: A Selection of Maps Used in the Publications of the 1950 Censuses of Population and Agriculture.* Government Printing Office, Washington, D.C.
Bell, E. Q.
    1867   In Lieu of Labor. *DeBow's Review* 4(n.s.):69–83.
Boeger, E. A., and E. A. Goldenweiser
    1916   *A Study of the Tenant Systems of Farming in the Yazoo-Mississippi Delta.* United States Department of Agriculture, Bulletin 337. Government Printing Office, Washington, D.C.
Bogue, A. G.
    1963   *From Prairie to Corn Belt: Farming on the Illinois and Iowa Prairies in the Nineteenth Century.* University of Chicago Press, Chicago.
Bogue, M. B.
    1959   *Patterns from the Sod: Land Use and Tenure in the Grand Prairie, 1950–1900.* Illinois State Historical Library, Springfield.
Brainerd, G. W.
    1951   The Place of Chronological Ordering in Archaeological Analysis. *American Antiquity* 16:301–313.
Burwell, W. M.
    1880   Our Black Peasantry. *DeBow's Review Monthly* 1(4):1–40.
Calhoun, J. A.
    1855   Management of Slaves. *DeBow's Review* 18:713–719.
Catts, W. P., and J. F. Custer
    1990   *Tenant Farmers, Stone Masons, and Black Laborers: Final Archaeological Inves-*

tigations of the Thomas Williams Site, Glasgow, New Castle County, Delaware. Delaware Department of Transportation, Dover.

Cooper, T.
1837   *The Statutes at Large of South Carolina.* A. S. Johnston, Columbia.

Cruzat, H. H.
1918   Sidelights on Louisiana History. *Louisiana Historical Quarterly* 1:87–153.

Doran, J. E., and R. F. Hodson
1975   *Mathematics and Computers in Archaeology.* Harvard University Press, Cambridge.

Ferguson, L.
1992   *Uncommon Ground: Archaeology and Early African America, 1650–1800.* Smithsonian Institution Press, Washington, D.C.

G. A. N.
1867   Laborers Wanted. *Southern Cultivator* 15(3):69.

Gates, P. W.
1941   Land Policy and Tenancy in the Prairie States. *Journal of Economic History* 1:60–82.
1945   Frontier Landlords and Pioneer Tenants. *Journal of the Illinois State Historical Society* 38:143–206.

Hagood, M. J.
1939   *Mothers of the South: Portraiture of the White Tenant Farm Woman.* University of North Carolina Press, Chapel Hill.

Hahn, S., and J. Prude
1985   Introduction. In *The Countryside in the Age of Capitalist Transformation: Essays in the Social History of Rural America*, edited by S. Hahn and J. Prude, pp. 3–21. University of North Carolina Press, Chapel Hill.

Hargrave, T. L., (reporter)
1905   Harrison v. Ricks. *North Carolina Reports* 71:5–11.

Herndon, G. M.
1969   *William Tatham and the Culture of Tobacco.* University of Miami Press, Coral Gables.

Hobbs, S. H., Jr.
1930   *North Carolina: Economic and Social.* University of North Carolina Press, Chapel Hill.

Holland, C. C.
1990   Tenant Farms of the Past, Present, and Future: An Ethnoarchaeological View. *Historical Archaeology* 24(4):60–69.

Jackson, H., (reporter)
1912   Thomas K. Appling v. Stephen Odom and A. J. Mercier. *Georgia Reports* 46:583–585.

Joseph, J. W., M. B. Reed and C. E. Cantley
1991   *Agrarian Life, Romantic Death: Archaeological and Historical Testing and Data Recovery for the I-85 Northern Alternative, Spartanburg County, South Carolina.* New South Associates, Stone Mountain, Georgia.

Jurney, D. H., and R. W. Moir (editors)
1987   *Historic Buildings, Material Culture, and People of the Prairie Margin: Architecture, Artifacts, and Synthesis of Historic Archaeology.* Richland Creek Technical Series, Vol. V. Archaeology Research Program, Southern Methodist University, Dallas.

Kennedy, J. C. G., (compiler)
1864   *Agriculture of the United States in 1860.* Government Printing Office, Washington, D.C.

Kerridge, E.
    1973   *The Farmers of Old England.* George Allen and Unwin, London.
Langsford, E. L., and B. H. Thibodeaux
    1939   *Plantation Organization and Operation in the Yazoo-Mississippi Delta.* United
        States Department of Agriculture, Technical Bulletin 682. Government Printing
        Office, Washington, D.C.
Maguire, J.
    1975   *On Shares: Ed Brown's Story.* W. W. Norton, New York.
Marx, K., and F. Engels
    1937   *The Civil War in the United States,* edited by R. Enmale. International, New York.
Mendenhall, M. S.
    1937   The Rise of Southern Tenancy. *Yale Review* 27:110–129.
Merrill, A. P.
    1869   Southern Labor. *DeBow's Review* 6 (n.s.):586–592.
Moir, R. W., and D. H. Jurney (editors)
    1987   *Pioneer Settlers, Tenant Farmers, and Communities: Objectives, Historical Back-
        ground, and Excavations.* Richland Creek Technical Series, Vol. IV. Archaeology
        Research Program, Southern Methodist University, Dallas.
Orser, C. E., Jr.
    1981   Clues from the Recent Past: The Emergence and Development of American
        Historical Archaeology. In *Guide for Historical Archaeology in Illinois,* edited by C. E.
        Orser, Jr., pp. 1–23. Loyola University, Chicago.
    1988a *The Material Basis of the Postbellum Tenant Plantation: Historical Archaeology
        in the South Carolina Piedmont.* University of Georgia Press, Athens.
    1988b Toward a Theory of Power for Historical Archaeology: Plantations and Space. In
        The Recovery of Meaning: Historical Archaeology in the Eastern United States, edited
        by M. P. Leone and P. B. Potter, Jr., pp. 313–343. Smithsonian Institution Press,
        Washington, D.C.
    1990   Archaeological Approaches to New World Plantation Slavery. In *Archaeological
        Method and Theory* Vol. 2, edited by M. B. Schiffer, pp. 111–154. University of Arizona
        Press, Tucson.
    1991   The Continued Pattern of Dominance: Landlord and Tenant on the Postbellum
        Cotton Plantation. In *Archaeology of Inequality,* edited by R. H. McGuire and R.
        Paynter, pp. 40–54. Blackwell, Oxford.
    1994a The Archaeology of African-American Slave Religion in the Antebellum South.
        Cambridge Archaeological Journal 4:33–45.
    1994b Corn Belt Agriculture during the Civil War Period, 1850–1870: A Research
        Prospectus for Historical Archaeology. In *Look to the Earth: Historical Archaeology
        and the American Civil War,* edited by C. R. Geier and S. W. Frye, pp. 141–160.
        University of Tennessee Press, Knoxville.
    1996   *A Historical Archaeology of the Modern World.* Plenum Press, New York.
Orser, C. E., Jr., and B. M. Fagan
    1995   *Historical Archaeology.* Harper Collins, New York.
Orser, C. E., Jr., and C. C. Holland
    1984   Let Us Praise Famous Men, Accurately: Toward a More Complete Understand-
        ing of Postbellum Southern Agricultural Practices. *Southeastern Archaeology* 3:111–120.
Orser, C. E., Jr., and A. M. Nekola
    1985   Plantation Settlement from Slavery to Tenancy: An Example from a Piedmont
        Plantation in South Carolina. In *The Archaeology of Slavery and Plantation Life,*
        edited by T. A. Singleton, pp. 67–94. Academic Press, Orlando.

Orser, C. E., Jr., A. M. Nekola, and J. L. Roark

1987   *Exploring the Rustic Life: Multidisciplinary Research at Millwood Plantation, A Large Piedmont Plantation in Abbeville County, South Carolina, and Elbert County, Georgia.* (three vols.) National Park Service, Atlanta.

Raper, A. F.

1936   *Preface to Peasantry: A Tale of Two Black Belt Counties.* University of North Carolina Press, Chapel Hill.

Robinson, W. S.

1951   A Method for Chronologically Ordering Archaeological Deposits. *American Antiquity* 16:293–301.

Rosengarten, T.

1984   *All God's Dangers: The Life of Nate Shaw.* Vintage, New York.

S.

1867   The Crops of the South of 1866 a Failure—Why! *Southern Cultivator* 15(5):40.

Schuler, E. A.

1938   *Social Status and Farm Tenure: Attitudes and Social Conditions of Corn Belt and Cotton Belt Farmers.* United States Department of Agriculture, Farm Security Administration, and the Bureau of Agricultural Economics, Social Research Report 4. Government Printing Office, Washington, D.C.

Singleton, T. A.

1991   The Archaeology of Slave Life. In *Before Freedom Came: African-American Life in the Antebellum South,* edited by E. D. C. Campbell, Jr., and K. S. Rice, pp. 155–175. Museum of the Confederacy, Richmond, and the University Press of Virginia, Charlottesville.

Smith, S. D.

1991   *A Comparison of the Documentary Evidence of Material Culture and the Archaeological Record: Store Ledgers and Two Black Belt Tenant Sites, Waverly Plantation, Mississippi.* Volumes in Historical Archaeology 12. The South Carolina Institute of Archaeology and Anthropology, Columbia.

Socolofsky, H. E.

1979   *Landlord William Scully.* Regents Press of Kansas, Lawrence.

Spillman, W. J.

1919   The Agricultural Ladder. In *Papers on Tenancy,* pp. 29–38. Office of the Secretary of the American Association for Agricultural Legislation, Bulletin 2, University of Wisconsin, Madison.

Taylor, H. C.

1938   What Should be Done about Farm Tenancy. *Journal of Farm Economics* 20: 145–152.

Tindall, G. B.

1967   *The Emergence of the New South, 1913–1945.* Louisiana State University Press, Baton Rouge.

Trinkley, M.

1983a   "Let Us Now Praise Famous Men": If Only We Can Find Them. *Southeastern Archaeology* 2:30–36.

1983b   Reply. *Southeastern Archaeology* 2:68–69.

Vance, R. B.

1929   *Human Factors in Cotton Culture: A Study of the Social Geography of the American South.* University of North Carolina Press, Chapel Hill.

1936   *How the Other Half in Housed: A Pictorial Record of Sub-Minimum Farm Housing in the South.* University of North Carolina Press, Chapel Hill.

Virginia Historical Society
   1895   The letters of William Fitzhugh. *Virginia Magazine of History and Biography*
          2:272–275.
White, E. V., and W. E. Leonard
   1915   *Studies in Farm Tenancy in Texas*. Bulletin 21. University of Texas, Austin.
Woofter, T. J., Jr., et al.
   1936   *Landlord and Tenant on the Cotton Plantation*. Works Progress Administration,
          Division of Social Research, Monograph 5. Government Printing Office, Washing-
          ton, D.C.
Worthy, L., (editor)
   1983   *All that Remains: The Traditional Architecture and Historic Engineering Struc-
          tures of the Richard B. Russell Multiple Resource Area, Georgia and South Carolina.*
          National Park Service, Atlanta.

"A Bold and Gorgeous Front"

The Contradictions of African America and Consumer Culture

7

Paul R. Mullins

INTRODUCTION

In an 1880s tour of New York City neighborhoods, Jacob Riis (1971: 118) seemed perplexed that "even where the wolf howls at the door, [African America] makes a bold and gorgeous front." Much like the subsequent century of scholars, Riis presumed African Americans' genteel household material culture was an insubstantial facade contradicting their objective identity. Riis reduced commodities in African-American homes to a meaningless "front" which Black consumers fabricated to conceal their "authentic" racial identity. Consumer discourses explicitly and tacitly promised a host of material advantages, civil privileges, and social possibilities, yet Riis denied such rights to African Americans because he assumed consumer culture's prospects were exclusive to Whites.

Between about 1880 and 1930, American society's incongruities were tempered by an exponentially expanding abundance of Victorian exotics, pervasive advertising, credit sales, and public marketing outlets, such as department stores (cf. Fox and Lears 1983; Horowitz 1985; Edsforth 1987; Agnew 1990; Cohen 1990; Lears 1994). For many African Americans, the explicit and implied civil privileges of consumption harbored the potential to subvert a host of racist inequalities in political, labor, and consumer space. This commitment to material consumption was typical of turn-of-the-century Americans: Americans representing

Paul R. Mullins • Anthropology Program, George Mason University, Fairfax, Virginia 22030.

Historical Archaeologies of Capitalism, edited by Mark P. Leone and Parker B. Potter, Jr. Plenum Press, New York, 1999.

every possible social position consumed identical commodities, leading some observers, then and now, to see the origins of a potentially problematic mass culture (cf. Horowitz 1985: 134). A fundamental allure of mass-consumed commodities was that surface attributes like cost, function, and aesthetics were redefined by myriad consumers. Perceptive contemporaries like Jacob Riis pondered apparently familiar objects and material consumption patterns in African America but found those goods and patterns difficult to interpret because they contradicted the popular caricature of Black subjectivity. In his bewilderment, Riis was recognizing that the prosaic meaning of "White" goods belied distinctive material and social symbolism that reflected consumers' social positions, not their essentialized racial identity.

African Americans certainly were not alone in the symbolic manipulation of commodities, the conviction that consumption conferred fundamental citizen rights, or the optimism that mass consumption forebode an improved society or personal circumstance. However, commodity symbolism assumed a distinctive dimension among African Americans. In the face of racism, the ability to construct and veil their communities in opposition to racism was crucial to African America's social opportunity and to its very survival. Distinctive African-American consumption tactics reproduced and often concealed African-American differences while introducing beneficial material changes and demonstrating African America's suitability to the privileges of consumer citizenship. To many contemporaries African-American consumption appeared to be innocuous, yet many African-Americans contested anti-Black racism, appealed for civil privilege, and secured the idiosyncratic personal pleasures of material objects through this seemingly innocuous consumption.

It would be imprudent (if not naive) to celebrate African-American consumers' symbolic creativity and ignore racism's oppressive impact on African America. The vast majority of African-American material assemblages were dominated by mass-produced goods, but the symbolic resistance of commodity symbolism was fraught with the contradictions of racism. African America's participation in a racially structured marketplace unavoidably shaped social subjectivity in ways African-American consumers often did not intend or recognize. The dominant symbolism of mass-produced goods was rooted in (albeit not determined by) White racism, and even the most self-conscious African American found it difficult to utterly step outside racial subjectivity.

For a century, observers embedded in a racist society typically have assumed that African Americans were too impoverished to consume mass-produced goods, too culturally distinct to find those objects symbolically meaningful, or, at best, were peripheral to the mass vision of rights and desires that could be realized in consumption. Yet it is overwhelmingly evident that African Americans quite actively participated in consumer culture as laborers, marketers, and consumers, and that African America consciously pondered and debated the possibilities and hazards of consumer culture. Less clear, though, are the concrete tactics African Americans forged to influence their position in emergent consumer culture. African Americans were certainly part of consumer space, but they were suspicious of its promises, conscious of its anti-Black contempt, and keen to subvert many dominant social practices. In some ways, African Americans were typical consumers whose material consumption reflected African America's desire for the equity of full citizenship; in others, they developed quite distinctive tactics that bespoke their aspiration to erase the racial exclusivity of consumer space. African Americans radically modified or abandoned some longstanding practices and shared increasingly more aspirations and material conditions with the burgeoning White and European working class, yet inevitably were distinguished by their consciousness of White racial privilege.

In *Black Reconstruction in America*, W. E. B. Du Bois (1935) argued that race was the central structuring mechanism of post-Emancipation American society. Du Bois contended that the failure of Reconstruction and the emergence of Jim Crow racism promoted an African-American "double consciousness." Double consciousness was based on the necessity to make something significant appear innocuous in order to avoid surveillance (cf. de Certeau 1986). To effectively minimize surveillance, African Americans cultivated a tactical consciousness built on the observation of White dominance, the recognition that the African-American community was constantly under White surveillance, and their own awareness of their shared experience.

Double consciousness makes African-American subjectivity a difficult thing to "see" archaeologically if analysis of commodity similarities stops at the surface appearance. Jacob Riis (1971: 118) stopped at appearances when he concluded that "In the art of putting the best foot foremost, of disguising his poverty by making a little go a long way, our negro has no equal." Riis assumed that a monolithic African-American racial identity (and associated attributes like poverty) lay beneath that material "disguise." An 1880 *Harper's Weekly* correspondent in Georgia admitted the same difficulty locating the essential Black subject when she observed that "the negro, *as he really is*, remains a misconception to the casual observer" (emphasis in original; "Inside Southern Cabins" 1880: 733). She viewed Black public behavior as a consciously contrived appearance, citing an African American who told her that "'We have been accustomed to look upon white people as beings to be conciliated at any cost, and so we hide ourselves behind a mask that *reflects their moods and opinions.'*"

Riis and the *Harper's* correspondent reduced African-American material symbolism simply to an artificial front concealing an essential underlying identity. This paper, in contrast, examines that symbolism as a product of consumers' negotiation of, and resistance to, social position, neither purely imposed by dominant racist institutions nor inherited in cultural tradition. African-American consumption harbors aspiration to civil and material opportunities, intentional misrepresentation, reproduction of distinctive cultural practices, and various articulate and inchoate forms of resistance. This situational consumption complexity frustrates the archaeological assumption that discrete subject entities (e.g., cultural, regional, or ethnic groups) will have distinct material assemblages reflecting their deep-seated differences. Rather than probe for an essential Black subject, an analysis of African-American consumption should focus on how African-American consumers actively reproduced, mediated, and defied social position against a backdrop of racial assumptions about the nature of Blackness and, by extension, Whiteness (cf. Roediger 1991).

This chapter attempts to sidestep caricatures such as assimilation and segregation, producer and consumer, and Black and White to examine African-American consumption as a complex negotiative process. African-American consumption was not ideologically directed emulation of White society, nor was it wholly willful resistance of racism. Instead, it was a dynamic process in which African Americans constantly evaded and subverted White racism and attempted to forge new social subjectivities and possibilities. Rather than paint it primarily as the satisfaction of functional needs or mechanical displays of identity, African-American consumption instead focused on a complex range of social aspirations and individual desires that were believed realizable through consumption. The rights and pleasures that were promised or implied in consumer goods often proved somewhat disappointing: no commodities ever dismissed racism or worked a dramatic cause-and-effect transformation in African-American social position. Yet it would be shortsighted to dismiss the meaningfulness of such aspirations, suggest that they had absolutely no impact on African-American social consciousness, or deny the significance of African-American anti-racist discourse on American society.

Clearly some of our most fundamental assumptions about radical "racial" differences appear to be completely undermined by the functional and aesthetic similarity between "Black" and "White" archaeological assemblages. Yet an analysis that embeds commodity symbolism in African-American consumers' negotiation of racism inevitably will reveal the distinctiveness of African America's experience in consumer culture. African-American consumption does not provide a straight-forward picture of domination by, or resistance to, various threads of racism; rather, it is one of situational negotiation, subtle tactics, persistent aspiration, and constant circuitousness. Obviously material symbolism was so complex—and many of our assumptions about social difference so mechanical—that archaeologists still misconstrue the distinctive social subjectivity African Americans negotiated within and against consumer culture.

This chapter focuses on the consumption tactics reflected in the archaeology of three African-American sites in Annapolis, Maryland. The most extensive excavations were conducted at the Maynard–Burgess House, a circa 1850–1980 African-American residence (Mullins and Warner 1993). Purchased in 1847 by the free African-American family of John and Maria (Spencer) Maynard, the house standing today at 163 Duke of Gloucester Street was built between 1850 and 1858. The Maynards sold the home to boarder Willis Burgess in 1914, and Burgess' family lived in it until the 1980s. Located on a block interior three blocks from Maynard-Burgess, Gott's Court was a group of 25 connected frame buildings that were rented by African-American working families from 1907 into the early 1950s (Warner 1992; Mullins 1996: 188–189). The Courthouse Site was a circa 1850–1970 African-American neighborhood in Annapolis (Warner and Mullins 1993; Aiello and Seidel 1995: 1:148). Covering a single contiguous block, the Court-house Site contained some privately owned houses, rented homes, and Bellis Court, an 1897–1939 central block "alley" housing complex similar to Gott's Court (Mullins 1996: 177–178). The socioeconomic heterogeneity of these households, which included well-connected aspirants like the Maynards, as well as marginalized laborers like the Gott's Court families, provides a sound insight into a range of consumption tactics within one African-American community.

ENVISIONING A RACELESS MARKET: BRAND-NAME CONSUMPTION

In 1932, African-American consumption researcher Paul Edwards (1969: 152) noted that "In the sale of grocery products, the evolution from bulk to brand has been rapid." Indeed, virtually any commodity could be sold by brand: fruits and vegetables, for instance, were individually stamped and wrapped, and dry foods, from beans to flour, were sold in packages. Widely marketed after about 1870, brands catered to consumers' desire to see themselves within an affluent consumer society that conferred a host of concrete benefits and implied privileges (Schlereth 1991: 162). Producers hoped brands would evoke and enhance consumers' desires for, among other things, genteel consumer subjectivity, moral and bodily disciplines, and membership in a consuming nation. Placing commodities within symbolically enigmatic packages amplified desire by linking a commodity with arbitrary brand symbolism and postponing consumption (cf. Willis 1991: 4–5). The predictable quality and uniform aesthetic imagery of brand goods also provided stability in a rapidly changing society: despite modest design changes in packaging and advertising, brands maintained the same motifs (e.g., Aunt Jemima) and provided an unchanging product in the face of a rapidly changing society (Willis 1991: 3; Miller 1997: 57).

Edwards found that African Americans in the urban South consumed very little wild or bulk foods by the 1920s. Instead he found that most of their households were quite committed to single brand-name grocery items. In a survey of 359 African-American households, the mean expenditure on food was 27.2% of household annual earnings, greater than any other single expense (including housing); the expenditure on brand foods was particularly significant because brands were universally more expensive than loose goods (Edwards 1969: 41–42). In contrast to brands, bulk goods varied in quality, and adulteration of locally produced, unpackaged goods was commonplace. The central explanation for African-American brand devotion, Edwards (1969: 159) argued, was that these consumers were "often taken advantage of by unscrupulous merchants": White merchants routinely sold inferior quality, overpriced goods to African-American customers. Acknowledging the market deceptions routinely aimed at African Americans, a 1905 advertisement for an African-American-owned drugstore in Washington emphasized that "I can save you 50 per cent discount on all prescriptions—you don't have to take them where the doctor tells you.... Have it filled where you get Fresh goods compounded by licensed men only and where you are not robbed" (*The Bee* 1905, 17 June: 5). The pitch promised what African-American consumers rarely got: equitable material exchange conditions. Brands emphasized their superior quality, they were sold by a single price determined by their producers, they were sealed outside the local market, and their production was standardized to ensure optimum product consistency. Consequently, brand names provided African-American consumers an effective mechanism to evade local marketers' racism.

The Maynard–Burgess household had begun to consume brands by the late-nineteenth century. Of 87 glass vessels recovered from the 1889 *TPQ* (*terminus post quem*, i.e., date after which) Maynard–Burgess cellar (79 bottles, 8 table vessels), none were from Annapolis area bottlers or pharmacists, but the assemblage contained 26 nationally advertised brands. The mean production date of the assemblage (1882.21) is quite close to the cellar *TPQ* (1889), indicating that most of the vessels were manufactured, purchased, and discarded in a relatively short span of time. Several brands were represented by multiple vessels (e.g., eight bottles of the medicinal gin Udolpho Wolfe's Aromatic Schnapps), indicating that the household identified several preferred brands. The assemblage of 54 glass bottles and table vessels from Gott's Court also included no Annapolis pharamacists or bottlers. Three late-nineteenth and early twentieth century assemblages from the Courthouse block (total 122 vessels) included four bottles with Annapolis embossments, but all post-date 1904 (Aiello and Seidel 1995: 1:224, 243; Mullins 1996: 603–604).

The four vessels from the Courthouse block were the sole archaeological evidence for consumption of locally bottled goods, and they reflect both national brand preference and the modest size and growth of Annapolis' bottling industry. In 1873, an Annapolis brewery and bottlery was established by J. B. Coolahan, an operation that continued on West Street until at least 1910 (*MRSCA* 24 May 1873: 3; Gould and Halleron 1910: 29); two Coolahan vessels were recovered from privy and sheet refuse at the Cathedral Street site on the Courthouse block. Wine and liquor dealer Charles Weiss was operating a bottlery by 1896 (Johnson Publishing 1896: 72), and a vessel from his brother Edward Weiss' business was recovered from the Cathedral Street yard refuse. Consequently, there was a modest local bottlers' trade which was not completely circumvented by African-American consumers, but it certainly did not provide significant quantities of goods to African-American households. Pharmacists often contracted to factories for embossed vessels, but the extent of such practice among Annapolitan pharmacists is unknown; in any case, no locally embossed pharmacists' bottles were recovered from any African-American assemblage.

Many brands were heavily advertised, but the genuine impact of advertising on African-American brand devotion is questionable. Indeed, in 1932 Edwards (1969: 194) found that many African Americans consuming brands had absolutely no recognition of the most pervasive advertising images. African-American consumers likely considered many social factors in brand preferences, but brands' symbolic roots in a "national" market certainly were a fundamental influence. Even the most scrupulous local White marketers were hard-pressed to escape the perception of racist complicity, whereas the racial sentiments of national producers were not typically betrayed by brand packaging (notwithstanding a few well-known exceptions, like Aunt Jemima). Consumption of the "best brands" also stimulated African Americans' sense of socioeconomic advance and genteel accomplishment, verifying their distance from economic, social, or racial marginalization. Despite consistent brand consumption across all African Americans, Edwards (1969: 44–45) identified slightly higher brand consumption among the most wealthy "business and professional class" in his study: for instance, 92.27% of African-American "business and professional class" consumers bought coffee by the brand, as compared to 82.69% of "common and semi-skilled labor." This hints at class differences, but the modest difference reflects consistent brand preference across classes and likely indicates the racism inflicted on African Americans of all socioeconomic standings.

Another major influence on African-American brand consumption was domestics' extensive experience using brands for their White employers (Edwards 1969: 58). In 1936, *The Brown American* ("The Negro Woman goes to Market," 1936: 13) recognized that domestics likely shaped both White employers' and African-American laborers' brand consumption, observing that "the less fortunate sisters, who have gone into Domestic Service ... must have powerful voice in the spending of many more millions by those who are really able to buy.... [A] product disliked by a cook seldom reaches a table twice." Furthermore, racist surveillance in stores probably made many African-American consumers less likely to browse, a critical activity for any discerning consumer. Because of this retail-space surveillance, Edwards (1969: 168) argued that, to "the Negro, window-shopping is perhaps more vitally important than to whites." Window displays invariably showcased a merchant's high-end brands, so African-American brand consumption may have been amplified by window shopping.

The commitment to bottled brand goods was mirrored by consumption of canned foods, which stressed their superior quality, carried uniform prices, and were produced outside the community, much like bottled brands. The Maynard–Burgess cellar, for instance, contained at least 792 tin fragments from canned foods. Archaeology does not indicate that African-American Annapolitans were preserving foods at home while they consumed these canned foods: Annapolis assemblages contained sparse evidence of home food preservation in either ceramic or glass vessels. The Maynard–Burgess cellar contained 79 bottles and nearly 800 can fragments, but just two Mason-type preserving jars and one stoneware crock were included in the assemblage. The Bellis Court privy contained just two glass preserving jars in an assemblage of 52 bottles and five coarse stonewares among 36 ceramic vessels (Mullins 1996: 602). No preserving jars were recovered among the 42 glass bottles excavated at Gott's Court (Warner 1992). Specialized curation of preserving jars could result in somewhat lower quantities than that for other bottled goods (which were usually disposed of once their contents were consumed), but the very low percentages from Annapolis sites argues that jar curation alone does not explain their scarcity.

One reason for the paucity of home-preserved foods was likely the ready availability of canned foods. The Chesapeake Bay region was a focus for the canning industry in the final quarter of the nineteenth century, with fish, vegetables, fruits, and shellfish sealed in canneries throughout the region (Heite 1990: 19). Despite the counsel of some ascetics who championed "self sufficiency," many household manuals advocated the consumption of canned foods. Marion Harland (1908: 258), for example, indicated that "there are many reasons why it is no longer advisable to put up the huge quantities of these things that our mothers and grandmothers did. The drudgery of putting them up is great and ... it is now possible to buy good canned fruit and jellies from the factories though one must know and be sure of the brand." Harland probably identified one of the most significant influences on decreased African-American home canning: particularly for African-American women who did strenuous domestic labor during the week, the arduous labor of canning was willingly rebuffed in favor of professionally prepared canned foods.

DESIRE AND AFRICAN-AMERICAN CONSUMPTION

Brand consumption illuminates the complex social aspirations and personal desires reflected in consumption itself. Material consumption is fueled by the desire for new social possibilities and individual pleasures which consumers believe will mediate (or evade) various social contradictions. This diverges somewhat from the standard assumption that consumers "need" various goods for utilitarian purposes, to satisfy an artificially created demand (i.e., a desire created by advertising), or as a compulsion to "display" their identity (e.g., socioeconomic status, ethnicity, etc.). Utilitarian need, advertiser-fanned demand, and the narrow public-display function of goods do not explain a great deal of consumption, particularly since non-utilitarian mass materialism has characterized consumption since the early eighteenth century.

Victorians' desire for goods may seem to be a radical break from previous consumption, but the general mechanics of consumer desire were already well-established. Colin Campbell (1987: 86) argues that a "modern self-illusory form of hedonism" arose during the eighteenth century, an emotional state in which desiring an object and its imagined symbolic qualities was the most gratifying element of consumption. This daydreaming hedonism, familiar to any window shopper, differed sharply from "traditional" consumption, which attempted to satisfy need through the material attributes of commodities and the possession of an object. Modern hedonism, in contrast, introduced a permanent, unfocused longing. That longing was driven by contradictions between opposed Romantic and Puritan values, such as instant gratification/ deferred satisfaction, self-interest/altruism, spending/saving, and imagination/reality. Campbell sees consumers' mediation of such symbiotically productive contradictions as the vehicle that drives consumerism, rather than a petty bourgeois parroting of the elite, the overwhelming influence of producers, or innate acquisitiveness.

Intensified production, restructured distribution and marketing, increased wages and leisure, and swelling sociocultural diversity were among the structural changes that fanned late-nineteenth century Americans' rethinking of personal and societal subjectivities. Americans developed the threads of publicly shared social expectations, and commodities began to be seen as a tangible harbinger of improved mass standards of living. By the late 1930s, American identity would be more firmly situated in material consumption than in any other social or moral discourse (Susman 1984; Agnew 1990; Lears 1994: 235–236). As Jean-Christophe Agnew (1990) stresses, consumer culture never afforded a concrete sociopolitical alternative to the objective inequality of capitalist consumption, but its many "have-nots" clearly criticized the unequal distribution of consumer goods (cf. Susman 1984: xxix; Edsforth 1987: 223–224). Despite such critique, marginalized consumers remained fervently committed to the potential of mass affluence and the notion that consumer affluence would reach them. That process unavoidably illuminated fundamental structural inequalities of American society, and African-American consumers' material aspirations negotiated and critiqued the profound racist contradictions that restricted the privileges of affluence.

COMMODITY-SPECIFIC CONSUMER TACTICS

Brand and canned food consumption suggest that African-American Annapolitans were committed to evading racism in local consumer space, securing the symbolic status of consumer in a national market, and obtaining goods with genuine functional benefits (e.g., canned foods that minimized household food production). Yet consumption tactics were in many cases commodity-specific; i.e., different sorts of goods were consumed and given symbolic meaning based upon different production and retail relationships and the social significance of the class of goods (Fine 1995: 142). Distinctive aspirations and contradictions were negotiated in the consumption of different commodities, and such aspirations and contradictions clearly could vary from one area to another.

The Chesapeake Bay and its numerous inlets contained a vast range of shellfish and fish that was readily available from the shoreline or small boats. Consequently, it is not surprising that many people living along the Bay considered household-caught fish and shellfish a dietary staple. In 1899, for instance, a dietary study of 19 African-American households in Elizabeth City County, Virginia, identified extensive fish consumption: the researchers estimated that over 20 percent of the households' total protein came from fish (Frissell and Bevier 1899: 40). The earliest Maynard–Burgess deposit suggests that household-caught fish accounted for a significant portion of the household's diet. An accumulation of refuse around the house's rear door was sealed by a rear addition built between 1874 and 1877, preserving 3885 bones (excluding wet screen and scales) (Warner 1998). Mark Warner (1998) analyzed the assemblage and identified a number of individual specimens (NISP) count of 678 fish elements (17.45 percent of assemblage NISP, excluding 229 trowel-recovered fish scales and 209 fish bones and 1322 scales recovered from wet screening). The assemblage contained 18 different species, and only one element (sea bass) was exclusively available from a deep-water context. Some of this fish probably was caught by household members or neighbors, and some likely was purchased from African-American hucksters. One African-American woman who grew up in Annapolis obtained fish from such hucksters, indicating that "We had horse and wagon hucksters going up and down the streets selling their wares, and that's where you bought your fresh vegetables. Winter and summer, and fish, mostly off wagons" (Goodwin et al. 1993: 11).

Yet the remaining African-American assemblages in Annapolis include very modest amounts of fish. For instance, the Bellis Court privy contained 355 bones, but it did not include any fish (Aiello and Seidel 1995: 226–228). At Gott's Court, 18 fish elements were recovered from an assemblage of 678 bones (Warner 1992). Only one fish element was recovered from sheet refuse in backyards of Cathedral Street homes in the same block (NISP 742). At Maynard–Burgess, the 1889 *TPQ* cellar had a fish NISP of 68 (7.11 percent of assemblage NISP), and the fish NISP for the 1905 *TPQ* privy was 79 (7.61 percent), both significantly lower than that from the 1874–1877 assemblage. Formation processes (e.g., sheet refuse, differential preservation) certainly influenced archaeological quantities, but it is unlikely that such variation accounts for a total or nearly total absence of fish from all the deposits postdating the Maynard–Burgess rear addition.

The decline of inexpensive, readily available fish in some African-American homes was driven by a variety of factors, but the availability alone clearly was not enough to sustain consumer demand. Overfishing and the ravaging of oyster beds led to dramatic price decreases in the 1870s, and then a rapid ecological decline of the Bay in the late-nineteenth century, but fish was always relatively plentiful in local markets and waterways, despite the Bay industries' self-inflicted wounds. Beyond market shifts, declining post-Reconstruction African-American fish consumption likely reflected the social stigmatization of fishing and fish consumption. Popular commentators disparaged fishing as a Black and rustic activity associated with caricatured racial attributes, such as laziness and a resistance to "hard work." Travel writer Julian Ralph observed in 1896 that "Somebody has called fishing 'idle time not idly spent,' that must be how the Southern colored people regard it, for they seem to be eternally at it wherever they and any piece of water, no matter how small, are thrown together" (Ralph 1896: 376). African Americans intent to avoid such caricatures and secure the status of genteel consumers would be particularly inclined to decrease fishing and fish consumption.

Although it is difficult to evaluate, the racialization of regional labor likely had an impact on fish consumption as well. In positions as cooks, waiters, and domestics, African Americans witnessed the apparent benefits of consumer citizenship. The racialization of domestic labor in White homes, restaurants, and other public venues forged a consumer space in which commodities like fish were delivered by a continuous chain of African-American fishing laborers, cannery workers, transporters, and domestics who prepared (and often shopped for) such foods. The notion that consumption conferred genuine privileges could not have been more evident to these African Americans who made White consumption possible in the first place. African Americans likely were particularly aware of the relative symbolic significance of consumption patterns, such as household fishing versus market purchase. Keen to avoid the stigmatization of household-based consumption, they may have viewed public acquisition (i.e., shopping itself) as a significant element of consumption's symbolic meaningfulness. This would mean that simply possessing an object did not secure all the material and social possibilities held out by consumer culture: a market-purchased fish and a household-caught fish had different symbolism.

CERAMICS AND MARKET CIRCUMVENTION

Ceramic consumption suggests yet another range of tactics which circumvented the retail market and disregarded the idealized material requirements of a genteel table. The 25 ceramic vessels from the Maynard–Burgess cellar (1889 *TPQ*), for instance, were older ware and decorative types (e.g., three pearlware vessels) that included no matching vessels. The Bellis Court privy (1920 *TPQ*) contained a minimum of 36 ceramic vessels that reflected a similar consumption pattern (Aiello and Seidel 1995: 223). The privy was excavated in three levels, and a mean ceramic date (MCD) was computed for each level using production dates based on criteria such as ware (e.g., white granite), decorative technology (e.g., printing), specific design (e.g., Willow), or potter's mark. Even using these methods, mean ceramic dating provides only suggestive dating (cf. Majewski and O'Brien 1987: 170–172). Nevertheless, even suggestive dates indicate that most of the ceramics were manufactured long before the privy's 1920 *TPQ*: the lowest level MCD was 1849.21, the middle level MCD was 1858.67, and the uppermost MCD was 1868.48 (all proveniences combined MCD was 1864.95). The privy contained eight vessels with polychrome decals, a decorative technique introduced in the 1890s (Majewski and O'Brien 1987: 146–147), so the mean date belies the wide range of production dates included in the assemblage: these vessels were almost certainly purchased over a long period. A few vessels may well have survived such a long period of use, but it certainly seems unlikely that these ceramics were all purchased new by the households who eventually discarded them. The notion that a significant number of these ceramics were display-piece heirlooms is implausible, because virtually all of the vessels in the assemblage were highly worn.

Matching vessels were almost completely absent. Like the Maynard–Burgess cellar, Bellis Court did not include any matching vessels. Sheet refuse deposits from early twentieth-century yard spaces on neighboring Cathedral Street included a pair of undecorated white granite vessels with identical marks, but this was the only evidence of sets from the Courthouse Site, Maynard–Burgess, or Gott's Court. The complete absence of matching vessels suggests that most of the ceramics were acquired in small quantities. Other archaeologists have analyzed small-quantity ceramic consumption and convincingly divined gradual efforts to assemble matching or similar wares in lieu of set purchases (e.g., Miller 1974; Klein and Garrow 1984: 221). However, there is no indication of such piecemeal consumption in any of these assemblages: there are no consistent colors, decorative preparations, functional types, or wares.

The mélange of decorative preparations and vessels' age suggests that many ceramics were obtained through informal exchange forms, such as barter, gift-giving, and inheritance. Furniture, flowers, food, craft skills, and labor were among the many goods and services exchanged among African-American Annapolitans. For instance, one African-American woman recalled that "I don't remember us having any good china sets, you know ... I think a lot of stuff was passed down from grandparents to parents" (Jopling 1991). This sort of exchange certainly was not unknown among other consumers, but African-American reciprocity was quite insular because of the boundaries of, and resistance to, racism in public space.

Unlike bottled goods, ceramics may have been more amenable to secondary exchange because sets themselves were not essential to African-American consumers' gentility. The genteel symbolism and genuine functional benefits of bottled goods were only conferred by their consumption, but much of the genteel symbolism of dining behaviors could be retained in the absence of matching wares (and matched ware had no functional advantage over unmatched vessels). The archaeologically recovered vessel forms do not preclude genteel dining etiquette, even though the table aesthetics would have been quite unlike the etiquette-book ideal. The mix of ceramics suggests that these households felt little compulsion to reproduce the idealized material trappings of dining etiquette; they may well have been quite genteel in their behaviors, but disinterested in the material ideals of genteel dining. Some consumers may have rejected or ignored Victorian dining ideologies altogether, but such resistance often recognized and subtly aspired to a consumer ideal. For instance, an African-American who grew up in the Courthouse neighborhood remembered that his mother "used to pride herself on a set of dishes she bought at S&N Katz [department store].... The stuff we used through the week was maybe a lot of odd stuff. You wouldn't have a whole set. The plates might be different" (Jopling 1991). This contrast of sets and everyday dishes indicates recognition, if not total adherence, to genteel table etiquette.

SURVEILLANCE AND BLACK CONSUMPTION CARICATURES

Whites legitimized consumer space's racial exclusivity by projecting a range of Black caricatures onto African-American consumption. The most superficially benevolent of these caricatures cast African Americans as innocents who required the munificence of the superior race. This paternalism was most commonly invoked by White institutions or employers who sanctioned the African-American consumption of White material discards. The Naval Academy, for instance, supplied their African-American and White workforce with a vast volume of discarded clothing and other supplies. One African American who grew up in the Courthouse neighborhood during the 1930s observed that "Anyone who worked there was given stuff and they brought home shoes, anything that was worn—shoes, shirts, ties and pants. In the main they would re-do them.... they would take off the buttons and re-do them for good use." Discarded goods also were openly or surreptitiously acquired by African-American laborers at local workplaces like hotels, and domestics were often given uneaten food to take home to their families. In 1896 Julian Ralph (1896: 385) noted this pervasive movement of goods from White employers to African Americans, indicating that "white men and women give their clothing to the colored people—to servants or dependents—when it is no longer serviceable.... it seems to me that every man or woman is accustomed to make this use of his or her discarded goods, and that every white family has at least one colored family in charge this way." Ralph romanticized such salvage as White benevolence, ignoring the labor and civil implications of having an African-American family "in charge." Such systematic, but publicly unacknowledged, movement of goods clearly was intended to reproduce African-American labor and social subordination.

Buttons reflect this movement of goods from employers to African-American consumers and the racialization of the service-labor force. At Maynard–Burgess, for instance, 290 buttons were recovered, including 6 Navy buttons and 2 Army buttons manufactured between 1820 and 1845 (Bomback 1993). Like a vast number of African-American women, Maria Maynard and Martha Maynard each appeared as a "washerwoman" in the 1860 census, so many of the buttons likely were lost during washing in the yard. In 1910, 19 African-American women living on the Courthouse block were recorded in the census as laundresses, and 104 buttons were recovered in Phase II testing at the site, including several with military motifs (similar button frequencies are noted by Cheek and Friedlander 1990: 55).

The gatekeepers of White space hyperbolized African-American theft to legitimize African-American labor surveillance, social marginalization, and racist violence, but some goods clearly were acquired surreptitiously. One African American recalled that "If it wasn't for the Naval Academy and Carvel Hall [a local hotel], people would have starved. The food that came out of those two places. People would bring it out, had to ... they would hide it inside their clothes, and they would sell it. You might get six, seven, ten pounds of meat. That's going to last you a long time. Meat, butter, different things, clothes, handkerchiefs, shirts, shoes" (Jopling 1991). The extent of such petty pilfering is unclear, but Whites insinuated that it was a rampant dilemma rooted in Black racial nature. In 1884, for instance, a household author pining for the days of enslaved domestics lamented that "the colored servant grows steadily worse.... She robs me unsparingly to feed her children, or her sisters, or her friends, or to give away" (Peirce 1884: 171). Pilfering certainly did not have a significant economic or moral impact, but the assumption of rampant thievery provided White employers a socially acceptable rationale to discipline and patrol African-American laborers.

FRAGMENTS OF AFFLUENCE:
AFRICAN-AMERICAN BRIC-A-BRAC

In 1919, Francis Taylor Long examined the effect of increased World War I incomes on African Americans in Clarke County, Georgia. Long decried African-American consumers' "extravagance ... shown with reference to rugs, pictures, china, bric-a-brac, and other articles," believing he had discerned Blacks' universal attraction to "the superficialities, the tinsel and glitter of life, [rather] than by its permanent benefits and durable satisfactions" (Long 1919: 54–55). Oddly enough, this puritanical reproach of African Americans' "lavish and unwise expenditure of money" focused on seemingly innocuous material culture: household decorative trinkets, furniture, clothes, and groceries, none of which seemed likely to disrupt Southern racial structure. Nevertheless, Long saw profound racial shortcomings, as well as cause for White apprehension, in African-American consumption.

Long's critique barely concealed a common White apprehension of African-American materialism. Long was disturbed to find that the silk shirts, brand groceries, mahogany chairs, and parlor rugs prescribed for genteel White homes were also in the homes of African-American tenant farmers, waiters, and domestics. Rather than see such goods as insignificant, Long understood that they harbored a foothold into consumer culture and threatened to undermine the assumed White exclusivity of consumer space.

Among the objects Long singled out was bric-a-brac, a gloss for a host of statues, vases, figurines, chromolithographs, and assorted curios that decorated working-class and elite homes alike. Manufactured abundantly at the turn of the century, such objects generally featured exotic motifs from the colonized world, nature, or a romanticized classical or historical past. Bric-a-brac has been found on each of the African-American sites in Annapolis. The Maynard–Burgess cellar, for instance, contained two porcelain knick knacks: a match holder and a female peasant figurine. Merely two objects may seem insignificant, but quantity alone cannot provide a definitive measure of symbolic significance. That significance is suggested by the vigilant curation of bric-a-brac. One African-American Annapolitan acknowledged his mother's conscientious care for such objects, observing that "we had knick knacks in our living room. In fact, we had quite a few of them. We weren't allowed to touch them. My mother didn't like to see her stuff broken up. She was so proud of her things. It was there for you to look at it. We weren't barred from the living room, we just weren't allowed to touch them" (Jopling 1991).

Bric-a-brac was in the Maynard home by the time John Maynard died in 1875: the 1876 probate inventory of Maynard's possessions included entries for "Wat Not" (i.e., "what not") valued at $0.75 and six "pictures" (chromolithographs) valued at $6.00 (Anne Arundel County Inventories 1876: 553–554). The bric-a-brac and pictures were located in a front room that was clearly the Maynards' showplace social space. In addition to the decorative objects, the appropriately genteel parlor contained a sofa, parlor carpet, sideboard, marble-top table, and a set of mahogany chairs that, taken as a room ensemble, accounted for 62.55% of the inventory's total value (cf. Schlereth 1991: 117–120).

Jacob Riis (1971: 118) believed inexpensive knick knacks were used to create a cluttered appearance of abundance in African-American homes, noting that "The poorest negro housekeeper's room in New York is bright with gaily-colored prints of his beloved 'Abe Linkum,' General Grant, President Garfield, Mrs. Cleveland, and other national celebrities, and cheery with flowers and singing birds." Yet bric-a-brac—like all material culture—was not purchased simply for contrived "public" display (cf. Glennie 1995: 178). Archaeologists often focus on public displays of material "status," but most mass-produced knick knacks retailed for a nickel or less, making them poor vehicles to display buying power or celebrate exchange value. Furthermore, there is relatively little evidence that consumers saw household goods like bric-a-brac primarily as exchange value displays. In 1882, for example, a household manual noted that it was possible "to carry the 'civilizing influence of the beautiful' even into the homes of the humblest at the minimum of expense" (Facey 1882: vi). An 1885 manual concurred that "there has been a complete revolution in the whole domain of house-furnishing and decoration, a revolution which has thrown opportunities in the way of everybody, rich and poor alike" (Sypher and Company 1885: 18).

Knick knacks made their consumers symbolic participants in colonization, a romanticized past, an affluent industrial America, or the taming of Nature. Bric-a-brac wholesale catalogs featured exotic goods including Japanese fans, biblical figurines, casts of Lincoln's death mask, and classical cherubs (cf. Linington 1880). One catalog's line of exotic motifs even included "Baskets of Darkies;" these porcelain figurines of caricatured Black children reinforced a household's investment in dominant racial structure (Spelman 1883: 137). Such objects defied valuations like purchase price or utility, instead serving as vehicles of consumers' desire to see themselves within an idealized society and world. For instance, an 1885 household manual suggested that Americans "take a very great interest in other peoples and in other countries, an interest so great that it has affected our whole way of living; not only our houses show it, but our pictures, our amusements, our books, our newspapers, and our dress. In our houses we give our love of adventure free play, and like to be reminded at every turn, of the fact that America, big as is her territory, is but a small part of the world" (Sypher and Company 1885: 6).

Objects like the Maynards' peasant-girl figurine placed the household within a society whose roots lay in a bucolic past; this certainly redefined (or ignored) the social and labor foundation of the agrarian South. In this way, bric-a-brac could accommodate utopian aspirations for the shape of society to come (or quixotic visions of the oppression that lay behind). Souvenirs did much the same thing, providing a material object that idealized a consumer's experience (or desired experience) (Stewart 1993: 147). Significant social desires were reflected in bric-a-brac consumption in the most unpretentious contexts: for example, Charles Orser (1988: 218) argues that the household of a South Carolina tenant farmer idealized its links to "the outside world" by the possession a medallion from the 1887 Ice Carnival held in Saint Paul, Minnesota. Seemingly mundane and often disregarded by archaeologists, such objects were modest, yet significant, symbolic rethinkings of a household's position in consumer culture. When Francis Taylor Long saw African-American consumers' demand for these sort of seemingly mundane objects, he understood that their consumption signalled the erosion of Whites' exclusive privilege to aspiration.

Bric-a-brac was not simply a creative symbolic redefinition of African Americans' social position. The everyday exotics in African-American homes indicate one way many African-American women were implicated in consumption. Bric-a-brac often was given by White women to their African-American domestics. For instance, one man's mother obtained bric-a-brac from various Whites for whom she did housework: "She would bring them off jobs. People would give them to her. Sometimes the people who she worked for would go away and when they came back they would bring a little gift" (Jopling 1991).

It would be naive to think that the trinkets White gave to African-American domestics sprang from unadulterated Christian benevolence. The strategy was instead a White effort to encourage reliability, legitimize African-American subordination, and discourage defiance ranging from theft to quitting the job. African Americans might see a mass-produced exotic as a mechanism that redefined their material world, but a White employer could view the same object as a reproduction of White domination. By distracting attention from social inequality, apparently trivial bric-a-brac could reproduce those very social relations.

THE CONTRADICTIONS
OF CAPITALIST MULTIVALENCE

African-American consumption emphasizes that material culture could be defined along a spectrum of possibilities ranging from conscious resistance to the masked reproduction of inequality. The notion that material culture has such "multivalent" symbolism dependent on consumers' social position assumes that objects are defined within an encompassed range of material and social possibilities (cf. Tilley 1989). Multivalence, though, is a concept that has been slow to flourish in historical archaeology (cf. Perry and Paynter 1998). Orser (1992) argues that the hesitancy to embrace multivalency reflects archaeologists' reduction of objects to monolithic surface attributes, such as function or price. That reduction of objects to all-encompassing meanings has been mirrored by constructions of totalizing systemic or "identity" parameters for material meaning (e.g., capitalism, ethnicity). There certainly are such dominant influences on human decision-making: in this study, for instance, it is reasonable to situate racial ideology at the heart of an analysis of African-American consumption. However, that focus does not assume how racism looked in every given time and place: like all contextual factors, racism was defined in myriad ways by labor dynamics, class relations, market structure, and any other number of local considerations. Capitalist economics might reasonably be accorded a similarly qualified centrality to much (if not most) historical archaeological analysis, but consumer experiences clearly varied in particular capitalistic production and consumption spaces. Consequently, there were not universal racist structures or capitalist economic processes (e.g., rational optimization of profit) that produced monolithic Black or capitalist subjects (cf. Orser 1998). Racism, consumption, and capitalism alike "work" so well precisely because they have so many diverse forms and extend (or promise) genuine benefits to select people: if race or capitalism were universally oppressive, self-evident processes, it is unlikely they would be so historically resilient.

Multivalence destabilizes totalizing categories like race as a mechanism to acknowledge dominant social processes and consumer agency alike. Unfortunately, multivalence has tended to be reduced to a pair of polarized caricatures that stress one or the other. On one hand, some analysts have popularized a dizzying sense of material multivalency adapted from various veins of hermeneutics, post-structuralism, and post-modernism (e.g., Baudrillard 1975). These thinkers suggest that people continually deconstruct material symbols within disparate sociocultural niches, essentially "making" endless heterogeneous identities through consumption. Such arguments provide some ingenious insight into Disneyland and the spectacles of mass-consumer society, and inevitably appeal to scholars intent on celebrating anonymous agents' defiance of dominant social formations (cf. the critique by Miller 1987: 173). However, this approach risks fixating on the cacophony of consumer symbolism and slighting (if not utterly ignoring) dominant social and economic structures.

On the other hand, some researchers reject multivalence as an illusion masking consumers' objective oppression (e.g., Ewen 1988). Rather than see material consumption as a critique of inequality or a meaningful appeal to social and material privilege, mass-produced goods instead loom as monolithic assimilators that reduce all consumers to commodities. In this bleak vision, consumer culture appears as a sort of ideological wasteland that homogenizes "authentic" identity (e.g., culture) and produces subjects more interested in the willing self-oppression of shopping than the fabrication of critical consciousness.

Either characterization exaggerates genuine tendencies and implications of consumption. All consumers construct meaningful symbols at the very moment they risk (or even accept) being confined by the society that produces such goods. Consumption would be unimaginable without such contradiction: contradiction between the idealized benefits of consumer capitalism and its ambiguous everyday reality forms an abyss that consumers persistently attempt to bridge with commodities. The multivalent symbolism of consumer goods provided African America rich possibilities to contemplate the restructuring of American society in general, and their local spaces in particular. While some of the tactics in this study may be specific to Annapolis, it seems probable that virtually all African-American aspirations focused on resistance to racism: through a wide range of tactics, African Americans sought to dismantle the racist boundaries to consumer space and civil privilege. African-American consumption was a complex negotiation of the contradictions between genteel subjectivity and Blackness, expressing desire for the privileges of American civil and consumer citizenship and the freedom to define their own individual and social subjectivities.

African-American material consumption was a richly textured effort to negotiate the contradictions of a society structured by race. Not surprisingly, these complex contradictions left no monolithic African-American experience of consumer culture in their wake, but they did promote a rich and distinctive range of social aspirations, personal pleasures, and individual negotiations of social position. An archaeological focus on material consumption tactics and their relationship to social positioning harbors a unique insight into African-American consumption as both resistance against, and an appeal for, privilege within American consumer culture.

Acknowledgments

This paper was given considerable direction by all the participants in the seminar. Marlys Pearson and Bob Paynter read numerous versions and contributed significantly to my ideas and their clarity. Mark Warner provided faunal data from his dissertation and gave me ideas based on his own research. Helan Page, Daniel Horowitz, Neville Thompson, and Chuck Orser read various versions, provided specific suggestions, and helped focus the arguments. Newpaper research and minimum vessel counts were funded by a predoctoral grant from the Wenner-Gren Foundation. Victorian popular literature was researched through a Winterthur Museum Research Fellowship. The ceramic analysis for Maynard–Burgess was performed through a grant-in-aid from Sigma Xi, the Scientific Research Society. I borrowed, and in some cases adapted, original research from Eric Larsen, who performed the Courthouse Phase III glass analysis; Hannah Jopling, who directed the oral history project; and Jane McWilliams, who performed initial Maynard–Burgess documentary research. Neither they nor anyone else named here bears responsibility for any shortcomings of this paper.

REFERENCES

Agnew, J.
1990 Coming Up for Air: Consumer Culture in Historical Perspective. *Intellectual History Newsletter* 12:3–21.
Aiello, E. A., and J. Seidel
1995 *Three Hundred Years in Annapolis: Phase III Archaeological Investigations of the Anne Arundel County Courthouse Site (18AP63), Annapolis, Maryland.* Submitted to Spillis Candela/Warnecke, Washington, D.C. Archaeology in Annapolis, Annapolis.
Baudrillard, J.
1975 *The Mirror of Production.* Telos Press, St Louis.
The Bee [Washington, D.C.]
1905 Stafford Drug Store advertisement. 17 June: 5. Washington, D.C.
Bomback, R.
1993 Button Analysis. In *Final Archaeological Investigations at the Maynard–Burgess House (18AP64), An 1847–1980 African-American Household in Annapolis, Maryland,* edited by Paul R. Mullins and Mark S. Warner, Appendix III. Submitted to Historic Annapolis Foundation, Annapolis, Maryland. Archaeology in Annapolis, Annapolis.
Campbell, C.
1987 *The Romantic Ethic and the Spirit of Modern Consumerism.* Basil Blackwell, Oxford.
Cheek, C. D., and A. Friedlander
1990 Pottery and Pig's Feet: Space, Ethnicity, and Neighborhood in Washington, D.C., 1880–1940. *Historical Archaeology* 24(1):34–60.
de Certeau, M.
1986 *The Practice of Everyday Life.* University of California Press, Berkeley.
Cohen, L.
1990 *Making a New Deal: Industrial Workers in Chicago, 1919–1939.* Cambridge University Press, New York.
Du Bois, W. E. B.
1935 *Black Reconstruction in America.* Harcourt Brace, Cleveland.
Edsforth, R.
1987 *Class Conflict and Cultural Consensus: The Making of a Mass Consumer Society in Flint, Michigan.* Rutgers University Press, New Brunswick, New Jersey.
Edwards, P. K.
1969 *The Southern Urban Negro as a Consumer.* (Reprint) Negro Universities Press, New York. Originally published 1932. Prentice-Hall, New York.
Ewen, S.
1988 *All Consuming Images: The Politics of Style in Contemporary Culture.* Basic Books, New York.
Facey, J. W., Jr.
1882 *Elementary Decoration: A Guide to the Simpler Forms of Everyday Art as Applied to the Interior and Exterior of Dwelling-Houses Etc.* Crosby Lockwood and Company, London.
Fields, B. J.
1985 *Slavery and Freedom on the Middle Ground: Maryland During the Nineteenth Century.* Yale University Press, New Haven.
Fine, B.
1995 From Political Economy to Consumption. In *Acknowledging Consumption: A Review of New Studies,* edited by D. Miller, pp. 127–163. Routledge, New York.

Fox, R. W., and T. J. J. Lears (editors)
  1983   The Culture of Consumption in America: Critical Essays in American History, 1880–1980. Pantheon, New York.
Frissell, H. B., and I. Bevier
  1898   Dietary Studies of Negroes in Eastern Virginia in 1897 and 1898. Bulletin of the U.S. Department of Agriculture No. 71. Department of Agriculture, Washington, D.C.
Glennie, P.
  1995   Consumption within Historical Studies. In Acknowledging Consumption: A Review of New Studies, edited by D. Miller, pp. 164–203. Routledge, New York.
Goodwin, R. C., S. L. C. Sanders, M. T. Moran, and D. Landon
  1993   Phase II / III Archaeological Investigations of the Gott's Court Parking Facility, Annapolis, Maryland. Submitted to the City of Annapolis, Maryland. R. Christopher Goodwin and Associates, Inc, Frederick.
Gould, F. E., and P. R. Halleron
  1910   Annapolis City Directory. Gould and Halleron, Annapolis.
Harland, M.
  1908   The Housekeeper's Week. Bobbs-Merrill Company, Indianapolis.
Heite, E. F.
  1990   Archaeological Data Recovery on the Collins, Geddes Cannery Site, Road 356A, Lebanon, North Murderkill Hundred, Kent County, Delaware. Delaware Department of Transportation Archaeology Series, No. 83, Delaware Department of Transportation, Wilmington.
Horowitz, D.
  1985   The Morality of Spending: Attitudes Toward the Consumer Society in America, 1875–1940. Johns Hopkins University Press, Baltimore.
Inside Southern Cabins
  1880   Harper's Weekly 26(1246):733–734.
Johnson Publishing Company
  1896   Johnsons' Annapolis Directory 1896–1897. Johnson Publishing Company, Wilmington.
Jopling, H.
  1991   Oral History Interview Transcripts. Manuscript on file, Archaeology in Annapolis, Annapolis.
Klein, T., and P. H. Garrow (editors)
  1984   Final Archaeological Investigations at the Wilmington Boulevard Monroe Street to King Street Wilmington, New Castle County, Delaware. Delaware Department of Transportation Archaeology Series, No.29, Delaware Department of Transportation, Wilmington.
Lears, J.
  1994   Fables of Abundance: A Cultural History of Advertising in America. Basic Books, New York.
Linington, C. M.
  1880   5 and 10 Cent Counter Supplies. Franz Gindele, Chicago.
Long, F. T.
  1919   The Negroes of Clarke County, Georgia, During the Great War. Phelps-Stokes Fellowship Studies Vol. 19, No. 8. University of Georgia, Athens.
Majewski, T., and M. J. O'Brien
  1987   The Use and Misuse of Nineteenth-Century English and American Ceramics in Archaeological Analysis. In Advances in Archaeological Method and Theory, Vol. 11, edited by M. B. Schiffer, pp.97–209. Academic Press, Orlando.
Maryland Republican State Capital Advertiser [Annapolis, Maryland]
  1873   Messrs. Coolahan & Bro. 24 May 1873:3. Annapolis, Maryland.

Miller, D.

1987 *Material Culture and Mass Consumption*. Basil Blackwell, New York.

1997 *Capitalism: An Ethnographic Approach*. Berg, New York.

Miller, G. L.

1974 A Tenant Farmer's Tableware: Nineteenth-Century Ceramics from Tabb's Purchase. *Maryland Historical Magazine* 69(2):197–210.

Mullins, P. R.

1996 *The Contradictions of Consumption: An Archaeology of African America and Consumer Culture, 1850–1930*. Ph.D. dissertation, University of Massachusetts, Amherst. University Microfilms, Ann Arbor.

Mullins, P. R., and M. S. Warner

1993 *Final Archaeological Investigations at the Maynard–Burgess House (18AP64), An 1847–1980 African-American Household in Annapolis, Maryland*. Submitted to Port of Annapolis, Inc., Annapolis, Maryland. Archaeology in Annapolis, Annapolis.

The Negro Woman goes to Market

1936 *The Brown American* 1(1):13.

Orser, C. E., Jr.

1988 *The Material Basis of the Postbellum Tenant Plantation: Historical Archaeology in the South Carolina Piedmont*. University of Georgia Press, Athens.

1992 Beneath the Material Surface of Things: Commodities, Artifacts, and Slave Plantations. In *Meanings and Uses of Material Culture*, edited by Barbara J. Little and Paul A. Shackel, pp.94–104. *Historical Archaeology* 26(3).

1998 Epilogue: From Georgian Order to Social Relations at Annapolis and Beyond. In *Annapolis Pasts: Historical Archaeology in Annapolis, Maryland*, edited by P. A. Shackel, P. R. Mullins, and M. S. Warner, pp. 307–324. University of Tennessee Press, Knoxville.

Peirce, M. F.

1884 *Co-operative Housekeeping: How to Do It and How Not to Do It*. James R. Osgood, Boston.

Perry, W., and R. Paynter

1998 Epilogue: Artifacts, Ethnicity and the archaeology of African Americans. In *I, Too, Am American*, edited by Theresa Singleton. Smithsonian Press, Washington, D.C. (in press)

Ralph, J.

1886 *Dixie, or Southern Scenes and Sketches*. Harper and Brothers, New York.

Roediger, D. R.

1991 *The Wages of Whiteness: Race and the Making of the American Working Class*. Verso, New York.

Riis, J. A.

1971 *How the Other Half Lives: Studies Among the Tenements of New York*. (Reprint) Dover, New York. Originally published 1890, Charles Scribner's Sons, New York.

Schlereth, T. J.

1991 *Victorian America: Transformations in Everyday Life, 1876–1915*. HarperPerennial, New York.

Spelman, W. A.

1883 Novelties and Bric-a-brac. *Spelman's Fancy Goods Graphic*. 3(3):137.

Stewart, S.

1993 *On Longing: Narratives of the Miniature, the Gigantic, the Souvenir, the Collection*. Duke University Press, Durham, North Carolina.

Susman, W. I.

1984 *Culture as History: The Transformation of American Society in the Twentieth Century*. Pantheon, New York.

Sypher and Company
  1885   *The Housekeeper's Quest: Where to Find Pretty Things*. Sypher and Company, New York.
Thom, W. T.
  1901   *The Negroes of Litwalton, Virginia: A Study of the "Oyster Negro."* Bulletin of theDepartment of Labor No. 37. Department of Labor, Washington, D.C.
Tilley, C.
  1989   Interpreting Material Culture. In *The Meaning of Things*, edited by Ian Hodder, pp.185–194. Unwin Hyman, London.
Warner, M. S.
  1992   *Test Excavations at Gott's Court, Annapolis, Maryland (18AP52)*. Submitted to Historic Annapolis Foundation, Annapolis, Maryland. Archaeology in Annapolis, Annapolis.
  1998   *Food and the Negotiation of African-American Identities in the Chesapeake*. Unpublished Ph.D. dissertation, Department of Anthropology, University of Virginia.
Warner, M. S., and P. R. Mullins
  1993   *Phase I-II Archaeological Investigations at the Courthouse Site (18AP63), An 1870–1970 African-American Neighborhood in Annapolis, Maryland*. Submitted to Historic Annapolis Foundation, Annapolis, Maryland. Archaeology in Annapolis, Annapolis.
Willis, S.
  1991   *A Primer for Daily Life*. Routledge, New York.

Ceramics from Annapolis, Maryland: A Measure of Time Routines and Work Discipline

8

Mark P. Leone

With the assistance of Marian Creveling and Christopher Nagle

INTRODUCTION

The archaeological record for ceramics is one of the most complete and informative available to historical archaeologists. Ceramics are widely used, easily breakable, not recyclable, and do not decompose. Therefore, changes in the use of dishes and crockery, and in their styles, are well-documented, although interpretations of these changes vary. James Deetz (1977; 1996) argues that change in colonial ceramics is caused by the more or less uniform entry and acceptance of a Georgian, or modern, worldview. George Miller, (1991: 2–3; n.d.; Miller, Martin, and Dickenson 1994) suggests that change is a function of externally derived price, which determines use. The purpose of this chapter is to present an alternative reason for the changes in the use of dishes, their styles, and their functions. The hypothesis offered here is that changing orderliness in ceramics at the table is caused by the advent of the time routines and work disciplines of capitalism.

The research here is drawn from five sites in Annapolis, Maryland, from the mid-eighteenth century to the early twentieth century. The work uses only minimal vessel counts and subdivides sites stratigraphically to create a chronology. The hypothesis used here is an effort

Mark P. Leone • Department of Anthropology, University of Maryland, College Park, Maryland 20742-7415.

Historical Archaeologies of Capitalism, edited by Mark P. Leone and Parker B. Potter, Jr. Plenum Press, New York, 1999.

to introduce the idea that ceramic use and change in eighteenth- and nineteenth-century households was heavily influenced by participation in a wage-labor and profit-making economy. Such an economy represents not only how people saw the world, as Deetz points out, but also how people were drawn into an economy that created surplus value.

For the purposes of this chapter, capitalism is defined as a way of creating profit that treats relations between people as though these were things: interchangeable, modular, and reproducible. An increasingly landless workforce characterizes capitalism, with people emerging whose only means of earning a living is by selling his or her labor. Land is privately owned, as are all other ways of earning a living. Continuous changes in technology, expansion of labor sources, sources for raw materials, and expansion of markets for goods ensure profits.

While this is a standard definition of capitalism, worked out for archaeologists in McGuire (1992: 82–83), the specific hypothesis I use is derived from E. P. Thompson's (1967, 1974) ideas on work and time discipline and from Michel Foucault's (1979) work on personal or individual discipline. My view is that as wage work and market fluctuations for the prices of raw and finished goods came to dominate any local area, people in any one household decided to either leave for a different area to escape difficult economic circumstances or adjust to where they were by trying different work strategies. These strategies included how they used work, measured time, and were willing to see themselves compensated. These adjustments, when they accommodated capitalism, are best defined by E. P. Thompson and are embodied in his terms "time routines" and "work discipline." Even though these routines appear self-descriptive, the reasons people provided for learning and imposing them are ideologies in the Marxist sense.

As can be seen from Table 1, which summarizes the findings of this chapter, there is a serious need to go beyond the work of Deetz and Miller. The figures in this table create an index of variation from combining numbers of whole vessels, numbers of forms, and numbers of types. The index comes from a formula used to measure Type Variant, and the variables in the formula can be rearranged to measure Function Variant. Both uses of the formula are available in Table 2 through Table 6. The formula used here has the same aim as that of Paul Shackel (1993: 30–42), but is played out to stress changing functions, as well as types, of ceramics. My formula is an experiment to measure, on the one hand, how orderly a table was, and, on the other hand, to see how such a dining pattern taught people time, etiquette, and the rules of producing labor in a profit-making economy. Neither the results predicted by interpreting Deetz nor Miller occur. Rather, the variation in ceramics is not one of inevitable cognitive modernity, as Deetz suggests, nor of ever

Table 1. Index of Ceramic Variability in Five Sites in Annapolis[a]

Time range	Hyde/Thompson House (O'Reilly 1994, Appendix A)	Victualing Warehouse (Pearson 1991, Appendix D)	Jonas Green Printshop (Cox and Buckler 1995, Appendix A)	Maynard–Burgess House (Mullins and Warner 1993:114–115)	Charles Carroll House (Kryder-Reid n.d., Appendix A)
c. 1700–1750	9				
c. 1750–1800	96		64		
c. 1800–1850	11	4	80		11
c. 1850–1900	89	26		24	1

[a]This table is a summary of the most important results found in Table 2 through Table 6. It rounds off the results using the Type Variant Index on tableware so that the overall pattern produced by the index is apparent.

The Hyde/Thompson House was home to professionals. The Victualing Warehouse was occupied by poorer people. The Jonas Green printing shop was attached to the house of the Greens, who were middle class printers. The Maynard–Burgess House was home successively to two free, middle-class, African-American families. The Charles Carroll of Carrollton house was occupied by renters.

The numbers in the table were derived from the following formula: $\frac{V}{F} \times W$.

This formula creates an index to ceramic variation, where V = total vessels present in minimum vessel count, F = number of different vessel forms present, W = number of ware types plus primary decorative techniques. Where described fully, the formula becomes:

$$\frac{\text{Total vessels present in minimum vessel count}}{\text{Number of different vessel forms present}} \times \text{Number of were types plus primary decorative techniques}$$

For example, using the information from the Hyde/Thompson house, 1757–1798, the formula becomes:

$$\frac{32 \text{ (total vessels in MVC)}}{7 \text{ (number of different vessel forms present)}} \times 21 \text{ (Number of ware types plus primary decorative techniques)} = 95.99$$

greater use of ever cheaper ceramics, as Miller predicts. Moreover, the pattern is certainly not a verification of poorer households emulating "better-off" neighbors. Table 1 shows that households vary over time and from each other.

In order to make the case that contradicts both Deetz and Miller, it is essential that their own hypotheses be described adequately. Deetz's ideas on material culture are very well-known and have not outlived their usefulness. He aligns architecture, gravestones, and ceramics, arguing that despite surface differences in their forms and overt purposes, they all illustrate the change in culture of the late seventeenth century to the beginning of what can now be best called a modern view of the world. Modern, also termed Georgian (the name of the era derived from the ruling British sovereigns), refers to centering society on the individual. The individual was the locus of responsibility, action, and rights. The individual was the social atom and was potentially equal to all others, in that he or she could command a place, privacy, earn merit, and expect a monument to his or her special history describing unique relationships and achievements.

This idea, or cognitive pattern, became well-established in New England in the course of the eighteenth century. By the middle of that century, archaeological sites there showed a pattern of individual ceramic plates, which meant they were beginning to be used as sets, each person at a table getting his or her own plate. Later, there was an increase of chamber pots as well, an index to privacy and of compartmentalized behavior, since elimination was done in a special place, alone.

> A one person: one dish relationship is symmetrical …. Balance and a greater importance of the individual characterize this new view of life …. In the 1780's, complete services of porcelain, creamware, and stoneware appear in some inventories. (Deetz 1977: 59–60)

Inventories also show sets of forks, tea sets with identical cups, and even sets of napkins. These same events can be seen from Annapolis inventories at the same time (Russo 1983; Leone and Shackel 1987; 1993). Inventories from New England, taken on a room-by-room basis, also show that the function of each room varied, as opposed to earlier in the seventeenth century, when many activities were piled together in one large common area.

> By 1760 significant numbers of New Englanders and their counterparts in other colonies partook of this new world view. Mechanical where the older was organic, balanced where the older had been asymmetrical, individualized where the older had been corporate, this new way of perceiving the world is the hallmark of … [the later 18th century], which lasts to the present and accounts for much of the way in which we ourselves look out upon reality. (Deetz 1977: 39–40)

Deetz's explanation for these changes is usually thought to be a cognitive one. That is, the change was situated in the way people saw reality and acted on what they thought. It was, he said, a change in worldview (1996: 63). But if the mind was its locus, a change in economic conditions was its context.

> New England, a theocracy before 1650, saw the loss of power by the clergy and its assumption by the merchants as the seventeenth century drew to a close.... The change in the character of New England society from religious to mercantile not only reflects the secularization of life but the legitimacy of wealth and personal possessions .... (Deetz 1977: 134–136)

One other concern is important. Deetz assumes uniformity in the view of the world he describes. Although it comes into effect gradually, and does not affect everyone in New England, especially African Americans, it does gradually and completely characterize all Europeans in New England and their descendants. Deetz does not specify how or why the ideas of modernity spread, nor does he allow for partial or gradual use of these ideas or rejection of them. Even though, to be fair, he probably never thought of it this way, he sees the Georgian order as becoming all pervasive once the notion of the individual and the technologies that support the concept have been acquired.

Over the years, George Miller has been building a sophisticated argument that explains that ceramic change stems from

> a continuous fall in the prices for English ceramics which had a great impact on demand and the choices made by consumers.... I would argue that falling prices had much more impact than social emulation in increasing consumption.... the consumer revolution was driven more by supply than demand ... because falling prices ... affected a much larger segment of the population that did the process of social emulation. (Miller n.d. 10)

Falling prices, in turn, were created because "supply was increasing faster than demand for the wares ... from 1660 to 1820" (Miller n.d. 1). Miller creates a historical setting of conditions in England that describes competing potteries, price fixing to stabilize prices, and constant innovation in style to keep prices up, yet ever-falling prices that produced a glut on colonial markets that saturated demand and drove potteries out of business. Implicitly, George Miller argues that costs and prices, not changes in local world views, are the basis of the reason ceramic styles, forms, and numbers of vessels in use change. By social emulation, George Miller employs the idea that richer people in a stratified society demonstrate their position through show, and that styles spread and become popular because taste creates a bond between the more wealthy and the less wealthy, whereby, the less well-off copy, or emulate, the rich. This may imply that all users share a world view of the kind Deetz describes, but the argument is based on the assumption that the rich and well-off automatically produce those who want to be like them. And to be alike, most of the not-so-well off buy similar things, even if not in similar quantities at the same time or shortly thereafter.

My own argument is somewhat different. It is based on the hypothesis that the idea of the individual has its reflection in ceramics because of the confluence of the use of wages for labor, the payment of rents and interest, price fluctuations for crops and finished goods, and the general unpredictability of income in a setting typified by early capitalism. This is what I intend Table 1 to show (in greater detail in Tables 2–6). There should be differential participation in, and subjugation to, a wage-labor system as people shift into classes and are either impoverished or become owners. There should be fluctuations in the use of matched ceramics from household to household as people rent or buy, become debtors or lenders, are workers or owners, or are in or out of the market, since cooking, eating, and associated acts of cleanliness mark the disciplines needed to produce wage earners and rent payers. So, I ask, how are debtors and laborers produced and how do dining habits produce them?

TIME ROUTINES, WORK DISCIPLINE, AND SELF-SURVEILLANCE

How are workers trained to work? Why do they train their children to do likewise? And, thus, why is there variation in ceramic use? Since a profit is defined as extracting some of the value from the labor of the worker, and because this is often an exploitative relationship, we must deal with why people work under such conditions. I depend on the work of E.P. Thompson (1967, 1974) for the needed reasoning that links capitalism to ceramics.

Thompson (1967, 1974) focuses on the Industrial Revolution in two key essays, and uses the ideas of time, routines, and work discipline in order to solve the problem of how individuals were tied to modern labor practices. He assumes that the individual is itself a modern concept of personhood. Thompson argues that the individual is a social creation, and that those people who realize their lives within the notion of individualism are not individuals as they conceive themselves to be, but rather are the interchangeable units of a society that makes its profit from selling the labor of persons who come to be seen as duplicates. Thompson explores eighteenth-century institutions "which enabled the rules to obtain, directly or indirectly, a control over *the whole life* of the laborer, as opposed to the purchase, *seriatim*, of his labor power" (Thompson 1974: 382, emphasis in original).

Time and time-discipline for Thompson are indicators of a new way of organizing production within all of society.

> And this culture includes the systems of power, property-relations, religious institutions .... Above all the translation is ... to industrial capitalism .... What we are examining here are not only changes in manufacturing techniques which demand greater synchronization of labor and a greater exactitude in time-routines in any society; but also these changes as they were lived through in the society of nascent industrial capitalism. We are concerned simultaneously with time-sense in its technological conditioning, and with time-measurement as a means of labor exploitation. (Thompson 1967: 80)

Here Thompson is describing the conditions of the late eighteenth century, in which workers were faced with manufacturing conditions consisting of repetitive actions to make large numbers of products, often sold at low prices. Working involved long hours, little protection, and a persuasive—and new—sense that faithful, regular work was a given, regardless of how much labor and time were involved. The new conditions involved putting the product first and the effects of work on the worker second, with a right on the part of the owner to expect the worker to share this priority because of the wage paid. Wages were compensation for all aspects of the work because the objects produced, not the relationship between the worker and the wage payer, were the purpose of work.

While Thompson was dealing with early factories and the other environments of mass production, Deetz was not when he described New England in the seventeenth century. He was, however, dealing with the early stages of a profit-making system in the early eighteenth century. The capitalism of that period involved trans-shipments of massive amounts of natural products and, in the case of the Chesapeake region, the labor-intensive production of tobacco leaves and the return of manufactured goods and slaves whose cost was controlled elsewhere (Kulikoff 1986). In the early eighteenth century, less capital was involved, and less minted or printed money, no banks, and only feeble credit systems were the rule. But the same gross fluctuations in market prices and, thus, incomes also existed. The people whom Deetz described lived through the successful building of a North Atlantic market, run under mercantilist conditions and laws. While archaeology tends to see the backyard, the labor spent there, the money made there, and the goods whose broken pieces were thrown out there, all were controlled as much, and more, by the Atlantic trade than by independent home manufacture.

I argue that the labor practices of New England from 1680 to 1800 are early versions of those E. P. Thompson describes for factory life in late eighteenth-century Britain. Yet wage work, the payment of rent and interest, and an inability to escape price inflation for goods, or price degradation for products, are the same. The question is how these conditions were created and sustained without widespread and constant violence.

Thompson sets out to describe the working habits of this new world, in which he wants to learn about:

> The inward apprehension of time of working people ... [was there] severe reconstruction of working habits—new disciplines, new incentives, and a new human nature upon which these incentives could bite effectively—how far is this related to changes in the inward notation of time? (Thompson 1967: 57)

Thompson begins with records of working clocks. He proposes that clocks were essential for teaching punctuality and the discipline that comes from beginning and ending tasks according to an amount of time, rather than a quality of work. He connects this particular function of the clock to productivity. To turn to Annapolis momentarily for illustration, clocks appear in probate inventories around 1700, in the houses of the richest and poorest people simultaneously (Shackel 1993: 180, Table A18). While the richest used more clocks and watches, it is clear that people from all ranges of income began to use them at the same time. Thus, if we assume that timekeeping is a discipline, some of the poor begin to observe it at the same time as the richer, not later. The number of people affected are not the same, but the change is not due to status, worldview, or price of the item.

I believe that clocks and watches can create moments of continually repeated measurement. Thompson calls this "time-thrift among capitalist employers" (Thompson 1967: 78). He then observes that the Industrial Revolution created people "ready to weigh and measure any parcel of human nature, and tell you exactly what it comes to [with their] deadly statistical clock ... which measured every second with a beat like a rap upon a coffin lid" (Dickens, quoted by Thompson 1967: 96).

Clocks could function in this way because they were used in the home, where telling time was taught. It is at home and during childhood that the production of individuals must occur, in preparation for an adult life of work. It is in this locale that we can expect individualism, as well as many of the attendant disciplines that affect life, to be taught. Into this argument (Foucault 1979), I would place dishes. If dishes can be seen this way, then cooking, eating, and waste disposal can also be seen as habits taught and learned as disciplines in childhood. I argue that analyzing ceramics and their location, which is usually the archaeological house lot, is a primary way of discovering the daily time routines that Thompson describes. We can see from Thomas Wedgwood, Josiah's son and the factory owner, how industrial production and the practices of child rearing could coincide:

> Thomas Wedgwood ... designed a plan for taking the time and work-discipline of Etruria into the very workshops of the child's consciousness: .... Let us suppose ourselves in possession of a detailed statement of the first twenty years of the life ... what a chaos of perceptions! ... How many hours, days, months have been a ... mass of confusion.... In the best regulated mind of the present day, had not there been, and is not there some hours every day passed in reverie, thought ungoverned, undirected? (as quoted in Thompson 1967: 96–97)

For Wedgwood and for all those involved in designing and enforcing factory life, the disciplines of life, including time routines, could be imposed on individuals in order to maintain order and productivity.

While Thompson's ideas reveal a world built around workers, Foucault (1979) focuses on the world built within the individual worker. Foucault explains in detail how the disciplines began to be imposed on every niche of an individual during the eighteenth century. This discussion leads from the classroom to home, hospital, library, school, and prison, and describes how these institutions created a personal conscience for an individual. Through time routines, which Foucault shows are embedded in self-surveillance, a form of power was built that is still used by the modern state. Such power is based on an organized home with structured eating habits, but also on all other forms of watchful institutions.

To create individuals who behave properly and produce and reproduce each other, Foucault begins with childhood and home life:

> In a disciplinary regime ... individualization is "descending": as power becomes more anonymous and functional, those on whom it is exercised tend to be more strongly individualized; it is exercised by surveillance ,... by observations, by comparative measures that have the "norm" as reference ,... by "gaps" rather than deeds. In a system of discipline, the child is more individualized than the adult, the patient more than the healthy man, the madman and the delinquent more than the normal ... when one wishes to individualize the healthy, normal and law-abiding adult, it is always by asking him how much of the child he has in him, what secret madness lies within him, what fundamental crime he has dreamt of committing. (Foucault 1979: 193)

The material culture connected to these disciplinary regimes can first be found in Annapolis around 1700 (Leone and Shackel 1987: 45–61). Yet it is only found in probate inventories, and not archaeologically this early, and includes clocks, sets of eating utensils, scientific and musical instruments, and teaware. Because eating and waste disposal are rule-bound and leave archaeological traces later, the indicators are matched cups and saucers, and even cuts of meat and chamber pots, as reported in Table 1 through Table 6.

Foucault focuses on schooling from an early age, but by the eighteenth century, all the practices he describes were routinely taught at home. We can see them archaeologically through the degree of orderliness at the table, in the kitchen, and throughout the trash pit. By reading Foucault's description of the classroom, we can imagine the home:

> ... an assistant teacher taught the holding of the pen, guided the pupil's hand, corrected mistakes and at the same time marked down troublemakers; another assistant teacher had the same tasks in the reading class; the intendant who supervised the other officers and was in charge of behavior in general also had the task of 'initiating new comers into the customs of the school' .... We have here a sketch of an institution of the 'mutual' type in which three procedures are integrated into a single mechanism: teaching proper, the acquisition of knowledge by the very practice of pedagogal activity and a reciprocal, hierarchized observation. A relation of surveillance, defined and regulated, is inscribed at the heart of the practice of teaching, not as an additional or adjacent part, but as a mechanism that is inherent to it and which increases its efficiency. (Foucault 1979: 176–177)

Foucault points out that teaching and watching are two sides of the same operation and was a form of power that linked people to the economy. Teaching and watching, or surveillance, created a network of relations from top to bottom throughout society, with everybody perpetually supervised. He characterizes a society of workers from the eighteenth century onwards as run by the disciplines that actually operated through "the uninterrupted play of calculated gazes" (Foucault 1979: 176–177).

When found in a specific locale, like a home, school, or hospital, these gazes were cast along lines of sight, from viewing platforms, through mirrors, from towers for watching, according to periods of assessment, using rules for observing, and postures for being observed. These, of course, all can be found in places such as those just listed, as well as in factories, state offices, prisons, churches, plantations, and forts. Foucault emphasizes that watching required the development of a conscience. It was through developing a conscience that the disciplined child grew into the subject or citizen who willingly watched himself or herself and was able to monitor anything and everyone.

COLONIAL AMERICAN ECONOMICS

While merchants and their calculations of profit did not emerge as the most powerful class in New England until the 1680s, the Chesapeake colonies were oriented to London and European markets from their beginnings in the early seventeenth century. By mid-century, Maryland, like Virginia (Isaac 1982: 266–68), was stratified, with slaves and a gentry of landowners with established control over land, courts, legislature, and public offices. In the middle was a populous group of whites who were, by 1700, permanently subject to rents, interest rates, and small plots of poorer land. By 1770, this group was financially closer to slaves, indentured servants, and disfranchised Native Americans, while being lifted above all these and tied together ideologically to the gentry through the imagined benefits of similar skin color (Epperson 1990: 29–36; 1993; n.d.).

When we look at the emergence of class in Annapolis, one of the small cities of the Chesapeake, we can see the environment of emergent capitalism. I argue that Annapolis is the early version of the time and work disciplines of E. P. Thompson and Foucault that we see through inventories and Table 1 through Table 6. Annapolis became the capital of the colony of Maryland in 1694, and by 1705 a previously homogenous population had become stratified by wealth. By 1720, 20% of the population held over half of the wealth, and by 1775 this elite controlled 85% of all the wealth (Russo 1983). Larger and larger numbers of people in this small city held fewer and fewer resources, and the group of impoverished people continuously expanded (Russo 1983; Leone and Shackel 1987: 61). The only earning power they had was their labor. How could the creation of such unequal wealth accumulation go unprotested? Deetz, Thompson, and Foucault either infer or say directly that time routines and disciplines of thinking and acting were the vehicles to achieve this in New England, England, and the Continent, respectively.

Ceramics from sites in Annapolis will help address this question and, I believe, show the same process there. Tableware, tea sets, kitchen equipment, and chamberpots, dating from 1760 to about 1900, come from five sites, as reported in the tables. Two patterns emerge, whether one looks at decoration, which we call type, or forms, like plates and bowls. All Annapolis households eventually used matched table settings and multiple forms for serving, although the amount varied at each site. Secondly, there is so much variation in this overall pattern at any one time that neither Deetz's Georgian worldview, nor Miller's price fixing that created inexpensive and ever newer styles, can be the explanation for the variation in ceramic use.

The explanation for variation, rather, is likely to come from the economic history of the family living in the house and their relation to the economy of Annapolis. For example, the Hyde/Thompson House, seen in Table 2, (Shackel 1986; O'Reilly 1994, Appendix 4) was lived in by upper-middle-class people for all its history, and thus its index rises

Table 2. Ceramic Variation at the Hyde/Thompson House

	Type	Function[a]	
Stratum 1718–1757			
Tableware	9.0	1.0	(3/3 × 1 = 1.00)
Teaware	2.0	2.0	(2/2 × 2 = 2.00)
Food preparation[b]	1.0	1.0	(1/1 × 1 = 1.00)
Personal use[c]	1.0	1.0	(1/1 × 1 = 1.00)
Stratum 1757–1798			
Tableware	96.00	10.67	(32/21 × 7 = 10.67)
Teaware	20.00	6.67	(12/9 × 5 = 6.67)
Food preparation	12.00	8.33	(10/6 × 5 = 8.33)
Personal use	36.00	1.00	(6/6 × 1 = 1.00)

	Type	Function[a]	
Stratum 1798–1864			
Tableware	10.80	7.50	(9/6 × 5 = 7.50)
Teaware	3.00	5.00	(5/4 × 4 = 5.00)
Food preparation	1.00	1.00	(1/1 × 1 = 1.00)
Personal use	1.00	1.00	(2/2 × 1 = 1.00)
Stratum 1864–1929			
Tableware	89.25	12.95	(34/21 × 8 = 12.95)
Teaware	120.00	12.11	(38/22 × 7 = 12.11)
Food preparation	4.80	7.50	(6/4 × 5 = 7.50)
Personal use	32.00	2.00	(8/8 × 2 = 2.00)

[a]The function column reports results when the formula stresses ware types over function, and reads: $\dfrac{V}{W} \times F$.

$$\frac{\text{Total vessels present in minimum vessel count}}{\text{Number of ware types plus number of primary decorative techniques}} \times \text{Number of different vessel forms present}$$

[b]Food preparation is bowls, churns, crocks, jugs, and pans. Standard classification for ceramics was used, including method for calculating minimum vessel counts.
[c]Personal use includes chamberpots, basins, and spittoons.

Table 3. Ceramic Variation at the Victualing Warehouse

	Type	Function	
Stratum 1790			
Tableware	4.00	4.00	(4/4 × 4 = 4.00)
Teaware	6.67	5.33	(8/6 × 4 = 5.33)
Food preparation	3.00	3.00	(3/3 × 3 = 3.00)
Personal use	16.00	1.00	(4/4 × 1 = 1.00)
Stratum 1790–1810			
Tableware	25.67	7.64	(14/11 × 6 = 7.64)
Teaware	12.00	3.00	(6/6 × 3 = 3.00)
Food preparation	4.00	4.00	(4/3 × 3 = 4.00)
Personal use	4.00	4.00	(2/2 × 1 = 1.00)

and stays high. We infer that the family living in the Victualing Warehouse, seen in Table 3, (Pearson 1991; Appendix D) was poor, as it was a warehouse on the docks and only secondarily a home. Its index is low. The Jonas Greens, seen in Table 4, (Little 1987; Cox and Buckler 1995, Appendix A) were middle class, but always struggling to stay in that position, and their index value is fairly stable. The index places them with the merchant, Mr. Hyde, and the physician, Dr. Thompson. The Maynards and Burgesses, in Table 5 (Mullins and Warner 1993: 114–115), were both free, middle-class African-American families and the index shows them to be different, but probably still middle class. Paul Shackel (1993: 21–29) provides a description of these households and their circumstances, insofar as historical information is available.

Hyde was a successful merchant and Jonas and Anne Catherine Green were established, although never wealthy, printers. Carroll's

Table 4. Ceramic Variation at the Jonas Green Print Shop Foundation

	Type	Function	
Stratum 1769–1820			
Tableware	64.00	4.00	(Counts used to calculate the formula are not available for this location.)
Teaware	24.00	3.38	
Food preparation	2.00	2.00	
Personal use	9.00	4.00	
Stratum 1820–1840			
Tableware	80.00	3.20	(Counts used to calculate the formula are not available for this location.)
Teaware	15.75	5.14	
Food preparation	3.75	6.67	
Personal use	1.00	4.00	

Table 5. Ceramic Variation at the Maynard–Burgess
House

	Type	Function	
Stratum 1860–1910			
Tableware	24.00	2.67	(8/6 × 2 = 2.67)
Teaware	22.00	6.67	(12/9 × 5 = 6.67)
Food preparation	2.00	2.00	(2/2 × 2 = 2.00)
Personal use	2.00	2.00	(2/2 × 2 = 2.00)

(Kryder-Reid n.d., Appendix A) renters, seen in Table 6, and the anonymous family in the Warehouse were not able to buy many dishes, and
were on the margins of purchasing power, judging by the archaeology.
The Maynards and Burgesses, who by 1860–1910 were not completely
affected by these routines, were nevertheless middle class (Mullins
1996). Since we do not know any of these peoples' stories well, one
inference from the index is that we investigate through associated
documents whether they were inside as well as outside the market.
Mullins (1996) has done this thoroughly for the Maynards and Burgesses and constructed their life both within, and in opposition to,
racism. The index at the Maynard–Burgess House is not an index to
poverty; it is an index to the degree to which they were outside the
pattern of buying with a wage, laboring for a wage, paying rent and
interest, and owning property.

The Annapolis we are discussing was one of many small cities
around Chesapeake Bay, including Williamsburg, Chestertown, Alexandria, and Georgetown. It held a little over 1000 people by the Revolu-

Table 6. Ceramic Variation at the Charles Carroll of
Carrollton House and Garden

	Type	Function	
Stratum 1790–1852			
Tableware	11.08	4.40	(11/10 × 4 = 4.40)
Teaware	45.92	11.50	(23/16 × 8 = 11.50)
Food preparation	9.00	4.00	(6/6 × 4 = 4.00)
Stratum 1852–1929			
Tableware	1.0	2.0	(2/2 × 2 = 2.00)
Teaware	4.50	2.0	(3/3 × 2 = 2.00)
Food preparation			

tion, and was both an administrative center and international port. It was highly stratified and was not a market town for the region. From this city, residents extracted a living from manufactured goods, ship-building, rents, interest payments, sales of slaves, and of things sold to slaves.

In this setting, Paul Shackel (1993) provided an understanding of the place of dining etiquette, public appearance, and civil orderliness, for which the eighteenth century is famous. Shackel linked sets of dishes, the notion of the individual, and time and work disciplines. He was concerned with the production and reproduction of labor in the setting that includes the routines of eating in Annapolis. Shackel's work cited here was proceeded by our joint work (Leone, Potter, and Shackel 1987: 283–302), which also contains an early version of the formula I report here.

Shackel's historical perspective shows that from the Renaissance onwards, the rules for dining became more precise:

> With this changing behavior came an increase in the forms of material cul-
> ture .... Individual drinking vessels and plates replaced shared goblets and
> trenchers. Several forks, knives, and spoons were added to the single knife ....
>
> The patterns of growth of new and varying material goods related to dining
> in Annapolis and Anne Arundel County were similar to that found among the
> mercantile classes of Western Europe. The types of material goods, such as
> sets of dining items are found in both regions. The difference is that these
> prescribed behaviors found in courtesy books do not appear in the Chesa-
> peake until about [the] 1710's and the 1720's .... The introduction of this
> modern discipline in the Chesapeake, based on the presence of etiquette
> books and new disciplining material goods, appeared suddenly during a time
> of social and economic instability .... (Shackel 1993: 152)

The etiquette books that Shackel speaks of appear in Annapolis book collections as early as the 1720s, according to probate inventories. Associated with these etiquette books were new types of material goods, such as leisurely dining items and sets of objects [dining and toilet] (Shackel 1993: 143).

Shackel shows that a whole range of items associated with people who saw themselves as individuals appeared in the early eighteenth century. Clocks, sets of dishes, sets of eating utensils, napkins, mirrors, chamberpots and other items that require rules of public use, or eti-quette, appear together. They were used by individuals who undertook to improve themselves or to demonstrate merit. Merit was seen, at the time, as punctuality, cleanliness, numeracy, manners at table, literacy, and other rationalized traits important to modern notions of produc-tivity.

In particular, sets of dishes have two qualities that are captured by counting uniformity of decoration and variety of forms (Leone, Potter, and Shackel 1987: 289). In the classification of ceramics used here, decoration means those characteristics usually called types, such as creamware or pearlware, and how they were molded, hand-painted, dipped, underglazed, transfer-printed, engine-turned, or shell-edged. Forms include plate, bowl, cup, saucer, and so on. Matched sets include very little decorative variety but the possibility of a great deal of variation in form, since all the pieces on a table would be decorated the same way. Over time, these forms proliferated to serve various functions at a meal. Along with the use of sets, plates began to come in different sizes, and so did bowls and serving dishes. Our measure does not count how many pieces were in a given category, but only presence or absence of the shape.

Our formula (Leone, Potter, and Shackel 1987) contrasts decoration with form and does so, by tableware, or teaware, or kitchenware, not for a whole assemblage taken together. Further, we separated out chamber pots, wash basins, and spittoons. We did this because different rules, routines, or disciplines were employed for all these items, which came into play at different times.

This chapter employs Christopher Nagle's updated version of Shackel's formula, which recognizes that ceramics reflect at least two centuries of change. In the early eighteenth century, there were relatively few types, few decorative techniques, and few forms. By the mid-nineteenth century there was, simultaneously, a multitude of forms and often fewer decorative types in a domestic assemblage.

Since the index is an experiment, my point is to argue that the variation it reports is created by the degree to which a household is integrated into the market. The variation reported from Annapolis is too great to illustrate the advent of a coherent worldview or the uniform effect of price fixing in Britain.

This paper includes five sites spanning a period from about 1750 to about 1910. The occupants, all known historically, but in rather sketchy ways, range from upper-middle class to lower-middle class, and European American to African American. What are the consequences of research that shows an uneven and episodic entry into the market, like the early nineteenth century at the Hyde Thompson House or the Carroll House? Deetz described a profound society-wide change in worldview expressed through the made and built world. Miller sees a consumer revolution that introduced more and more mass-produced goods at cheaper prices, copied or emulated by the rest of society as prices fell.

The cause, then, as I see it, of the changing use of ceramics is neither a universal change in world view or in the universal availability of dishes through declining prices. Deetz and Miller agree that there were transitions over time, and Deetz recognizes that African Americans were involved in a different way. On the other hand, Deetz, Miller, Thompson, Foucault, and I are dealing with the social mechanisms through which internal changes within capitalist societies came about. We all agree that these changes can be seen in the material culture associated with the routines of daily life. On the other hand, the research I report shows that there is great difference within and between households, which was unexpected. Households do not change in only one direction, and all households do not show the effects of any trend equally.

CONCLUSIONS

Investigations in historical archaeology and interpretations of material culture are important to the study of the origins and evolution of capitalism. Through the materials we excavate, people once learned to work productively, go to school, watch the clock, and eat with a fork and spoon from a mass-produced, modular plate. Inventories indicate that a few of the poor in Annapolis even did this before 1720. I interpret this as the discipline that produced a willingness to work, pay rent and interest, and respect the property rights of owners, as well as to accept poverty.

Capitalism's success at generating wage workers and those who pay interest willingly depends upon individuals who are interchangeably employable. Paradoxically, it is the material culture of individualism that makes everyone similar: Everyone has a plate, but all the plates are the same; everyone has a clock, but all clocks can be set to the same time. Modular dishes and clocks were attractive to eighteenth-century Americans, not because the gentry used them first, nor because they were cheap, but because they represented and reinforced the concept of people as individuals. Individuals were defined as having freedom, making progress, and improving their conditions. Individuals could take opportunities and could own property, things, and skills that produced actions that purchased rewards. It is the use of this concept, which is an ideology (Althusser 1971: 127–186), that caused change in ceramics, rather than a change in worldview, lower prices, or social emulation.

The ideology of individualism is at the heart of why people work

within the exploitation that capitalism often produces. It is why there
was little violence in Annapolis. Individualism is Deetz's Georgian order, Thompson's work discipline, and Foucault's modern citizenship.
The creation of the various versions of a self occurred at differing rates
from household to household and community to community, either as
capitalism penetrated or as people withdrew from it. And people came
into and went out of the market at varying rates, as they were subject to
its conditions.

Individualism, in Marxist terminology, is an ideology (Althusser
1971: 127–186; Barnett and Silverman 1979: 39–81). An ideology is a
given that disguises the economic and political conditions of existence
and creates false consciousness. Ideology creates a sense of freedom,
choice, or value that is not actually true when measured against, or
compared to, daily economic or political reality. Because these daily
conditions can be exploitative in many different ways and can appear
to be inescapable—and sometimes are truly inescapable—ideology
blinds or masks these conditions by offering either divine or naturalistic
explanations for them. Such explanations admit both how bad reality is
and provide reasons for it—sometimes invoking the person's own responsibility for the conditions. This process is called false consciousness,
and the notion of individualism is part of it.

The higher the index for orderliness at a table, the greater the
likelihood that individualism and its etiquettes were operative in the
household. These beliefs and practices were examples of ideology,
both because they were usually held as givens and were usually undis-
cussed. They could have been both deeply held and deeply incorrect at
the same time. They lead to false consciousness when those within them
also saw, from time to time, that they were themselves captives of the
attendant practices. Seeing oneself as an individual, in turn, likely leads
to beliefs such as personal merit, opportunity for all, a clockwork uni-
verse, private property, and slavery and poverty as natural conditions.

While individualism was, and is, an ideology, its component practices, such as etiquette, the demonstration of merit, or the observance
of punctuality, produced workers and their work. When someone saw
that paying interest was a "necessary evil," or that slavery produced
"happy Negroes" and "caring masters," that person worked or lived
consciously in an oxymoron, and thereby perpetuated the status quo.
These ideas not only helped explain how people worked, but also why
they continued to.

The case of African Americans who were free may be an important contribution to understanding the effectiveness of ideology. The

Maynard–Burgess House has a collection of nineteenth- and twentieth-century ceramics that shows the usual types, but with a low index of matched sets. This is not unusual, as Steven Shephard (1987) showed in his work across the Potomac from Annapolis, in Alexandria, Virginia. One interpretation of using odd pieces of ceramics is called "making do." This is a standard notion among some people in the African-American community that says creative, but economically poor, people use what is available to achieve their own purposes.

Paul Mullins, in this volume and elsewhere (1996; 1998: 7–34), describes how middle-class, free black people avoided market conditions by using a number of strategies. They bought national brands with guaranteed prices and uniform quality. They fished Chesapeake Bay, raised some of their own food, and bought from street vendors. They also knew how to feign ignorance, use varying punctuality, and varying skill in literacy as they desired (Fields 1985). The disciplines they were teaching at the table certainly were related to understanding market conditions, but did not include the same direct involvement with the ideology of individualism and its etiquette that a high index would show. Setting a middle-class or Victorian table may have been to demonstrate that they knew what white folks wanted to see, or it could have meant that the table's orderliness contradicted racist assertions that black people could not be orderly or punctual.

I conclude with some unanswered questions. If a low index of matching ceramics for an African-American household could mean an ability to exempt themselves from the ideology of individualism, and thus of some market pressures, does a similar index mean the same within another household that is poor but white? Further, does a low index mean that people can exempt themselves from the market, or that they were just too poor to own the ceramics needed to meet the requirements of the index?

Since dishes were normally cheap, the important question is how market forces operated to absorb more and more people for low wages, and then how Victorian mores sent them out as customers for goods paid for by those wages. A low index should cause an archaeologist to look at the rest of an assemblage and the associated documents for clues that were not previously noticed about the condition of the family or household. The renters of the Carroll House were living in a colonial mansion, but no one has looked either at the house's condition at that time or at the circumstances of the renters. Now we have reason to do so.

Capitalism in the eighteenth and nineteenth centuries did not absorb every family. People left for frontiers, joined utopian communities, or engaged in symbolic violence, as did many enslaved Africans. Attempts at self-sufficiency could be a temporary way for people to exempt themselves from the effects of price fluctuations, wage rates, availability of goods, and the cost of credit. But these very practices, which are not mysterious at all on their surface, are the ways that, person by person, and household by household, capitalist practices operate to draw people into a market. Their action constitutes the penetration of capitalism. Their action creates markets, creditors and debtors, and profits reinvested as capital, as well as people who have too little to save and can only labor, and who do so without violent resistance.

It certainly should not come as any surprise that the depth of any one household's absorption within a profit-making system should vary. But no one in archaeology has said this before, nor perhaps, has there been occasion to. In the experiment I have tried here, I have seen the opposite result from what I expected. And that result, if for no other reason than that it was not expected, deserves notice. Once one can accept the counts and simple formula that I employed (and I acknowledge that there may be errors and that the samples may be too small or incommensurable) then one can see that Deetz's cognitive process coincides with the operation of the Atlantic market on New England's Puritan utopia, and that Miller's description of English marketing procedures is part of how workers were produced. Both scholars see the operation of parts of culture the way the archaeological world did before Lewis Binford reminded us that culture is participated in differentially. Participation is not uniform. Capitalism, which I see as a series of practices operating within cultures, does not operate uniformly, especially in a highly stratified, slave-holding, unstable society, like Maryland. My result, then, should be taken, not only as a measure of the variable operation of the etiquette–ideology–wage-labor mechanism, but also as a chance to examine other sources to verify whether or not such variation could have been true.

Acknowledgments

Christopher Nagle wrote the program for the index of variation used in this paper and changed Paul Shackel's formula as well. Marian Creveling organized the data from the minimal vessel counts and ran the program. Paul Mullins did all the minimal vessel counts for all the sites used here. The paper was read carefully and critiqued by Paul Mullins, Paul Shackel, Michael Lucas, George Miller, and Joan O'Donnell. Kevin Hardwick originally lead me to E. P. Thompson's essays.

REFERENCES

Althusser, Louis
  1971   Ideology and Ideological State Apparatuses. In *Lenin and Philosophy*, pp. 127–
    186. Translated from the French by Ben Brewster. Monthly Review Press, New York.
Barnett, Steve, and Martin G. Silverman
  1979   Separations in Capitalist Societies: Persons, Things, Units and Relations. In
    Ideology and Everday Life, pp. 39–81, edited by Steve Barrett and Martin G. Silver-
    man. University of Michigan Press, Ann Arbor.
Cox, C. Jane, and John J. Buckler, compilers
  1995   A Summary of Archaeological Excavations from 1983–1986 at the Green Family
    Print Shop, 18 AP 29, Annapolis, Maryland. Historic Annapolis Foundation, An-
    napolis.
Deetz, James
  1977   *In Small Things Forgotten*. Anchor Books/Doubleday, Garden City, New York.
  1996   *In Small Things Forgotten*. Expanded and revised. Anchor Books, Doubleday,
    New York.
Epperson, Terrence W.
  1990   Race and the Disciplines of the Plantation. *Historical Archaeology* 24(4):26–39.
  1993   *'To Fix a Perpetual Brand': The Social Construction of Race in Virginia, 1675–
    1750*. University Microfilms, Ann Arbor.
  n.d.   Constructing difference: the social and spatial order of the Chesapeake planta-
    tion. In *Studies in African American Archaeology*, edited by Theresa Singleton.
    University Press of Virginia, Charlottesville.
Fields, Barbara J.
  1985   *Slavery and Freedom on the Middle Ground: Maryland During the Nineteenth
    Century*. Yale University Press, New Haven.
Foucault, Michel
  1979   *Discipline and Punish*. Vintage Books, Random House, New York.
Isaac, Rhys
  1982   *The Transformation of Virginia 1740–1790*. University of North Carolina Press,
    Chapel Hill.
Kryder-Reid, Elizabeth
  n.d.   *Final Report on the 1987, 1988, 1989, and 1990 Excavations on the Charles Carroll
    of Carrollton Garden and House*, or *The St. Mary's Site, 18 AP 45*, Historic Annapolis
    Foundation, Annapolis.
Kulikoff, Allan
  1986   *Tobacco and Slaves: The Development of Southern Culture in the Chesapeake,
    1680–1800*. University of North Carolina Press, Chapel Hill.
Leone, Mark P.
  1995   A Historical Archaeology of Capitalism. *American Anthropologist* 97(2):251–268.
Leone, Mark P., Parker B. Potter, Jr., and Paul A. Shackel
  1987   Toward a Critical Archaeology. *Current Anthropology* 28(3):283–302.
Leone, Mark P., and Paul A. Shackel
  1987   Forks, clocks and power. In *Mirror and Metaphor*, edited by Daniel W. Inger-
    soll, Jr. and Gordon Bronitsky, pp. 44–61. University Press of America, Lanham,
    Maryland.
Little, Barbara J.
  1987   *Ideology and Media: Historical Archaeology of Printing in 18th Century An-*

napolis, Maryland. PhD. dissertation, SUNY Buffalo. University Microfilms, Ann Arbor.

McGuire, Randall H.

1992   *A Marxist Archaeology*. Academic Press, New York.

Miller, George

1991   A Revised Set of CC Index Values for Classification and Economic Scaling of English Ceramics from 1787–1880. *Historical Archaeology* 25:1–25.

n.d.   *Demand Entropy as a Byproduct of Price Competition: A Case Study from Staffordshire*. Paper for the School of American Research Seminar, The Historical Archaeology of Capitalism, Santa Fe, New Mexico.

Miller, George L., Ann Smart Martin, and Nancy S. Dickerson

1994   Changing Consumption Patterns, English Ceramics and the American Market from 1770 to 1840. In *Everyday Life in the Early Republic 1789–1828*, pp. 219–248, edited by Catherine E. Hutchins. Winterthur Museum, Winterthur, Delaware.

Mullins, Paul R.

1996   *The Contradictions of Consumption: An Archaeology of African America and Consumer Culture, 1850–1930*. Ph.D. dissertation, University of Massachusetts, Amherst. University Microfilms, Ann Arbor.

1998   Expanding Archaeological Discourse: Ideology, Metaphor, and Critical Theory in Historical Archaeology. In *Annapolis Pasts*, pp. 7–34, edited by Paul A. Shackel, Paul R. Mullins, and Mark S. Warner. University of Tennessee Press, Nashville.

Mullins, Paul R., and Mark S. Warner

1993   *Final Archaeological Excavations at the Maynard-Burgess House (18 AP 64), An 1847–1980 African American Household in Annapolis, Maryland*. Historic Annapolis Foundation, Annapolis.

O'Reilly, Carey

1994   *Archaeological Excavations at 18AP44: 193 Main Street, Annapolis, Maryland 1985–1987*. Historic Annapolis Foundation, Annapolis.

Pearson, Marlys J.

1991   *Archaeological Excavations at 18 AP14: The Victualing Warehouse Site, 77 Main Street, Annapolis, Maryland, 1982–1984*. Historic Annapolis Foundation, Annapolis.

Russo, Jean

1983   The Structure of the Anne Arundel County Economy. In *Annapolis and Anne Arundel County, Maryland: A Study of Urban Development in a Tobacco Economy, 1649–1776*. Lorena S. Walsh, editor. NEH Grant Number RS-20199-81-1955. Historic Annapolis Foundation, Annapolis.

Shackel, Paul A.

1986   *Archaeological Testing at the 193 Main Street Site, 18 AP44, Annapolis, Maryland*. Historic Annapolis Foundation, Annapolis.

1993   *Personal Discipline and Material Culture*. University of Tennessee Press, Knoxville.

Shephard, Steven J.

1987   Status variation in antebellum Alexandria. In *Consumer Choice in Historical Archaeology*, edited by Suzanne Spencer-Wood, pp. 163–198. Plenum, New York.

Thompson, E.P.

1967   Time, Work-Discipline, and Industrial Capitalism. *Past and Present* 38:56–97.

1974   Patrician Society, Plebeian Culture. *Journal of Social History* 7:382–405.

Beyond North America | IV

For the final chapter in this book, Matthew Johnson has designed a viable set of principles for an international historical archaeology. He builds on ideas examined by others, particularly Charles Orser, whose work followed that of James Deetz, who also laid down ideas for a comparative historical archaeology.

Matthew Johnson has begun to help us understand that, whatever the British brought to North America, it was not medieval, nor Elizabethan, nor probably Renaissance. He points out that all these homogenizing terms hide the tensions in seventeenth-century English culture, and that what arrived here was a set of conflicts revolving around a profound crisis in English society expressed through Puritanism and republicanism, and which attempted to define how a person was to be a member of a household, a community, and a commonwealth. Nothing fixed arrived in North America, but a lot arrived here that needed to be fixed. Therefore, we are excavating the remains of conflict and contradiction, not uniform structure, cognition, or culture.

The following essay uses an understanding of capitalism's development that shows its operation to be uneven; it ebbs and flows. Capitalism's early development in England, as Johnson has shown in his *An Archaeology of Capitalism*, has early manifestations in the fifteenth and sixteenth centuries, with management of the landscape for profit occurring even earlier. But with out-migration, capitalism can be interrupted, escaped, and reformed, but not avoided for long. This essay focuses on the crises within social development in England that were imported into the New World, which were expressed through material culture.

Johnson also calls attention to two points that need far more debate in historical archaeology than the field has been willing to sustain. The first is that complex explanations that use context, including documentary evidence, must not do so at the expense of considering root causes. Life does not just occur, and explanations are not just contextual. Explanations that are comprehensive, local, and historical do not have to be so blunted that they appear untied to the concrete conditions in which people live.

Second, explanation is either implicitly or explicitly tied to action—political action. Like all the authors in this volume, Johnson eschews the model of neutral explanations for a historical archaeology of capitalism.

9

Historical, Archaeology, Capitalism

Matthew Johnson

INTRODUCTION

In this paper I want to support the central thrust of this volume, namely the call for a historical archaeology of capitalism. Writing such an archaeology is a complex and difficult task, and I seek to explore some of the general problems raised by such a call as explored both in my own work and in the papers published here. My paper will concentrate its comments on several distinct, but clearly related, issues: space, time, context, material culture, and politics. Aspects of these issues have been raised before in the context of an archaeology of the modern world (Orser 1996), but I want to argue here that such concepts are not only central to an archaeology of capitalism, they are themselves central to the practice of archaeology in all areas and places, and as such can be considered the basic building blocks of archaeology as a whole. An archaeology of capitalism is, consequently, much more than an "off-shoot" of more traditional archaeological concerns; it is situated at the core of the discipline of archaeology conceived in a holistic sense. I will discuss this relationship between historical and other archaeologies further in the conclusions.

1. Space: How do we relate studies of local contexts, at a very small scale, to the wider structures of a system that is, by its very nature, global?
2. Time: How far do the changes of the seventeenth, eighteenth and nineteenth centuries, many of which are explored in this

---

Matthew Johnson • Department of Archaeology, University of Durham, Durham DH1 3LE, England.

Historical Archaeologies of Capitalism, edited by Mark P. Leone and Parker B. Potter, Jr. Plenum Press, New York, 1999.

volume, need to be traced back to more distant antecedents and
preconditions to be fully understood?

3. Context: Should we view capitalism as a total system, within
   which all aspects of cultural life and the archaeological record
   should be included in a contextual study, or should its study be
   delimited to certain key or "essential" features?

4. Material culture: How do objects, spaces, and buildings come
   to carry meanings? Are the meanings of objects, spaces, and
   buildings fundamentally similar to, or different from, those
   carried by written texts, and if so in what way? How does this
   process of signification change under the specific, changing
   conditions of nascent and developed capitalism?

5. Politics: Given general agreement that we do not write in a
   social and cultural vacuum, how do we engage with the contemporary context of our research?

SPACE

One of the central thrusts of archaeological theory in the last
twenty years has been the idea that we should be looking at local
contexts. Such a concern for locality and the small scale has also been
expressed in terms of a need to investigate agency and "the individual."
This move has been all the stronger because it has come from a variety
of theoretical positions, not simply "the radical critique." Far from being
just another postprocessual slogan, there has been interest from a variety of theoretical quarters in "agency theory," in the archaeology of
gender and of the household, and in methodological individualism.

The result of this stress has been a new concentration on particularity, on local contexts, and on an insistence that the "big questions"
of evolution in the broadest sense, from the rise of social complexity to
the origins of capitalism, must be rooted in these contexts. For Elizabeth
Brumfiel, gender, class, and faction steal the show (1992); for John
Barrett (1994), antiquity lies in fragments rather than in aggregates.
The small scale and the individual has almost become "motherhood
and apple pie."

I feel there is a tension here within archaeological thinking as a
whole that is worth exploring. Even as we stress the individual and the
local, we can only do so against a backdrop of global structure; even as
we look at the small scale and the particular, we fit these into large-
scale processes. Even when Yentsch (1991) and Beaudry (1996) stress
the need for fine-grained studies of particular contexts, they justify such

studies by pointing out how these cases illuminate broader processes. As Wylie points out in this volume, we have inherited a particularizing/ generalizing opposition from the nineteenth century that, in practice, archaeologists of all areas and periods transgress.

The way this wider shift in archaeological thinking has impacted on historical archaeology is far from straightforward. The classic example is Deetz's original thesis of the Georgian Order. Deetz's model has frequently, and justly, been criticized for allowing no room for the individual and for applying a blanket model to particular contexts. Just as orthodox structuralism lacks a theory of practice, so the large-scale changes delineated by Deetz lack any account of how individuals re-interpreted and renegotiated either the "pre-Georgian" or the "Georgian" mindset. I suggest that such a criticism is justified in theory, but needs to be qualified in practice; it is striking that Deetz's original text begins with an account of localized, concrete, individual episodes. In other words, Deetz's work moves beyond the limitations of the theoretical model it is using.

I think that the question of scale raised here is absolutely critical for a historical archaeology of capitalism for two reasons: the nature of capitalism itself, and the historical nature of the period we study. Capitalism is nothing if not a global structure. However we wish to define capitalism, in its developed form it is absolutely dependent on a series of links spanning the surface of the world. One does not have to accept Wallerstein's views on the operation of world systems to acknowledge the point that, under capitalism, the actions of a slave in the West Indies are bound up with the American colonies, with merchants in Liverpool, England, with West Africa, and with other contexts as well.

The nature of the documentary records for the period historical archaeologists study accentuates this difficulty. For the first time in many areas, the people who made the things we look at are not anonymous; though the fact that they have names does not mean that we necessarily have a more secure grasp on their supposed individuality. Indeed, one of the central contributions of the Annapolis school was to link the development of capitalism to changing notions of the self, in part through the technologies delineated in Mark Leone's chapter in this volume. If the thesis that capitalism works through more developed ideas of the self holds any weight, the individuals we see will change through time; these "individuals" exist in a dialectical relationship with global structures, which themselves are changing rapidly.

Of course, all these issues have been raised in recent debates over "globalization theory," and are raised in part though Mullins' and others' discussions of changing consumption patterns. One of the central insights I shall take away from these papers is the way in which very local and particular practices of consumption can be read into assemblages of mass-produced products.

How should archaeologists grasp this interplay of global and local at a theoretical level? Charles Orser (1996) has suggested that the way to understand such a relationship is to adopt a "mutualist" approach, derived from the work of Michael Carrithers (1992); others have turned to the more familiar work of Giddens and Bourdieu, or have utilized various versions of neo-Marxist theory. All such theories have, in my view, unresolved problems reconciling structure and action. For example: How, precisely, do individual actions aggregate to, affect the stability of, or lead to, change in the structure of society? And under what conditions do actions lead to structural transformation rather than continuity? These questions are nettles that have never fully been grasped by modern social theory.

I have already hinted at a more fundamental problem. Notions of agency and individual action are by definition predicated on certain ideas of the self; that is, how we act or pursue certain social strategies will depend, in part, on our view of our own being and selfhood. Now it is a truism that such views are socially conditioned and are historically variable, in particular. If notions of the self are in flux during our period of study, as they surely are if our period really does involve the "rise of the individual," then we have a problem. *Adoption of a cross-cultural definition of the individual* from the work of social theorists, whether Giddens or Carrithers, whose primary task is to explain the individual identities and global structures of the present, *may be counterproductive in the study of a period when those very identities and structures are in the process of being fashioned*. This is a point to which I shall return.

TIME

For Purser (this volume), we should not end our studies with the capitalist boom, and should take our work forward into the twentieth century; I agree, but add the corollary, that we should extend our analyses further back in time.

Put very crudely, when does a historical archaeology of capitalism start? Chapter 1 mentions Renaissance Europe; Orser (1996) and Andren (1998) provide valuable reviews of varying definitions; and studies in this volume concentrate on the eighteenth and nineteenth centuries, the central period of industrialization. It has recently been argued by some historians that we should abandon a simplistic concept of the

Industrial Revolution starting around 1750; more general historical thinking has stressed a variety of antecedents to the industrialization of the later eighteenth century. A "Consumer Revolution" of the period c.1650 to 1750 has been delineated, which has had a dual effect. First, the dates of change have been pushed back and the period of "transformation," however defined, has been lengthened; second, attention has been focused away from production-oriented, top-down models of the rise of "heavy industry," towards more bottom-up models looking at the cultural preferences and actions of the consumer. My own work (Johnson 1996) has urged that we locate the origins of agrarian capitalism in the sixteenth century, and that even then careful attention has to be paid to medieval antecedents if we are to understand the nature of emergent capitalist structures.

I think that much New World research, including that discussed in some of the chapters here, has a problem dealing with these antecedents arising very simply from their empirical nature. To explore the antecedents of certain practices, one must move not just in time but in space, back across the Atlantic to the Old World. It is perhaps very tempting to see capitalism, or practices characteristic of capitalism, arriving as a package on the shores of east coast America, whether as a pattern book, between the ears of Puritan colonists, or as a job-lot of Staffordshire pottery. To explore those antecedents, and to combine such breadth with a theoretically informed approach, takes both boldness and courage, as Orser has recently demonstrated (1996).

It is necessary to add in the same breath that one of the main reasons why Orser's work in spanning the Atlantic world is so unparalleled by other archaeological scholarship is the theoretically backward nature of much British and European historical archaeology. It is difficult to point to European work that shows an awareness of the debates raised in this volume and a willingness to think about them with respect to seventeenth/eighteenth century, or earlier, material. A second reason for this lack of dialogue is European ignorance of the range and diversity of the work currently going on in North American historical archaeology: When European scholars do engage with this period, debates are still framed around a rather narrow view of the "Georgian Order" thesis (Courtney 1996). Where links across the Atlantic have been examined, they have tended to be discussed in terms of migration and continuity. A certain lifestyle or mindset is created in the Old World and arrives in the New, to be adapted or modified to the new, and often very hostile, conditions.

Leone hints at the inadequacies of a geographically limited view from either side of the Atlantic when he criticises Deetz's rather disembodied view of the 'Elizabethan' culture that the Puritans "brought with them" to New England; I would go further. Deetz's conception of a pre-Georgian mindset brought to the New World between the ears of the Puritan migrants was dependent on the assumption that such a mindset was a fixed, stable set of cultural values that had somehow passed directly from medieval England to the minds of the socially middling Puritans. The Renaissance, in this view, had not yet penetrated beyond polite culture.

It seems axiomatic, however, that the ships arriving on the shores of New England were symptoms not of cultural stability, but of change; that the Puritans' religious beliefs and their reasons for migration were tied up with a profound cultural and political crisis both at a national level and within village and town communities in England. The classic, if controversial, exploration of these issues is Underdown's (1985) study of the west country of England, where he finds Puritans active in uprooting and reforming traditional, "medieval" ways of life along principles of discipline and godliness. Where the opposition of the rest of the community to reform proved too strong, many Puritans chose the route of forming ideal communities of their own across the Atlantic. Migration, then, can be located in political failure.

If that is the case, then we must recognise that what the Puritans carried between their ears was only in part a blueprint for the recreation of a medieval or Elizabethan culture. It was also a set of tensions between individual and community, self and household, commonwealth and social order. These tensions were in part mediations of some of the forces of nascent capitalism in the Old World (for example, between self and community), far from being a "medieval" mindset (Johnson forthcoming).

If we are serious about writing an archaeology of capitalism, the preconditions of its emergence must be addressed. In the first place, we need to discuss core as well as periphery, sixteenth- and seventeenth-century Europe as well as its colonies. It is commonplace to observe that this period saw the cultural, economic, and political marginalization of the lower orders, dispossession of peasant land holdings and their transformation into landless laborers and an urban proletariat, and that the history of these subordinated groups fits with the history of colonial exploitation like a lock and key. It is also commonplace to observe that the rise of colonialism went hand-in-hand with a new materialism in the sixteenth century (Mukerji 1983).

We must go further than this, however. It is also a familiar point that as we move away from traditional models of Marxism, we must acknowledge that historical antecedent and the particularity of cultures must play a part in our explanations. One of the peculiar features of capitalism is the way it can take very different local cultures and sweep them up into a global network.

The concern with antecendent and historical particularity comes together when we consider the development of capitalism in different contexts. At a European scale, Robert Brenner (1985) has argued that we have to look at the divergent outcome of peasant/landlord class struggles in the fifteenth and sixteenth centuries. In England, he suggests, the landlord emerged victorious, and with the landlord, a landlord/tenant/laborer model of social relations in the countryside. Such a model facilitated capital accumulation and agricultural innovation, and played its part in the early emergence of fully-fledged capitalism in eighteenth-century England. By contrast, in France and other continental European countries, class struggle was resolved in favor of the peasant, leaving the restrictions of "traditional" agrarian regimes intact and leading in the long run to economic stagnation and "late" development of capitalism. Brenner's arguments are usually treated as a case study in "social" models of historical interpretation versus "environmental" models, but here I want to draw attention to their stress on contingency (political accident led to *this* resolution of class struggle in England versus *that* resolution elsewhere) and on regional variability.

But antecdent and particularity can be crucial at a still smaller scale. If we want to understand why certain forms of economic specialism and types of community developed in different areas of England in the sixteenth and seventeenth centuries, leading in turn to different forms of nascent capitalism, then we have to look at the different types of human landscape they inhabited. In some areas we find nucleated villages grouped around church and manor house, surrounded by open fields; in others, a more dispersed pattern, with enclosed or strip fields. These differences in landscape can be traced back to a much earlier period, possibly as far back as the eighth and ninth centuries A.D; in turn, they can possibly be seen as the outcome of different forms of feudal lordship and community. If we wish to account for the different development of agrarian capitalism in different areas of England, then an appreciation of enduring material and community structures first created under different social systems, and of regional difference in general, is absolutely critical.

A good example of the importance of understanding antecedents arises from Charles Orser's paper on "capitalist" farm tenancy. Orser mentions the medieval origins of farm tenancy in passing; what is interesting about this practice is that it was actually on the decline in later medieval England. Indeed, it is fascinating for me to read of its reemerging in seventeenth-century Virginia, as payment of rent in the form of labor services on the lord's land had been virtually absent from English agrarian practices for at least two centuries. From the thirteenth century onwards, such services had been commuted or changed into cash payments; for Marxists, this commutation and the introduction of a cash nexus into the very core of agrarian production is seen as a key moment in the transformation of agrarian practices and the demise of the classic feudal model.

Labor services of this kind are usually taken as a central component of Marxist definitions of feudalism, so to find them reemerging as props to a capitalist agrarian economy in the American South is both ironic and intriguing. There is a complex genealogy to be traced here that spans the Atlantic and a number of centuries; as there is also with the traditional medieval set of practices embedded in Epperson's contested commons. Orser himself has begun to explore aspects of this genealogy in his recent work on Ireland (1996).

CONTEXT

One of the central insights of much recent archaeological work on capitalism is almost too obvious to state, namely, that the study of its origins and development cannot be restricted to solely economic variables. Capitalism is a total system: It embraces lifeways, conceptions of the self and the individual, table manners, music, and bodily discipline.

If we wish to study capitalism, then, we must develop a truly contextual account of our period. The task of writing such an account introduces both practical and methodological problems. The practical ones are obvious: While one might be able to master a range of contextual data for Late Woodland Mississippi or for the European Bronze Age, such a mastery is difficult if not impossible for the period after c.1500. Add to this the necessity for a global scope and an interdisciplinary perspective, and the practical problem is compounded even further.

But the methodological and theoretical problems involved in contextual study are still more profound. If capitalism spans all aspects of life by definition, then the task of specifying core, defining features of the system becomes problematic. We cannot therefore specify with clarity what is base and what is superstructure, what is "economic" and what "ideological." As a result, we run the risk of a lack of focus in our object of study. Our study becomes diffuse, without defining features.

This of course is the problem of attempting to define and analyze capitalism in a postmodern world; one moves from fragment to fragment, noting links between things, but never really penetrating the surface or giving a satisfactory account of cause and effect. We find parallel patterns of order in both music and in accounting, but refuse to specify which came first or created the other. At the risk of sounding flippant, studies that eschew a narrowly mechanistic view of causality and that take a full and sensitive account of context run the risk of "having their cake and eating it." Such a view may fit in with the contingent and incomplete nature of research in a postmodern world, but if not treated carefully becomes a shallow exercise, avoiding the responsibility of the archaeologist to attempt explanation, however contingent. It is to the credit of the chapters in this volume that all attempt resolution, however provisional, despite being only too aware of the complexities of the task.

MATERIAL CULTURE

One of the strongest elements to come out of this volume is an insistence that the perceived sameness of material culture under capitalism—whether a transfer-printed dish or a babbitt—falls apart when we look at local and particular contexts, particularly at different patterns of consumption and discard. I mentioned above the central importance of studies of the consumer revolution to recent rethinking of the archaeology of capitalism. Two strands of thinking are involved here.

First, there is the empirical study by historians of the creation of new consumer goods and their arrival in the New World. Second, there is an increasing emphasis in the theoretical literature on the problematic way in which material things come to carry social meanings. In particular, it has been stressed how the peculiar conditions of capitalism change the conditions within which commodities are consumed. The most striking and influential discussion of the changing meanings of things as they are consumed under capitalism is the work of Danny Miller (1987).

Possibly the first writer to both think and act on the nature of material culture under capitalism was William Morris (Thompson 1967). Morris wrapped his penetrating critique of capitalism in the guise of a lament for a lost medieval utopia of free craftsmen yet to be alienated from their object of labor; his own company attempted to recreate these conditions. Of course, the attempt was naive at a very fundamental level; Morris sold his products to upper-class clients and a century later his designs are part of the symbolic capital of the upper-middle classes. It is not to demean Potter's account of his New Hampshire cows to say that his story is in some ways that of William Morris writ small. But the story of William Morris brings us inexorably on to praxis and politics.

POLITICS

It is now generally agreed (at least among the schools of thought represented in this volume) that archaeology is so intrinsically political that the basic arguments need not be rehearsed again. It is also generally agreed that a historical archaeology of capitalism plays a special part in the exploration of that political context, more so than the archaeology of other periods: as the Introduction stated in this volume, and amplified by Wylie, we study capitalism from a position within it, a position that brings its own special problems and possibilities to our discourse.

One of the central lessons of the last decade or so, however, is that such a political context is seldom easy to understand or to outline in a programmatic way. In particular, it is almost impossible to prescribe a praxis, how the self-reflective historical archaeologist should practice her or his craft, precisely how our studies should try to "illuminate the present" as the Introduction states. A view of ideology based on traditional materialism was easy to do and a little pat in practice. Just read off the ideological message from a given archaeological text, set its ideology against the realities or the outside world, and one had a recipe book for the critique of almost any period or school of thought one cared to specify. Such a procedure (which this author was as guilty of as anyone) was always a little intellectually lazy, though often a necessary first step in a deconstruction of the pretensions of neutral method.

Praxis became difficult for two reasons. First, we found that there were other stories to tell at least as valid as a story of class. The rise of feminist perspectives and the archaeology of gender militated against any straightforward class analysis in the traditional manner. The politics of race and ethnicity acted in a similar way to make our stories more sensitive and nuanced to the realities of the world, but also to make them more complex and less focused. In the second place, critical examination of how we might do a critical archaeology saw the project unravelling in front of our eyes. Potter's account of the Archaeology in Annapolis project (1994) and Leone's subsequent refocusing of the aims of that project shows this clearly.

I do think that on both sides of the Atlantic there is now a risk of becoming so self-reflective that we are not articulating a clear and coherent radical view of what we are doing. At times we can be so aware of the complexities and contradictions of our own position, so nuanced and self-critical, that we forget there is still a viciously right-wing majority out there. Wylie's "vicious myths" still cloak themselves in a mask of neutrality and objectivity, simply by ignoring all contrary arguments. One of the significant failings of the academic Left in the last three decades and on both sides of the Atlantic has been an inability to meet such apologists head-on, to allow the right-wing vulgarization of our past to go unchallenged.

For example, there has been an exciting radical critique in the past few years of the related notions of "England," "Britain," and "British-ness," a critique that resonates with Epperson's comments on the need for rethinking of the concept of whiteness. Historians like David Cannadine and Linda Colley have stressed that "Britain" is both a recent and an unstable concept, and self-critical "British" and "English" studies are currently virtually a growth industry. However, as intellectually stimulating and potentially subversive as such critiques are, they have largely failed to penetrate the popular consciousness. Last year saw the publication of Sir Roy Strong's *The Story of Britain*, a popular historical narrative that pursued its thesis of an essential and unchanging identity to Britain by simply ignoring all the contrary literature. Strong's book got mixed reviews but is selling well.

Chapter 1 treads a careful path through the minefield of politics and ideology and consciousness that I do not need to add to here. It rightly notes the difficulties surrounding the necessary advocacy that goes with an archaeology of capitalism. At a recent conference held in the north of England, I found myself giving precisely the opposite political message to that intended, through lack of thought about the context of my comments. I castigated industrial archaeologists for simply confining their studies to changing technology, ignoring the labor and other human relations that were present on such sites; the critique here was meant to be implicitly political, that an industrial archaeology that is exclusively technological in scope serves to obscure the realities of class oppression and to write working-class communities out of the story. But my comments were given a very different reading by many of the industrial archaeologists present. Several got up to proclaim their working-class origins, as if this justified their chosen method of study; how naive! I thought. It gradually dawned on me that I was the naive one; as a middle-class university-employed academic, my comments were seen as a threat to their chosen means of expression of identity.

Different contributors to this volume deal with the question of praxis in different ways. Potter delineates the response of one middle-class couple in New Hampshire. A notable absence, however, is a discussion of where, specifically, the politics of the Left should go, and how, specifically, historical archaeology can inform this enterprise. Danny Miller's work on consumption (1987) implies a politics of the consumer and an acceptance of the role of the free market in ensuring social justice; Raphael Samuel (1995) has delineated a new approach for historians and archaeologists to the concept of heritage.

Over the last few years I have become increasingly convinced that the theoretical inferiority of much of British historical archaeology, when compared with comparable North American work, is due in part to a lack of appreciation or critical engagement with the political context of our studies. Senior figures within the discipline can talk of "a climate in which the individual's freedom of the mind could flourish" in English culture in c.1600, apparently in ignorance of Ireland and other colonies, gender inequality, and a thousand other qualifications that render such a statement utterly meaningless (Tait 1997, 6). This is partly because the sharp edge of much British material is absent from the immediate context of explanation, whether it is a cotton mill relying on imports from Southern plantations or a country house dependent on income from Antigua; archaeologists can write about both cotton mill and country house and get away with a failure to engage with the other end of the line. Movement towards a more truly global historical archaeology will make it less possible to get away with such sleights of hand.

CONCLUSION: BEYOND CAPITALISM

One of the most striking features of all the chapters in this volume is their theoretical sophistication. All master complex bodies of interdisciplinary theory, from consumption theory, to postcolonial themes, to the politics of race, to critiques of essentialism. In this way a historical archaeology of capitalism does more than explore capitalism; it rewrites the discipline of archaeology as a whole.

Traditionally, prehistory has been treated as the proper and pure reserve of real archaeology; one learns one's techniques there, and then debates how far prehistoric techniques might be applicable to the archaeology of historic periods. Advances in archaeological theory and method has been driven forward by prehistoric studies. Traditional histories of the discipline have been dominated by accounts of the development of such prehistoric constructs as the Three Age System and the Midwestern Taxonomic Method. A checklist of the pivotal case studies in archaeological interpretation of the last 30 years is largely prehistoric: It might include pueblo social organization, the Mousterian question, the Hopewell culture, and megaliths of the Atlantic coast.

Until recently, historical archaeology, particularly of the period after c.1500, has remained peripheral to theoretical debates. More recent developments have begun to change thi's picture: Debates over ideology, over structuralism, and over the political context of our work have found historical archaeologists at the forefront of debates that change the way we think about archaeology as a whole (recall the Paca Garden and Georgian Order theses, and the African Burial Ground debate, respectively). In this volume, historical archaeology continues its move from the periphery to the core of the discipline.

Many of the reasons for this progress have been enumerated in this volume: the relevant epistemological issues are explored by Wylie, for example. But in conclusion I would like to note one gap in current theory that a historical archaeology of capitalism can be central in filling. Much recent theory depends on the assumption of a radical break between modern and pre-modern ways of knowing, thinking, and using material culture. Miller posits such a break with the advent of mass production and consumption; Shanks and Tilley invoke such a break in order to condemn theories such as optimal foraging theory as presentist in their assumptions of time budgeting and energy flows. And yet insofar as our discipline relies on the use of empathy, we assume continuity in the faculties of the human mind.

If historical archaeology can rewrite the changing nature of the subject from the later medieval period through to the twentieth century, we can not only accomplish the not inconsiderable task of rewriting the archaeology of capitalism, but can also investigate empirically a moment in time that has been posited as central by recent work in archaeological theory. In this way, a historical archaeology of capitalism becomes not just a central element in rethinking the archaeology of modern times, but a central element in a substantive reanalysis of our discipline as a whole.

Acknowledgments

The comments in this article benefitted considerably from critical comments by Mark Leone, Chuck Orser, and Rebecca Johnson.

REFERENCES

Andren, A.
   1998 *Between Artifacts and Texts: Historical Archaeology in Global Prespective.* Plenum, New York.

Aston, T.H., and C.H.E. Philpin (editors)
  1985 *The Brenner Debate: Agrarian Class Structure and Economic Development in PreIndustrial Europe*. Cambridge University Press, Cambridge.
Barrett, J.
  1994 *Fragments of Antiquity*. Blackwell, Oxford.
Brenner, R.
  1985 The agrarian roots of European capitalism. In *The Brenner Debate: Agrarian Class Structure and Development in Preindustrial Europe*, edited by T.H. Aston and C.H.E. Philpin, pp. 213–227. Cambridge University Press, Cambridge.
Brumfiel, E.M.
  1992 Distinguished lecture in archaeology: breaking and entering the ecosystem—gender, class and faction steal the show. *American Anthropologist* 94:551–567.
Carrithers, M.
  1992 *Why Humans Have Cultures: Explaining Anthropology and Social Diversity*. Oxford University Press, Oxford.
Courtney, P.
  1996 In small things forgotten: the Georgian world view, material culture and the consumer revolution. *Rural History* 7(1):87–96.
Johnson, M.H.
  1996 *An Archaeology of Capitalism*. Blackwell, Oxford.
  in press Genealogies of the Georgian order. *Historical Archaeology*.
Miller, D.
  1987 *Material Culture and Mass Consumption*. Blackwell, Oxford.
Mukerji, C.
  1983 *From Graven Images: Patterns of Modern Materialism*. Columbia University Press, New York.
Orser, C.E.
  1996 *An Historical Archaeology of the Modern World*. Plenum, New York.
Potter, P.
  1994 *Archaeology in Annapolis: A Critical Approach to Archaeology in Maryland's Ancient City*. Washington, Smithsonian.
Samuel, R.
  1995 *Theatres of Memory*. Verso, London.
Tait, H.
  1996 The great divide. In *The Age of Transition: The Archaeology of English Culture 1400–1600*, edited by D. Gaimster and P. Stamper, pp. 1–8. Oxbow, Oxford.
Thompson, P.
  1967 *The Work of William Morris*. Quartet, London.
Underdown, D.
  1985 *Revel, Riot and Rebellion: Popular Politics and Culture in England 1603–1660*. Oxford University Press, Oxford.

Index

Discipline (*cont.*)
  and execution, 84, 86, 89, 92, 93
  forts, 92, 204
  hospitals, 203, 204
  individual, 196, 202, 204, 206, 209,
    210, 211, 213, 224, 226
  jails, 84, 98, 203, 204
  law, 83, 90, 95, 99, 116, 130, 148, 149,
    150, 151, 160
  monumental architecture, 92, 204
  naming practices, 100, 101
  personal, 196, 198, 200, 203, 209, 210,
    213, 226
  religion, 89, 90, 91, 101, 203, 204, 212,
    224
  schools, 89, 203, 204, 206
  surveillance, 171, 176, 182, 183, 184,
    200, 203, 204, 206, 207
  time-discipline, 19, 70, 71, 113, 195,
    196, 200, 201, 202, 203, 205, 209,
    211, 212, 213, 226
  work-discipline, 113, 195, 196, 200,
    207, 209, 211, 212
Discourse, 22, 27, 34, 54, 64, 69, 71, 74,
    76, 103, 169, 210
Disfranchisement, 12, 145, 205, 224
Disneyland, 188
Documentary records, 3, 18, 23, 25, 28,
    29, 31, 32, 33, 34, 35, 37, 40, 44,
    65, 82, 86, 88, 92, 94, 127, 128,
    131, 132, 147, 154, 158, 177, 182,
    183, 185, 186, 198, 202, 203, 206,
    209, 211, 213, 214, 217, 220, 221
Dominance, 124, 171, 173, 182, 183, 186
Domination: *see* Subordination
Douglas, Mary, 123
Drake, St. Claire, 101, 102
DuBois, W.E.B., 102, 171
Durkheim, Émile, 59

Economic cycles, 144
  boom, 120, 121, 125, 135, 222
  bust, 119, 120, 121, 125, 130, 131, 132,
    135, 136
Economic expansionism, 4, 14, 66, 119,
    122, 125
Economy, *see also* Capitalism
  informal, 14, 16, 59, 129, 130, 148, 182,
    186–187
  scales, 14, 116, 117, 124, 135, 136, 220
  as worldview, 196, 199, 204, 206
Edwards, Paul, 173, 174, 175, 176

Elizabeth City County, VA, 179; *see also*
    Virginia
Emancipation of slaves, 146, 147
Empire, 119
  Mali Empire, 87
Empiricism, viii, 227
Engels, Friedrich, 45, 146
England, 121, 148, 199, 202, 205, 210,
    217, 221, 224, 225, 229; *see also*
    Liverpool, England; London,
    England
English studies, 229
Epperson, Terrence W., 226, 229
Epistemology, *see also* Historical archae-
    ology
  history–archaeology independence, 28,
    29, 30, 34, 35, 36, 37, 38, 39, 40,
    220
  history–archaeology similarities, 25, 34
  multi-disciplinary evidence, 36, 39, 40,
    41, 46
  production of knowledge, viii
Equality, 12, 159
Essentialism, 82, 100
  bias, 8, 91, 100, 101
  critique of, 9, 68, 100, 220, 229, 230
  and identity politics, 100, 101, 170,
    171, 186, 187, 188, 228, 230
  mutable nature of meaning, viii, 68,
    187, 227
  parallels to capitalism, 103
Ethnicity, 18, 123, 126, 131, 136, 177,
    228; *see also* Identity
  Basque, 115, 116, 125, 136
  Chinese, 136
  and classification, 87
  difficulty in discerning ethnicity on ba-
    sis of artifact assemblages, 154
  German, 136
  Italian, 125, 136
  rejection of monolithic categories, 94
  as social construct, 92, 94
  and state formation, 87
  and stereotyping, 87, 88
Ethnography, 58, 160
Etiquette, 182, 196, 205, 209, 212, 213,
    214, 226; *see also* Discipline;
    Segmentation
Europe, 205, 209, 225
Evans, Walker, 151
Evolution, 52, 64, 66
Experiment, 196, 210, 214